THE ROYAL NAVY AND THE SLAVERS

THE ROYAL NAVY
AND THE SLAVERS

THE SUPPRESSION OF THE ATLANTIC SLAVE TRADE

by
W. E. F. WARD
C.M.G., B.LITT., M.A.

with drawings and maps by
IAN T. MORISON, D.A.

PANTHEON BOOKS
A Division of Random House
New York

ACKNOWLEDGEMENTS

The author acknowledges with warm thanks the courtesy of the National Maritime Museum in seeking and permitting reproduction of the paintings in Plates I to VI and VII (a). Plate VII (b) is reproduced from *The Illustrated London News* by courtesy of the Trustees of the British Museum. Plate VIII is due to the kindness of the Fine Art Gallery, 25 Devonshire Street, London. So is the self-portrait of Captain Buck, on the title page.

Library of Congress Catalog Card Number: 69-18853

PRINTED IN GREAT BRITAIN
in 11 point Janson type
AT THE SHENVAL PRESS
LONDON, HERTFORD AND HARLOW

Preface

A few years ago, when working in the Public Record Office on West African history, I came across some exciting despatches from British naval officers describing their actions against slave ships, which I thought were too good to lie buried. In this book I have used these and similar materials as the basis for a history of the Navy's work in suppressing the Atlantic slave trade.

The Navy had a somewhat similar task in the Indian Ocean also, and in his book *The Navy and the Slave Trade*, Christopher Lloyd covers both oceans. I have chosen to limit myself to the Atlantic slave trade. This story has a certain shape to it. The early optimism of the abolitionists suffers a shock when foreign countries are reluctant to co-operate in suppressing the trade. A flurry of diplomatic activity produces some results, and the Navy is empowered to seize vessels equipped for slaving even though at the time of seizure no slaves are found on board. In the forties the Navy produces general alarm and despondency among the slavers by sending landing parties to destroy the barracoons in which the slaves are being stored to await shipment. This naval triumph is abruptly ended when the Navy is told that such action is illegal. But the naval men find a way round the difficulty: they make a series of treaties with African chiefs, prohibiting slave dealing and explicitly authorizing the Navy to use force if the treaties are broken. With the general advance in legitimate commerce along the Guinea coast, the slave trade is eventually pretty well stamped out there. But American sensitiveness over the right of search prevents the Navy from completely suppressing the trade further south, and only the final closure of the transatlantic slave markets puts an end to it.

The naval despatches cannot be understood except in reference to the diplomatic and general history of the time, and I have sketched in this background. But I have tried to remain faithful to my original impulse, which was not to write a general history of the slave trade, but to study what their orders meant to the officers and men of the Navy's West African squadron, and to tell the story of how they set about their task. The book is based throughout on original sources, some printed and some in manuscript. I have invented nothing; where the original despatch seemed to need amplification by details of wind, weather and the ship's course, I have taken these details from the captain's log. I have not provided an apparatus of footnotes, but have listed my authorities in an appendix. For the benefit of landsmen like myself, I have added a glossary of nautical terms used in the narrative.

The transcripts of Crown-copyright papers appear by permission of the Controller of H.M. Stationery Office. I am grateful to the staff of the Public Record Office, of the Commonwealth Office library, and of the library of the Ministry of Defence (Naval section) for their help; and also to Mr A. S. Fraser and Commander Keith Stephenson, RN, for their advice on sundry details.

W.E.F.W.

Contents

PREFACE   *page* 7

1. *Prologue in Parliament*   13
2. *The Men and the Ships*   22
3. *Opening the Campaign*   38
4. *Foreign Governments and Foreign Lawyers*   76
5. *Fighting Against Odds*   99
6. *The Equipment Clause*   119
7. *The Stars and Stripes*   138
8. *Triumph, Disappointment, Revival*   162
9. *The West Coast in the 'Fifties*   202
10. *The Close of the Campaign*   220

Table of Dates: The Progress of the Campaign   229
Glossary of Nautical Terms   232
List of Authorities   240
INDEX   241

Illustrations

PLATES

I The Midshipmen's Berth   *facing page* 32
II The Night Alarm   33
III The *Netuno* Beating Off the *Carolina*   80
IV The *Primrose* and the *Veloz Pasagera*   81
V The *Pickle* and the *Voladora*   128
VI The *Monkey* and the *Midas* Off Miami   129
VII (a) Slaves on the Main Deck   176
    (b) Captain Jones in the Solyman River   176
VIII The *Grappler* and the *Secunda Andorinha*   177

DRAWINGS

A full-rigged ship   *page* 26
A cutter and a brig   56
A schooner   72
A brigantine   108
A topsail schooner and a barque   142

MAPS

Africa   *page* 12
The Windward Coast   40
The Leeward Coast   41
The Coast from Benin to Molembo   42
St Thomas Island   51
The Rio Pongas   62
The Gallinas River   169
The Attack on Lagos   210

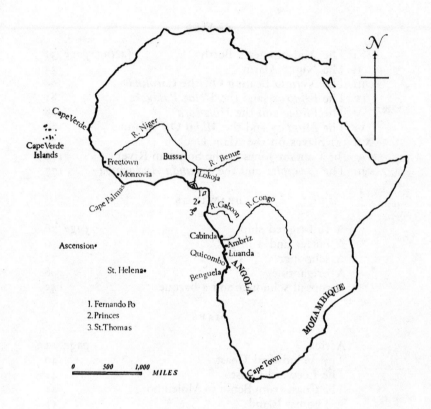

Cape Verde

Cape Verde
Islands

R. Niger

Freetown
Monrovia

Bussa

R. Benue

Lokoja

Cape Palmas

1
2
3

R. Gaboon

R. Congo

Cabinda
Ambriz
Quicombo
Luanda
Benguela

ANGOLA

Ascension

St. Helena

MOZAMBIQUE

1. Fernando Po
2. Princes
3. St. Thomas

0   500   1,000   MILES

Cape Town

AFRICA

Chapter One

PROLOGUE
IN PARLIAMENT

England was at war. It was the spring of 1807, and she had been at war almost continuously for fourteen long years. A year after Trafalgar, the leaders of the Anti-Slavery movement judged the time was ripe for them to introduce their abolition Bill into Parliament.

They introduced their Bill in the House of Lords. After passing in that House it came to the Commons; it was carried in the committee stage by 175 votes to seventeen, and came up for its third reading on Monday, March 16.

The arguments used against the Bill have a curiously familiar ring. The slave trade is a great nursery of seamen. Now that Britain has lost her American colonies, the West Indies are one of her chief supports. The planters are loyal to a man; they support us with men and money at a time when we need all the help we can get. This Bill will ruin them. They may even be driven to emigrate to Spanish America, leaving our colonies fatally impoverished. What have they done to deserve such treatment? The Negroes are better off working in a Christian country than being left in their native barbarism; and you have only to look at their smiling faces to see that they themselves realize it. We cannot legislate for foreign countries; if we pull out of the trade, they will carry it on, and we shall give up our profit without benefiting the Negroes.

Here is Mr Fuller, speaking in the committee stage:

'Those who are not[1] planters themselves may easily raise a
_____
[1] Hansard omits the word *not*; surely a misprint?

13

clamour against the cruelty of the planters; but I would have hon. gentlemen to recollect that the West Indies have been the support of the country for many years, both as to seamen and revenue. We might as well say, "Oh, we will not have our chimney swept, because it is a little troublesome to the boy", as that we should give up the benefit of the West Indies on account of the supposed hardships of the Negro.'

He was supported by Mr T. W. Plummer:

'I am as much an advocate for liberty as any man, but I think it very dangerous to propagate such an idea among the unenlightened Negroes. It is to be recollected how much Great Britain has already lost in her colonial strength by the discussion of these abstract principles . . .'

Mr Plummer is using the 'thin end of the wedge' argument: if you abolish the slave trade, you will then be asked to abolish slavery itself, and we have seen what has happened in America when people begin to claim that all men are created equal, and are entitled not only to life and the pursuit of happiness, but also to liberty!

Then there is The Man Who Knows. Mr Hughan delivers a maiden speech, a great deal longer and more controversial than would nowadays be thought suitable:

'. . . Having spent a considerable part of my life in the most important of our colonies, and having therefore some knowledge of the subject, I will endeavour to convey juster ideas of the present state of Negroes in these settlements than seem now to prevail. . . . I will tell the hon. members, from my own personal observation, that there does not exist a more happy race than the slaves in our colonies, if any trust is to be placed in outward appearances, which universally indicate cheerfulness and contentment. . . . With regard to the general tendency and the result of the measure, I will not hesitate to affirm that it must prove as little beneficial to the Africans themselves as it will be injurious –'

Mr Hughan's oratory seems a little confused here; he presumably means that the Bill will do little good to the Africans, but great injury to colonial interests, but this is not what he says –

'to the colonial interests and naval superiority of the empire. Throughout the whole discussion, cause and effect have been studiously blended: slavery with the slave trade. The slave trade in Africa is the result of slavery, and slavery is produced by the barbarism of the inhabitants. . . . . The proposed Act only abolishes the British slave trade. Will the French, the Dutch, the Spaniards, the Portuguese, or the Americans abandon it? . . . This measure will not produce any reduction of the number of slaves in Africa, and not one less will be exported from that continent. A temporary interruption of the trade may perhaps take place, and involve the objects of it in horrors on the coast, to which they are not, during its continuance, exposed.'

Mr Hughan had spent ten years in the West Indies, but he does not claim to have visited Africa. This does not stop him talking in the same authoritative tone about African barbarism as about the idyllic life of a West Indian slave. Other members follow him in pointing out that slavery had long existed in Africa. It does not seem to have occurred to them that domestic slavery in Africa was less of a hardship than plantation slavery in a foreign land after surviving the horrors of the middle passage. Nor did they consider that the white man's insatiable demand for slaves naturally stimulated the supply long after the African domestic market was amply satisfied.

Then there is the Government spokesman, full of elegant arguments for doing nothing. Mr Secretary Windham is against abolishing the slave trade, because the next logical step will be the abolition of slavery itself:

'On such a question, the House ought not to go upon abstract principles of right, but upon the consideration of the consequences of the measure, and the possible ruin of the British empire resulting from it. As to Africa, this measure will produce no benefit to that country, for there will not be less slavery after our abolishing the trade than before it. In the West Indies, it will tend to produce discontent among the Negroes; to individuals it will be a great loss and injustice, and will prove ruinous to numbers who have a claim to the protection of this country. France and other rival nations will most probably refuse to imitate our example, and will redouble this traffic to our ruin.

'Nor is this a time to venture such a dangerous experiment. We are engaged in a dangerous war with a powerful enemy. Is it not also a time to be strictly economical? Are we not called to attend to candle-ends and cheese-parings? And at such a time, should parliament think of throwing away such a resource as the West India islands? Do we not see empire after empire tumbling like so many nine-pins all around us? . . .'

Perhaps it is unfair to call Mr Windham a Government spokesman; for this was the Ministry of All the Talents, and Fox, though he took no part in the debate, was for the Bill. There seems to have been no Government line on the question.

Lord Castlereagh agreed with Windham; he feared that if the trade were made illegal, slaves would still be smuggled, and the mortality during the voyage would be still higher.

The champions of the Bill were confident that the House and the country were with them. They could afford to make shorter speeches and answer the objections. Mr Whitbread dealt with the point that the slaves were happy. One of his friends had bought a fine young slave, who seemed 'afflicted and sullen'. His owner expected that in time he would get over it; but before long another consignment of Negroes arrived,

'and the newly-imported Negroes, upon meeting with the former, prostrated themselves before him as their chief. The violence of his emotions, and the contrast between what he was and what he had been, drove him within twelve hours to commit suicide. One such instance as this is enough to show the iniquity of the traffic.'

Lord Howick answered the objection that the slave trade was a

great nursery of seamen. The mortality among the seamen
working in the triangular trade from England to West Africa
and thence to the West Indies and home was no less than eight
times the mortality among those who sailed straight backwards
and forwards between England and the Caribbean; so how
could it be said that to abolish the slave trade would cripple the
Navy? You could tell what the seamen themselves thought of
the business; for whereas everywhere else the Navy had to
press seamen, in the West Indies the men actually deserted
from the slave ships and voluntarily enlisted in the Navy as the
lesser evil! 'The tars themselves are with us to a man.' Lord
Howick also answered Mr Hughan and others who had pre-
dicted that France and other nations would continue the slave
trade if we abandoned it:

'Let us hope that France, which is contending with us for
power, when it sees us take the lead, may be ashamed to confess itself inferior to us in liberality and virtue. At all events,
this appears to be the most proper moment for effecting the
salutary measure; for the trade of France and Holland are
nearly annihilated; Denmark and America have already
abolished the traffic in slaves; Portugal alone continues it, and
her trade is not one-sixth part of ours. . . .'

Mr Henry Thornton denied Mr Hughan's statement that the
slave trade merely removed from Africa people who were
slaves already. Most of them were specially enslaved for sale
to the white men, and the Bill would 'have the effect of putting an end to the wars, crimes and kidnappings which are
resorted to in Africa to obtain slaves'.

There was not much left for Wilberforce himself to say in
his closing speech on the third reading. He pointed out that
the Bill merely proposed to abolish the trade in slaves: not, as
some had suggested, to abolish the status of slavery, immediately and without compensation to the owners. He treated
Mr Windham with light banter:

'My logical friend on the other side of the House must be in error. We are not to say that because a man has two wounds we should refrain from curing one because it is not in our power to heal up both wounds immediately.'

Unlike Lord Castlereagh, he saw no reason why it should not be as easy to stop the smuggling of slaves as to stop any other kind of smuggling. (And indeed, a landsman might well imagine that it would be easier for the Navy to control slave ships on the Guinea coast than for the revenue cutters to stop a Dieppe lugger from landing lace and brandy on a Sussex beach one dark night.) He admitted that the abolition of slavery itself was his ultimate aim:

'If this measure is to be shortly carried into execution, I shall think that my labour for these nineteen years past has been amply rewarded. But still, I must confess that I shall have another object after this in view, and that I look forward to a still more happy change in the state of the Negroes in the West India islands.'

He concluded by thanking the many great and enlightened statesmen – everyone must have thought especially of the two rivals Pitt and Fox – for

'the liberality with which they have set aside all lesser differences and united their efforts with this great measure for promoting the happiness of mankind. I hope that the cheerfulness with which it is supported by most of the leading members of the present administration –

with a side-long glance across the House at Windham –

'is a favourable omen of what may be expected from them at any time hereafter when questions are to be decided on the great and immutable principles of truth, justice and humanity.'

He sat down, and the House rang with cries of 'Question!' The gallery was cleared, the Speaker put the question, and the third reading of the Bill was carried without a division. The House then adjourned.

There is one point of interest that arises from a study of these debates. It is fashionable nowadays in some quarters to say that Britain abolished the slave trade because it was out-living its usefulness: that the industrial revolution was bring-ing about an enormous demand for palm-oil, and that British capitalists were coming to the conclusion that Africans were more valuable to them as free men growing palm-oil in Africa than as slaves growing sugar in the West Indies. This argument was not once raised in the debates on the Bill. Admittedly, in that unreformed parliament, the merchant interests were greatly under-represented. But the House shows itself well-informed. There is much citing of statistics showing the trade's importance in the British shipping world. Wilberforce and his friends do not attempt to deny that abolition will be a blow both to ship-owners and to planters; profits are being made, and those profits will be cut. Never do they say, 'Profits may be cut for a time, but we have reason to hope that the ships now engaged in the slave trade will find new openings in the palm-oil trade.' They argue their case on moral grounds: a Christian country should be glad to give up profits which are made out of human shame and misery. Windham and others twit the abolitionists with 'going upon abstract principles of right' and not facing facts. Wilberforce's peroration throws back the jeer, and stands firmly 'on the great and immutable principles of truth, justice and humanity'. It was these moral arguments which persuaded the British parliament to abolish the slave trade.

And yet this is not the whole of the story. The abolitionists were genuine in their idealism, and they succeeded in arousing the British public to respond. But they would have been much less successful had not the selfish or materialistic reasons for maintaining the slave trade been weakened. The trade was based on the need to supply labour for the large plantations of sugar in the West Indies, and tobacco and cotton in the Southern States of America. Immense fortunes were made when the West Indies went over in the mid-seventeenth century from small tobacco farms to large sugar plantations. By the economic ideas of the eighteenth century, Britain and her colonies were to be linked in a trading system devised partly for mutual benefit, but mainly for the benefit of the mother country. Britain would supply the colonies with manufactured goods and with slaves; the British West Indies would provide Britain and the mainland colonies with sugar, molasses and rum; the mainland colonies would send their tobacco and cotton and furs to Britain, and would supply the West Indies with provisions.

This snug closed system had been destroyed by two events: the emergence of the independent United States, and the decline of sugar production in the British West Indies. The United States refused to be bound by the old colonial system, and found that it could trade more profitably with other parts of the Caribbean. Slave labour is inefficient and therefore expensive; it needs large-scale production and a highly fertile soil if it is to be profitable. The soil of the British islands was becoming exhausted after 150 years of exploitation. Guadeloupe and Martinique, and still more Hispaniola, Cuba and Brazil, could produce bigger yields and could undercut the British West Indies. But they could do so only if they obtained enough slave labour to develop their land. If the slave trade continued, it would benefit these foreign countries at the expense of the British West Indies. If it were abolished, it would keep up the price of sugar and enable the older British colonies to keep going.

Thus in 1807, when Napoleon's continental blockade prevented Britain from exporting sugar to Europe, the economists had some reason for not conducting a vehement counter-campaign against Clarkson and Wilberforce. After 1815, things were different. The abolitionists hoped that foreign countries would respond to their idealism. But foreign countries were very slow to respond. They suspected that Britain was moved less by idealism than by self-interest: that she was anxious to prevent the younger countries from obtaining labour and competing effectively with Barbados and Jamaica. The import of slaves into Cuba and Brazil continued on a large scale, and thousands too were smuggled into the United States in spite of the federal prohibition. The ship-owners of France, Spain, Brazil and the United States made fortunes out of the revived slave trade. As the free trade movement developed, many powerful voices were raised in Britain against any interference with the slave trade, for it supplied the British public with cheap sugar and enabled the British sugar refiners to supply half Europe. But Britain, alone among the great maritime powers of the day, refused to allow her ships and seamen to carry slave cargoes, and after 1807 no slave ship dared to fly the Red Ensign. From time to time other nations contributed ships to the work of the anti-slavery patrol. But it was the Royal Navy which began the patrol, and which, in spite of all discouragements and frustrations, main-tained it unceasingly until the Atlantic slave trade was extinguished.

Chapter Two

THE MEN AND THE SHIPS

The Navy which embarked on the task of suppressing the slave trade was Nelson's Navy: the Navy of wooden sailing ships manned by crews consisting largely of pressed men. The Navy had been enormously expanded to guard against the enemy fleets (not only those of France and Spain, but sometimes also those of Holland, Denmark and the United States), to protect British commerce against enemy raiders, and to enforce the Continental blockade. At the close of the war, the Navy consisted of 240 ships of the line and 317 frigates, with large numbers of smaller vessels. When the wars were ended, there was, of course, a great reduction in the naval establishment; by 1835 the Navy was reduced to fewer than 300 vessels all told.

The anti-slavery patrol began during the war, when the enemy had broken up his battle fleets and was devoting his main effort to commerce-raiding. The strain on our manpower was at its height. Perhaps one man in four on the lower deck was a volunteer; about half the men had been secured by the press-gang; most of the remainder were provided by a rudimentary form of selective national service, the quota. By laws passed in 1795, every town and county in the land was compelled to provide its quota of men for the Navy, the figure being roughly based on its population. The quota-men were the least satisfactory part of a ship's crew, for local authorities naturally got rid of their undesirables, the men whom the district could best spare.

After 1815 these quota-men and pressed men were no longer needed. But until 1836, the Navy, like the merchant service, recruited its seamen on short service terms. They joined the Navy when a ship was commissioned, and left it when she was paid off. Since they were all volunteers, many of them no doubt renewed their engagements year after year and made the Navy their profession. This was certainly the case with those who obtained promotion. The gunner, boatswain, carpenter and other warrant officers stayed in one ship for years on end while ratings came and went. A series of reforms, beginning in 1836 and ending with the Naval Discipline Act of 1866, greatly improved the conditions of service on the lower deck; the Act of 1853 established a long-service system, and created the British bluejacket as we know him.

The commissioned officers already formed a regular profession, with security of tenure. For a century before 1815, the Government had accepted an obligation to keep a naval officer on the half-pay list if it had no sea-going employment for him. Once in the service, he rose in the seniority list as he does today. But there were two great differences between the position of a modern officer and that of his predecessor of Nelson's day. One is that in those days, promotion depended not only on seniority and merit, but largely also on interest or patronage. The other is that in those days an officer could not be retired. The Admiralty was not bound to employ him, but it could not take his name off the active list.

The bad old distinction between the gentleman officer and the 'tarpaulin', or professional of humbler birth, had disappeared by Nelson's day. The road to commissioned rank did not yet lie strictly, as it came to do in the nineteenth century, through a special naval college, though such a college did from time to time exist. Most young gentlemen who aspired to walk the quarter-deck entered the Navy by finding a captain who was willing to take them into his ship and see that they were given both practical experience and also the necessary instruction to enable them to pass their professional examinations. Before a young officer could be accepted as a lieutenant and commissioned, the Admiralty required the appropriate examination passes and satisfactory certificates from his commanding officers extending over a specified minimum period of service at sea. It was always possible for suitably qualified men from the lower deck to obtain commissions. Even after the war, when the establishment of commissioned officers was small, the Admiralty files contain many letters from captains recommending Their Lordships to grant a lieutenancy to some petty officer or warrant officer who has distinguished himself, and – very important and always stated – who has passed the necessary examinations.

In earlier times, an officer was commissioned to hold a specified post – such as captain or lieutenant in a particular ship – and reverted almost to civilian status when the ship's commission ended and she paid off. In 1815, the Navy was gradually passing from that system to the modern system, in which an officer is commissioned to hold a particular rank. In the Navy of Nelson's day, a lieutenant could count on retaining his rank and his pay or half-pay: pay if at sea, half-pay if unemployed. But however meritorious, he could not count on his promotion. For promotion, he needed interest or patronage. The critical step in an officer's career was his being 'made post', that is, being appointed to command a sixth-rate ship or better. Once he had achieved this step and become a post-captain, his promotion to admiral was merely a matter of time and seniority. It is true that after his first cruise as a post-captain, the Admiralty was not bound ever to send him to sea again. But as long as he was alive, and did not misconduct himself so seriously as to be dismissed the service, the Admiralty could not stop his rise in seniority and his eventual promotion.

When the war ended in 1815, the Navy thus found itself with immense numbers of officers on the active list: over 200 admirals and nearly 900 captains, with about 5,000 other officers, very few of whom could hope for anything but half-pay ashore in the reduced peace-time Navy. The scramble for sea-going employment was intense. It was not until 1847 that the Admiralty began to offer its ageing and superfluous officers inducements to accept voluntary retirement, the obvious inducement being promotion on the half-pay list.

THE SHIPS

'Hearts of oak are our ships,' says the song. The hulls of the ships were traditionally built of English oak, though by Nelson's time English oaks big enough for the great timbers of a ship of the line were becoming scarce. The Admiralty had to use some inferior continental timber, and experimented with teak and mahogany as well. The ships' spars were made of Scandinavian or North American pine.

Fighting ships were classified in grades or 'rates' according to their size and gun-power. The classification naturally varied somewhat in detail from time to time, but remained broadly the same throughout the era of wooden ships. First came the ships of the line, the 'line' being the line of battle. These ships, strong enough to take part in a fleet action, were classified in three rates, from the first-rate of a hundred guns or more and a crew of over 800 down to the third-rate of seventy-four guns.

Below the ships of the line came the frigates, ranging from the fourth-rate of fifty guns and about 350 men to the sixth-rate of about twenty-four guns and 175 men. In those days before radio, much depended on the sharp eyes of the midshipman or lieutenant of the watch to catch the first glimpse of a sail on the horizon or to read the string of signal flags fluttering at the admiral's masthead. The frigates were 'the eyes of the fleet', built for speed and never intended to join in the line of battle. Their business was to gather news and pass it speedily to the fighting squadron that could use it, running from any heavier opponent and fighting off any attack from enemy ships of their own class.

All these vessels, ships of the line and frigates alike, were full-rigged ships. The West African squadron never as a rule contained a ship of the line, though there was one year when for some reason it was dignified by the presence of a seventy-four. Its flagship was usually a fourth- or fifth-rate of forty to fifty guns, and it usually had one or two sixth-rates as well, light frigates of twenty-eight guns or so.

Below the frigates came the smallest class of full-rigged ship used in the Navy, the sloops of from sixteen to twenty guns. The sloop, like the frigate, was built for speed, though vessels designed primarily for use in the North Sea and the North Atlantic often found themselves outsailed in tropical

A FULL-RIGGED SHIP. 1, Outer jib. 2, Inner jib. 3, Jib. 4, Fore topgallant sail. 5, Fore topsail. 6, Foresail. 7, Main topgallant sail. 8, Main topsail. 9, Mainsail. 10, Mizzen topgallant sail. 11, Mizzen topsail. 12, Crossjack. 13, Spanker. 14, Main topgallant staysail. 15 Main topmast staysail. This vessel is 'under all plain sail'. If she had an ideal sailing breeze which was likely to continue, she would set studdingsails ('stuns'ls') on short extensions of the yards outside sails 4, 5, 7, 8, 10 and 11. She might also set additional staysails between mizzenmast and mainmast. In the nineteenth century, Naval ships adopted a fashion of dividing their topsails into two, an upper and a lower topsail, to make for easier handling. The spanker is sometimes called the driver. For some reason, the biggest sail on the mizzenmast was always called the crossjack ('cro'jack'), never the mizzensail. A larger ship would carry taller masts and would set additional sails (royals and skysails) above the topgallant sails.

waters by vessels specially built for tropical conditions. The sloops were the backbone of the West African squadron. They were fast enough to chase slave ships with some hope of catching them, carried enough guns to hammer them into surrender, and were light enough in draught even sometimes to edge themselves gingerly over the bars which obstructed the river-mouths. In the early days of the squadron, the word *sloop* had the meaning we have given it, and a clear distinction was drawn between sloops and brigs. In later years, the term came to be used more loosely to mean any vessel of about that size, and some large brigs were rated as sloops.

For smaller vessels the Navy made great use of brigs, which might carry anything from two guns to twelve. Commodores on the West African coast liked to have plenty of brigs, because they were less conspicuous among the merchant vessels. Three-masted vessels, whether full-rigged or barque-rigged, were uncommon in those waters; nearly all the slaving vessels we read of were two-masted, brigs, brigantines or schooners. The Navy brigs had this advantage of being able to move inconspicuously among the merchant vessels, and moreover they drew less water than the sloops, so that a brig could often enter a river while the sloop had to stay outside the bar. On the other hand, many of them were slow and unhandy. 'The worst vessel in the English Navy,' declared Captain Broadhead roundly in 1842, 'is an English ten-gun brig.' Not all brigs were slow. Captain Denman at the same time spoke enthusiastically of the fast brig he commanded. He said she was 'superior to the slavers; I never chased a vessel that I did not catch; some got away from darkness coming on, but I had the advantage in point of sailing in every instance'. The difference between Denman's brig and Broadhead's was in the design. The captain of a ship, like the pilot of an aircraft, is at the mercy of his designer. The chief naval designer from 1813 to 1832 was Sir Richard Seppings, who made valuable improvements in ship design, notably in strengthening the hull. But he was unfortunate in his ten-gun brigs, which though sturdily built were slow and clumsy. Denman had the good fortune to command one of the new brigs designed by Seppings's successor, Sir William Symonds. Symonds studied and adapted the lines of racing yachts; and the beautiful brigs he designed, such as Denman's *Wanderer*, Butterfield's *Fantôme* and Gardner's *Waterwitch*, were fast enough to catch anything afloat.

A sloop was nearly always commanded by a captain, anything smaller by a lieutenant or a commander.

When builders in the later middle ages first began to build fighting ships differently from merchant ships, they did so by erecting tall 'castles' in the bows and stern, which were garrisoned with soldiers. When bows and arrows were replaced by heavy guns, the castles lost most of their military value and diminished in size, though the seamen still saw some point in building up the bows and stern of a ship above the level of the waist to keep out the seas when the vessel was pitching in heavy weather. The fighting ship thus retained a low forecastle, and built up the stern in two steps, a quarterdeck and a poop. In the early nineteenth century, the forecastle and the quarterdeck were connected by two gangways running along either side of the ship above the guns. The beams supporting these gangways ran right across the ship from side to side; they were used also to support the spare spars which a ship must always carry. The gun deck was thus open in the middle to sun, rain and spray, but was covered over along both sides of the ship immediately over the guns. In the last days of the sailing Navy, the quarterdeck, gangways and forecastle were joined together into one continuous upper deck. The gun deck was thus completely enclosed, and received light and air only through the open gun ports.

The lower deck or gun deck, besides being the main fighting area of the ship, was also the crew's living space. The seamen spent their whole time between the guns. Their mess tables were hung close to the beams above their heads; and when the men were piped to dinner, down came the tables and up went the canvas screens which gave each mess some measure of privacy. At night the men slung their hammocks from the beams and slept closely packed; early in the morning the boatswain's pipe roused them to lash their hammocks and stow them for the day along the bulwarks of the upper deck. Each man had two hammocks, so that when one was being scrubbed and aired the other was in use. 'Scrubbed hammocks' is a regular entry in the captain's log to mark a quiet day.

In the first years of the nineteenth century the Admiralty made two changes which made a great difference to the men's health and comfort. It replaced the wooden water-casks by iron water-tanks which were bolted into position, and it replaced the sand or gravel ballast by heavy pigs of iron which were carefully fitted into the ballast space but which could be taken out and cleaned. The ship was well rid of the sodden and stinking gravel of the bilge. Even in northern latitudes, water from wooden casks can never have been very palatable. In the tropics, the wooden cask provided a congenial home for many kinds of aquatic plant and animal life: insects, crustacea, parasitic worms. The water quickly became thick and foul and a source of dysentery and other diseases.

A wooden ship was never very comfortable. The lower deck where the men lived must have been damp most of the time; rain or spray swept in from above, and the wooden beams and roof timbers sweated. The hammocks lashed along the bulwarks can seldom have been thoroughly dry. The men's food was uninteresting; it still consisted largely of salt beef or pork with dried peas and bread or biscuit. Occasionally we read of a captain who took advantage of a tropical port to 'issue oranges to the People', but the opportunity for even such a modest treat did not come very often. The large daily issue of Navy rum (too large for the crew's efficiency, some captains thought) was helpful in counteracting the monotony of the food and the foul taste of the water. It is understandable that drunkenness was one of the commonest offences against discipline.

THE SHIP'S BOATS

Since nothing must interfere with the firing of the ship's

broadside, a warship could not carry her boats ready slung in davits along the side. Most of them were carried (sometimes stacked one inside the other) on the spare spars which lay lengthwise above the gun deck. The boats were of several types. The biggest was the launch or longboat, a big beamy craft capable of carrying heavy gear like anchors or cannon. The cutter and the gig were long, narrow boats built for speed; the whaleboat was a light, fast boat with a centre-board. All these boats could be sailed or rowed. Other boats were meant for rowing only: the dinghy, the pinnace and the jolly-boat. These boats were distinguished by differences in line and proportions which the seamen's eye could see at a glance, but which need not concern us. The jolly-boat's name has nothing to do with merry-making. The word is the same as the word *yawl*, and the boat was a small one with a bluff bow and a wide square stern, usually hoisted at the stern of a ship and used for hack-work. If a cask had to be taken out to sea to be used as a target for gun-practice, or a man overboard had to be picked up, or a lieutenant had to be sent to inspect a ship's papers, the jolly-boat was ordered away to do the work.

For a cutting-out expedition, the larger boats could easily be armed with a light carronade in the bows. A flotilla of three or four boats, each carrying a six- or nine-pound carronade as well as musketeers, could provide a formidable body of fire as soon as they came within 200 or 300 yards. The danger they ran was of being enfiladed by small-arms fire from the river banks, and of being outranged by the enemy's long guns before their own short-range carronades could come into action. On occasion, two or three boats might be provisioned for some days to keep watch on a ship at anchor or on some spot of coast. They could easily be fitted with awnings for protection against sun and rain.

THE GUNS

The larger ships of the line were three-deckers; that is, they carried their guns on three decks, though they had at least two and often three other decks for living and storage space. The seventy-four was a two-decker; most frigates and all smaller vessels were single-deckers. This nomenclature refers solely to the number of gun decks. The broadside guns were fired through square ports cut in the vessel's side. The port had a hinged cover, which could cover the port completely in heavy weather, could be held horizontal to give air to the gun deck in fair weather, and could be hauled flat against the ship's side when she was going into action. A fighting ship bared her teeth for action by opening her ports and running out the loaded guns so that they projected beyond the ship's side. A ship did not always carry as many guns as she was designed to carry. One ship captured by the Navy was 'pierced for sixteen guns' but carried only four, and this sort of discrepancy was common: though not in the Navy itself.

The very smallest vessels, carrying only one or two guns, often mounted them on a pivot or swivel, so that they could be swung through a wide arc. Some merchant vessels with a weak broadside supplemented it with one or two swivel guns, though this does not seem to have been usual in the Navy. A fighting vessel carried nearly all her guns in her two broadsides, keeping only a few to be mounted on poop and forecastle to fire directly astern or ahead during a chase. Since the main armament was carried in the two broadsides, the normal formation of a fleet in action was in line ahead, one fleet firing its starboard guns and the other its port guns. It was unusual for a battle to develop into a mêlée, in which a ship might find herself engaged with an enemy ship on each side. Gun's crews were calculated on the assumption that only one broadside would be in action at a time. One gun's crew had charge of two guns, Number Three gun starboard and Number Three port, for example. If both those guns had to be in action together, each had to be shorthanded.

The West African squadron was never called upon to fight a fleet action. All the fighting in West African waters consisted either of boat work or of single ship actions. In a single ship action, the traditional method was to bring your vessel alongside the enemy and hammer away broadside to broadside. This is easily said; but there was great scope for tactical skill in bringing your vessel into position in differing conditions of wind and sea, so that you were able to damage the enemy without his damaging you. Once the two ships were alongside, one ship might have the good fortune to dismast the enemy or put a shot into his magazine. Apart from such luck, victory in an even contest would go to the ship with the most gallant and efficient gun crews: those who stood best to their guns and poured in four well-aimed broadsides to the enemy's three, or three to his two. It was in gunnery that the Royal Navy was most superior to its foes. The slavers often had the faster ships, they often had tough and well-disciplined seamen, but they usually seemed short of trained gunners.

Apart from this slogging match, there was an effective device which could be used by the faster or the handier ship: that of raking the enemy by doubling under his stern and firing down the whole length of his deck. This attack brought the whole broadside into action as each gun came to bear, while the enemy could reply only with his single stern gun. It could cause heavy casualties, and it increased the chances of crippling the enemy by bringing down his spars. But all captains were on the lookout for this manoeuvre, and it seldom succeeded unless one vessel was much faster or more agile than the other.

A raking attack was often feared by a vessel which was anchored by the head and was likely to be attacked by small boats from astern. In this position, the anchored vessel was highly vulnerable, for she had only her stern gun bearing on the enemy boats. Her remedy was to anchor 'with a spring on her cable': that is, with a slack rope from her stern attached to the anchor cable at her bow. If this slack rope were hauled tight, it would have the effect of swinging the vessel through a right angle and bringing her broadside to bear on the attacking boats.

An action fought broadside to broadside between evenly matched opponents was apt to leave the victor in almost as

I. THE MIDSHIPMEN'S BERTH

This is a large ship to carry so many midshipmen and give them so much space. Even so, daylight is scarce, and most of it comes from the opening in the roof. (*From the painting by Augustus Earle.*)

II. THE NIGHT ALARM

The men are stowing their hammocks, and many hooks are already vacant. Two of the crew of No. 6 gun are already at their posts, one carrying the sponge for cleaning the barrel after the gun has been fired. Another porthole can be seen on the left, but the hurrying men hide the gun from sight.

bad a state as the vanquished. It is true that some variation was possible in gunnery tactics. French and Spanish gunners usually aimed at the spars so as to cripple their enemy; British gunners aimed at the hulls and the decks so as to kill the crew and put the guns out of action. In an action fought at medium or long range, a British ship would suffer more damage aloft but lighter casualties than the enemy. But at close quarters this difference would be less marked; and it was the tradition of the Royal Navy to engage at close quarters. After a few broadsides had been fired, a captain, anxious to avoid having his ship badly knocked about, would often try to shorten the action by grappling with the enemy and calling away boarders. With his crew superior in numbers or discipline, he would hope that twenty minutes with cold steel would settle the matter and leave his own ship in good fighting trim. An enemy conscious of his weakness would reinforce his bulwarks with high netting to keep out boarders. One Spanish slaver successfully repelled an attack by such elaborate precautions of this kind that only one man at a time could possibly come on board his ship.

Until the end of the anti-slavery patrol on the West African coast, the Navy was still using smooth-bore muzzle-loading guns throwing round shot. Breech-loading guns were first tried in the 'forties, but they were unsuccessful. In the 'sixties, rifled guns came into use, and the rifled barrel led to the replacement of the spherical shot by cylindrical, with a great increase in range and accuracy. The first rifled guns were breech-loaders, but the breech mechanism was less successful than the rest of the invention, and for some time the Navy, though keeping the rifled barrel, went back to muzzle-loading. But these developments came too late for the West African squadron.

Besides solid round shot, the guns could fire grape shot, and canister or case shot. Both these replaced the one solid sphere by many small spheres for killing men instead of for smashing the ship. Canister was a thin metal shell filled with balls, which broke on impact and scattered its contents. The balls in grape shot were twice as big as those in canister, and were packed in three layers separated by metal plates. Explosive shells were used by the Russians in the Crimean war, but did not come into use in the Royal Navy until the West African patrol was nearly ended.

Gunnery in the 'thirties and 'forties was what it had been in Nelson's day, except that in the very last years of the Napoleonic war the Admiralty abandoned the system whereby the gunner measured out for himself the amount of propellant powder he needed from the shovelful handed him by the powder-monkey. This loose powder was replaced by prepacked cartridges of cloth or stiff paper, containing the correct charge for the appropriate weight of shot.

The guns were classified, from the three-pounder upwards, according to the weight of the shot they threw. The heaviest gun in a frigate was a 32-pounder. The word 'pounder' was omitted in speech, so that a ship's armament might be described as consisting of 'four nines and a long twelve'. A long gun had a somewhat longer range, and a good deal more accuracy of aim, than a gun of normal length. Long guns were commonly mounted in the bow or stern.

There was also a gun shorter than normal; this was the carronade or 'smasher', first made at the Carron iron works in Scotland in 1779. The carronade used a much smaller propellant charge than the normal gun, so that its shot had a much lower muzzle velocity. A shot from a normal gun might pierce the outer skin of the enemy's hull and embed itself fairly harmlessly in the wood, but the slower-flying shot from the carronade smashed the outer skin and sent the deadly splinters flying. The carronade had other advantages. Because of its small charge, it was much more thinly made and much lighter than a normal gun, and much more manoeuvrable. An ordinary 32-pounder weighed nearly three tons, the 32-pounder carronade weighed about 18 cwt, about the same as a long nine. The carronade thus needed fewer men to work it, and was light enough to be swung over the side with a block and tackle and mounted in the bows of one of the ship's boats.

Until thirty years before the West African squadron

34

began its work, the ship's 'great guns' were fired by a method which had long since been abandoned in small arms: the slow-match. On top of the barrel of the gun at the breech end was a touch-hole communicating with the explosive charge; this touch-hole was filled with gunpowder. The gunner held a length of slow-burning fuse; he laid a short train of powder on the breech of the gun leading to the touch-hole, lighted the train, and awaited developments. Shortly before the outbreak of the Napoleonic war, the first attempt was made to provide the gun with a flint-lock firing mechanism like that used in small-arms. Some form of flint-lock device gradually came into general use. It was not completely satisfactory. In the musket, the hammer was brought violently into play by a strong spring; but this was found impracticable in the great gun, for the concussion soon ruined the spring. The captain of the gun released the hammer by jerking a lanyard, but unless he had just the right knack, the hammer failed to strike a spark and the gun misfired. So great was the risk of an obstinately misfiring gun, that a lighted slow-match was always kept ready as a precaution.

The carronade had a range of 200 to 300 yards, the 32-pounder was effective at half a mile, and at extreme elevation could carry about 1,300 yards. Aiming the gun was a primitive affair. The gun was mounted on a wooden carriage running on four small wheels. The barrel could swing fairly freely in a vertical plane, but not sideways. The gun-layer could alter the elevation of the gun by knocking in or taking out wedges which were provided to fit between the barrel and the carriage. The only means of training the gun to right or left was to insert crowbars and handspikes under the carriage, lift the wheels clear of the deck, and lever the whole contraption round: no easy matter with a gun weighing from two to three tons. The gun on its four-wheeled carriage thus had the great disadvantage that it could be trained round only slowly and jerkily through a very limited arc. The elevation on the other hand could be altered with ease; and apart from any alteration desired by the gun-layer, the gun's elevation was constantly changing as the ship rolled. The gun-layer from his port-hole could see only the heaving water and the enemy vessel, and it was essential for him to know how his own highly mobile gun-platform was rolling. There were various devices to tell him this, the simplest being a pendulum swinging against a graduated arc. He aimed his gun by peering along the barrel, taking a quick glance at the roll-indicator, and firing when the elevation was right. Even as late as the Crimean War, there were some ships in the Navy with no more in the way of gun-sights than this. It was only with the introduction of rifled breech-loading guns that the range began to lengthen and elaborate gun-sights became essential.

The gun-carriage was carefully secured with heavy ropes to ring-bolts in the bulwarks, partly to absorb the recoil and bring the gun back to the loading position, partly to make sure that in heavy weather the carriage did not slide out of place and take the gun charging up and down the deck, imperilling life and limb and the safety of the ship.

THE COMING OF STEAM

The Navy acquired its first paddle-steamers in 1822, but the Admiralty did not welcome the steamship. As the nobleman in armour had disliked firearms because they destroyed his pre-eminence in the art of war, so the Admiralty disliked the steamship because it was likely to set at naught the skill and discipline of the British bluejacket in handling the beautiful sloops and frigates of the 'thirties. For that matter, the Admiralty was ill-disposed towards all mechanical innovations. Nelson's Navy had shown itself capable of beating the world in arms (except the Americans), and the Admiralty had the logical policy of accepting and adopting any inventions – shells, improved gun-sights, rifled breech-loaders, armour-plating – which were taken up by foreign navies: but not of taking the initiative itself in modifying the Navy which had served the country so well. It was not till the duel of the *Monitor* and the *Merrimac* in 1862 that the Admiralty realized that an epoch was ended, and set itself strenuously to reconstruct the Royal Navy to meet the new conditions.

The early steamship had plain disadvantages. It was slow; its coal-bunkers occupied valuable space; it consumed coal in huge quantities, and needed an elaborate organization of coaling-stations if it was not to be reduced to the humiliating and inefficient course of burning wood. Perhaps worst of all, its enormous paddle-boxes made broadside firing impossible. It is true that under power it could travel in a calm when sailing ships were motionless; but this advantage was hardly worth the price.

In 1842 the West African squadron contained five steamers, but it was not until 1845 that the Admiralty really began to take kindly to the new invention. In that year, the Admiralty set the screw steamer HMS *Rattler* to compete with the paddle steamer HMS *Alecto*. In the final test, the two vessels were fastened together stern to stern, and in a dead North Sea calm both engines were set going full speed ahead. The screw steamer towed her rival stern first at two knots, and the Admiralty decided to pin its faith to screws henceforth: the more willingly because it saw the broadside thereby restored. Throughout the first half of the century, all naval steamers carried a full set of sails, and used their engines as auxiliary power.

All the early steamers were built of wood, and many apprehensions were expressed about the risk of fire in putting a stokehold and furnaces into a wooden hull. The replacement of wooden hulls by iron and then by steel, the discarding of sails and the abandonment of the order, 'Down funnel, up screw!'; such changes as these belong to the new era of naval affairs which began in the middle of the nineteenth century. To the end of its days, the West African squadron of the Royal Navy used wooden ships and relied mainly on sails. It belongs to the old world.

Chapter Three

OPENING THE CAMPAIGN

Their speeches in parliament show that the abolitionists were optimistic. All the ports in the trade were well known, those from which the slaves were shipped, and those where they were unloaded to begin their new life. A vessel carrying some hundreds of slaves and following these recognized sea lanes would surely find it difficult to escape from the Royal Navy, whose captains had so many years of experience in intercepting enemy squadrons and in watching enemy ports from the Texel to Toulon. Denmark and America had already forbidden their people to engage in the slave trade. Revolutionary France, with its fine talk about the rights of man, would surely follow suit and prohibit a traffic which so manifestly contravened those rights; so would Holland. There might be difficulty with Spain and Portugal, which had plantations in the New World. But when the long war was ended, the general peace treaty could be made to include a general prohibition of the slave trade, and Spain and Portugal would surely not hold aloof.

Events showed that this optimism was not justified. The Congress of Vienna did certainly issue a general condemnation of the slave trade, but it would not prohibit it and draw up rules for enforcing the prohibition. These matters it left to individual states to arrange by a system of bilateral treaties. Britain found it difficult to persuade other countries to make these treaties, and when they were made they contained such loopholes that it was easy for slavers to carry on their business without infringing them. There was too much profit in the trade for Wilberforce's idealism to find much support among Spanish, Portuguese and American business interests.

Consequently, the Navy did not have to deal merely with a few desperadoes who were willing to risk defying their own country's laws. It had to deal with big business: with large firms owning fleets of vessels and secretly condoned by their own governments. To cope with slave-running on this scale the Navy would have needed scores of ships. But with the end of the war, the Navy, of course, was drastically cut down, and there were never enough ships available.

The problem was thus far larger than the abolitionists expected, and the Atlantic slave trade was not extinguished in a few years, as they hoped. First of all, the Foreign Office had to persuade foreign countries to enter into treaties prohibiting the slave trade and empowering British naval officers to arrest the slavers. Then, when the defects in the treaties became plain, the Foreign Office had to go to work again to secure supplementary treaties. This process, along with the incessant work of the Royal Navy, gradually weeded out the law-abiding and the faint-hearted. It left in the business the tough and desperate men, those who were prepared to fight their way through the naval patrol. It took thirty years to reach this stage.

In the 'forties, the naval squadron was strengthened, and some other countries were persuaded to co-operate by sending naval squadrons of their own. At the same time, the Navy decided that blockading ports and intercepting ships would never be completely effective; the only way of stopping the trade entirely was to cut off the supply of slaves. In the 'forties and 'fifties the Navy did this, both by destroying the stores where the slaves were kept to await shipment, and also by making treaties with the African chiefs. 'We will pay you,' said the Navy, 'a regular salary as long as you allow no foreign slave dealers to operate in your country. If you do allow them, not only shall we stop your salary, but we shall see to it that you receive no goods from Europe, and if you gather any slaves for sale, we shall come ashore and release them.' It was 1860 before this network of treaties was reasonably complete.

Meanwhile, at the other end of the sea lanes, the Navy

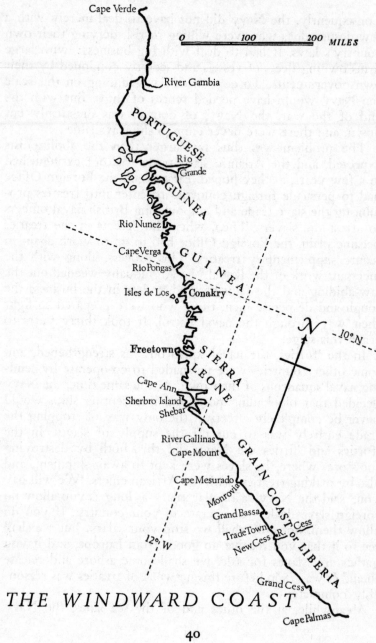

Cape Verde

River Gambia

SCALE: 0 — 100 — 200 MILES

PORTUGUESE

Rio
Grande

GUINEA

Rio Nunez

GUINEA

Cape Verga

Rio Pongas

Isles de Los Conakry

N

10° N

Freetown

SIERRA

LEONE

Cape Ann

Sherbro Island

Shebar

River Gallinas

Cape Mount

GRAIN COAST or LIBERIA

Cape Mesurado

Monrovia

Grand Bassa

12° W

Trade Town

New Cess R. Cess

Grand Cess

Cape Palmas

THE WINDWARD COAST

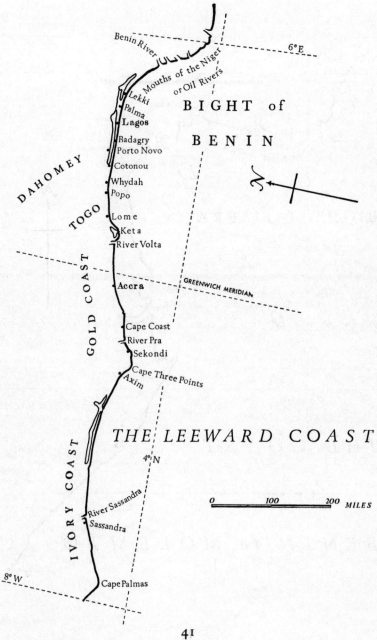

Benin River

Mouths of the Niger
or Oil Rivers

6° E

BIGHT of

BENIN

Lekki
Palma
Lagos
Badagry
Porto Novo
Cotonou
Whydah
Popo

DAHOMEY

TOGO

Lome
Keta
River Volta

GOLD COAST

Accra

GREENWICH MERIDIAN

Cape Coast
River Pra
Sekondi
Cape Three Points
Axim

THE LEEWARD COAST

4° N

0   100   200 MILES

IVORY COAST

River Sassandra
Sassandra

8° W

Cape Palmas

41

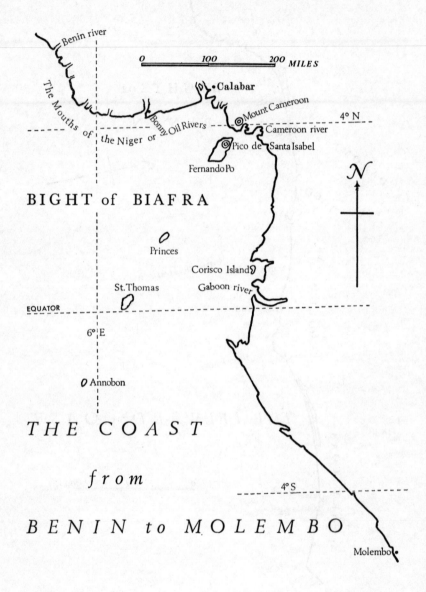

Benin river

0   100   200 MILES

•Calabar

The Mouths of the Niger or Bonny Oil Rivers

Mount Cameroon

4° N

Cameroon river

Pico de Santa Isabel

Fernando Po

BIGHT of BIAFRA

Princes

Corisco Island

St. Thomas

Gaboon river

EQUATOR

6° E

Annobon

THE COAST

from

4° S

BENIN to MOLEMBO

Molembo •

42

had taken energetic action in the 'fifties to close one of the three main transatlantic markets, Brazil. The second market, Cuba, was closed at length by the Spanish authorities there. The third, the United States, was closed by President Lincoln's emancipation of the slaves in 1862. It took nearly sixty years to abolish the Atlantic slave trade: sixty years of Foreign Office diplomacy and sixty years of incessant patrolling and fighting by the Navy.

The Abolition Act was passed in 1807, and next year, as a sort of trial run, the Admiralty sent the frigate *Solebay* and the sloop *Derwent* to cast an eye along the West African coast. But there could be no question of immediately stationing a permanent squadron on the coast to give effect to the Act. The country was still at war, and the Navy was fully stretched in the double task of protecting British commerce and of blockading the enemy ports. After a year or two the pressure eased somewhat. In 1809 Lisbon became available as a naval base, and the next year we captured Mauritius and Réunion in the Indian Ocean, nests of French commerce-raiders throughout the eighteenth century and a constant thorn in the flesh of the Honourable East India Company. In 1811 the Admiralty felt able to spare a squadron of five ships for an anti-slavery patrol on the West African coast. But next year the American war broke out, and again the Navy was fully stretched. It was not until the end of the war that Their Lordships found themselves with vessels to spare, and were able to establish a permanent West African anti-slavery squadron.

'*Admiralty Office,*
Whitehall

'You are hereby required and directed to put to sea, in the ship you command, as soon as she shall in all respects be ready to sail, and proceed without delay to the coast of Africa, for the purpose of visiting the several British forts and settlements on that coast and rendering them such assistance and protection as you may find them to require.

You are to repair in the first instance to Sierra Leone. . . . In proceeding down the coast you are diligently to look into

43

the several bays and creeks on the same between Cape de Verd and Benguela, particularly on the Gold Coast, Whydah, the Bight of Benin, and Angola, in order to your seizing such ships or vessels as may be liable thereto, under the authority of the several Acts of Parliament prohibiting the slave trade (abstracts or copies of which we herewith inclose for your information and guidance); and you are to use every other means in your power to prevent a continuance of the traffic in slaves and to give full effect to the Acts of Parliament in question.

With regard to the conduct to be observed towards the Portuguese ships and settlements, we send you herewith copies of two treaties between this country and Portugal, signed at Vienna on the 21st and 22nd of January 1815, and we hereby strictly require and direct you to govern yourself according to the instructions and stipulations contained therein. . . .

Given under our hands the 20th March 1816

J. S. Yorke

Geo. Haye

B. P. Blackford

BY ORDER *J. W. Croker*

Sir James Lucas Yeo, KCB,
Captain of His Majesty's ship
the *Inconstant*'

In these days of speedy communications, when Accra and Lagos are only a few hours by air from London, we need to make the effort to imagine the time-scale on which the Navy had to work 150 years ago. The sloop HMS *Bann* seems to have been a vessel of average speed. She left Spithead on Friday, December 8, 1815, under orders for West Africa. She called at Funchal in Madeira exactly a week later, on the 15th, and after a stay of only a few hours set sail for Freetown. On Saturday, December 30th, she was abreast of Cape Verde, and on Tuesday, January 9th, she arrived at Freetown. She was on the coast for four months, and then returned home, as most ships did in those days, via the West Indies; she left Sierra

Leone on May 1st and arrived at Barbados on May 28th, stayed there ten days, and then, leaving Barbados on June 8th, arrived at Spithead on July 4th. We may take it then that the three sides of this triangular voyage were roughly equal at a month each; but of course much would depend on the weather.

Their new orders set the naval officers on the Guinea coast a three-fold problem. First, they had to keep moving up and down the coast, providing a steady patrol along the whole length of their beat. Second, they had to find and catch the slave ships. Third, having caught a slave ship, they had to get it condemned by the court. Each aspect of the problem contained its own difficulties.

The orders we have quoted fixed the limits of the coast to be patrolled as Cape Verde and Benguela, that is, from 12 degrees north to 15 degrees south. In practice, the Navy seems to have ignored the northern and southern extremities of this long beat, and concentrated its attention on the stretch from the Isles de Los, off Conakry in the modern republic of Guinea, to the island of St Thomas off the mouth of the Gaboon river. This stretch of coast ran from about nine degrees north to the equator. It was well over 2,000 miles long, roughly equivalent to the British coast from John o'Groats through the Straits of Dover and up to the Clyde, or the Atlantic coast of the United States round the tip of Florida as far as New Orleans. There were good reasons for this concentration. The coast from Cape Verde to the Isles de Los was by no means one of the chief centres of the slave trade. Such trade as there was in this region was almost entirely in French hands, and France would not allow her ships to be touched. At the southern end of the coast, the Benguela region was one of the main sources of slaves. But Benguela was a Portuguese colony, and for many years, all the slavery treaties with Portugal reserved the right of Portuguese dealers to trade in slaves from territory south of the equator, especially from Portuguese territory. The Navy had to acquiesce in this part of the trade, so why bother to patrol the coast? There was quite enough work on the Guinea coast, where slave ships of half a dozen nations were jostling each other at the anchorages to secure their share of the precious cargo.

The two thousand miles of coastline patrolled by the Navy can be divided into four sections. The extreme north end, from the islands as far as Cape Mesurado, is a drowned coast like Chesapeake Bay or south Cornwall, cut up into long shallow winding inlets, with many branches. From Cape Mesurado to Lagos there is a sandy beach backed by low wooded cliffs, with little shelter for ships except in the river mouths and an occasional lagoon. Then comes the Niger delta, with hundreds of miles of creeks and lagoons, screened by islands and mangrove swamps so as to provide ideal hiding places. Beyond the delta there is another smooth coastline broken only by river estuaries.

The Navy's first problem was to show the flag regularly along the coast. A modern liner (and West African liners are not transatlantic flyers) takes only three or four days between Lagos and Freetown in either direction, with intermediate stops. But it was a very different matter in the days of sail. The journey is entirely within the tropics. Except for the short stretch north of Freetown, the whole of the Navy's beat lies for the most of the year within the belt of tropical calms. Sailing breezes are scarce, and the prevailing wind, when there is a wind, is westerly or south-westerly. Moreover, as unwary bathers on the shore find today, there is a current, sometimes quite a strong one, setting from west to east. Consequently, it is much easier for a sailing ship to sail from the islands eastward to the Gaboon than to return. The Portuguese were the first European sea-captains to burst into this silent sea. They were so impressed by this that for a time they made effective use of it to discourage foreign competition: they spread the exaggerated rumour that it was quite impossible for any ordinary vessel to beat its way out of the great gulf and sail home to Europe. But the difficulty was a real one throughout the days of sail. A ship could easily drop down from Freetown to Lagos in ten days or a fortnight; but in 1812, for example, Captain Lloyd in the sloop *Kangaroo* took more than five weeks, from April 7th to May 16th, to make a non-stop return passage against wind and current from Whydah (slightly short of Lagos) to Freetown. It was much easier if one was able to return to Freetown direct from St Thomas island, keeping well out to sea. On this voyage of 1,300 miles a ship picked up the south-east trade wind, and the trip could be done in ten days. But there was no chance of catching any slave ships on this route.

A ship's captain always feels happier on the high seas than in coastal waters. But the Navy found that close inshore patrolling was a much more effective way of throttling the slave trade than making wide sweeps on the sea lanes. This sort of patrol kept the Navy captains constantly creeping along an imperfectly charted coast, investigating estuaries whose mouths were blocked by sand bars, looking into swampy creeks and lagoons which might or might not contain slave ships but which were certainly full of fever. They had strict orders not to let their men spend a night ashore, for the night air was supposed to be deadly. No one then suspected that malaria was carried by mosquito bite. Keen young officers in command of a cutting-out expedition often kept their boats up the river till well after dark, so that their men got well bitten by mosquitos on the way downstream. There was a great deal of this river work. Slave ships gave a very wide berth to ports where there was a regular European settlement with law and order well enforced. They preferred the lonely creek, well screened from the open sea, with African villages which were under no European authority. It was here that the Navy must come to search for them, taking all precautions against spears and poisoned arrows, as well as against European musketry and gunfire.

This laborious creek-searching went on until the very end of the campaign. Here is an example from as late as 1852. Cdr Sotheby of HMS *Sealark* received information that a Spanish slave ship was lurking somewhere in the Rio Grande in Portuguese Guinea. He visited the river on March 4th and called on the local chief, who said, No, there was no Spanish slave ship in his river, nor did he deal in slaves. There was, indeed, a Spanish trader living there; but he traded in groundnuts and had no ship of his own; he sold his produce to other ships. Sotheby saw this man, Tadeo Vidul, and inspected his store, which seemed to have nothing suspicious about it. Still, the information that Sotheby had received was definite enough to keep his suspicions alive; and when he found that Tadeo Vidul had an alias, Juan Pons, he felt sure that he was on the track of something.

However, there seemed nothing to be gained by scratching any more at this particular hole, so Sotheby withdrew, and spent the next two days in making a thorough search of no fewer than eighteen other creeks. He found nothing. On the 7th he revisited the main river, and offered a reward of a hundred dollars for further information. This brought forward an African who undertook to show him the very ship he was seeking; and under his guidance, Sotheby's boat went further upstream and turned into a narrow side creek. Sure enough, there she was; for better concealment her masts had been taken out, and she was completely screened by the mangroves. Sotheby went on board; she was fully equipped for slaving, but there was no sign of her crew. She had evidently been lying there for some considerable time, and when Sotheby tried to warp her out of the creek, he found he could not move her. So he blew her up, and thus her voyage came to an end.

It was clear now that the chief and Tadeo Vidul, or whatever his name was, had been lying. Sotheby's African informant gave good value for his money; he showed him something else: a hut, which he said belonged to the chief, and which contained some loaded muskets and some slave shackles. Presently a man came out of the bush and joined the party. He said he was a slave; he and twenty others had been taken and held in captivity to await sale to the Spaniards. He had escaped, but the others were still being kept at the chief's town, which was three miles away in the bush.

This was good enough. Sotheby went back to his ship, and wrote a short letter to the chief demanding to have these slaves handed over to him. 'If they are not brought down tomorrow,' he added, 'I will burn your town.'

48

On the 9th, the twenty slaves were brought down to the beach; and Sotheby went to have another talk with Tadeo Vidul alias Pons. But he was not at home, and his store had been burnt down since Sotheby's earlier visit. Sotheby poked about among the ashes, and found several more slave shackles; and in the bush close by he found a ship's compass and a ship's carpenter's tool-chest. He felt more and more desirous of meeting Señor Vidul, and he went up to the chief's town to find him. Before he reached the town, he was met by a party of men bringing with them Vidul and another Spaniard as prisoners. The chief had decided the game was up; and he now admitted that he had sold all the slaves to Vidul, who was the supercargo of the Spanish slave ship. The rest of the crew were away visiting other neighbouring creeks to negotiate further purchases of slaves. Sotheby asked the twenty men who had enslaved them? They gave him the names of three local chiefs, every one of whom had signed a treaty abjuring the slave trade for ever. The slaves were taken to Freetown for liberation, and the Spaniards for trial.

This was small-scale, hole-and-corner stuff: nothing to compare with the big business carried on by Spanish or American firms who loaded seven or eight hundred slaves at a time into their specially built Baltimore clippers. But this routine policing of holes and corners had to be carried on all through the lifetime of the West African squadron. 'You are diligently to look into the several bays and creeks': these orders of 1816 remained valid for fifty years.

We need hardly emphasize the physical discomfort of the West African station. Its steamy heat can be very trying today. It must have been terrible in the cramped and ill-ventilated lower decks of a wooden frigate, on a diet of salt beef and pork, dried peas and weevily biscuit. The large glossy brown West African cockroaches seem to find breeding places even in a modern concrete house; they must have swarmed in the ships' mess decks.

A great part of the work was routine patrolling, with little excitement to enliven it. When we read of chases and actions, we must always set this part of the story against the long days

D

and weeks of strenuous inaction. For days on end the ship cruises without seeing a strange sail, and one day is much like another. The men on duty are sweating with the work of constantly trimming the sails to catch the shifting light airs. When taking his midday observation, the navigating lieutenant has the sun almost directly overhead. There is no shade; the white decks are dazzling and the guns scorching hot to the touch, and it is a welcome relief to all when the sails begin to cast their lengthening afternoon shadows. The calm sea is a soft blue, and the lazy ripple at the ship's bow sends now and again a shoal of flying-fish skittering away over the smooth surface. A few miles away the coast is slowly – so slowly – sliding past: a low line of greenery bordered by the glitter of the white surf, which the Atlantic swell throws up even on the calmest day. All on board are longing for a break in the monotony: for a real sailing breeze, or a squall of rain to cool the hot decks, or a school of dolphins to escort the ship, leaping and playing around her for an hour or so. Better still would be a strange vessel to challenge or a new bay or creek to explore, even though everyone knows that the new creek will be exactly like all the others.

Before we consider the Navy's problems of catching slave ships and getting them condemned, let us look at one routine cruise as an example. It comes from the early days, when these two problems were simpler than they afterwards became.

Captain Irby of HMS *Amelia* left his base at Freetown just after Christmas 1811. On December 31st he fell in with the Portuguese brig *Sao Joao*; she was loaded with slaves, and he sent her into Freetown for adjudication. On January 4th he stopped another Portuguese brig, the *Bom Caminho*. She had no slaves on board, but she had recently called at Cape Coast and had bought two canoes from the British authorities there. Why did she want canoes if she did not intend to go slaving? It was suspicious,[1] but there was no other evidence against her, so he let her go. But next day he wrote to the British Governor at Cape Coast, Edward White, to tell him that when boarding the *Bom Caminho*, he had found that

[1] Why? See page 120.

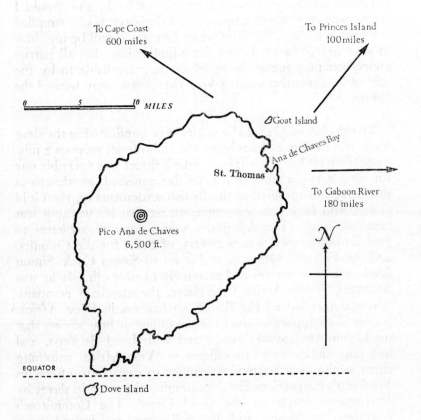

To Cape Coast
600 miles

To Princes Island
100 miles

0   5   10   MILES

⊘Goat Island

Ana de Chaves Bay

St. Thomas

To Gaboon River
180 miles

Pico Ana de Chaves
6,500 ft.

N

EQUATOR

◯Dove Island

St. THOMAS ISLAND
(SAÕ TOMÉ)

'she has been supplied with two canoes from Cape Coast Castle for the express purpose of carrying on the slave trade. From the orders I am acting under, I have deemed it indispensably necessary to send these canoes back; and should I again meet any vessel employed in the slave trade, supplied with canoes from a British fort or factory, it will be my duty to send her to Sierra Leone for adjudication, that all parties concerned may incur the penalties they are liable to by the Act of Parliament passed 14 May 1811, commonly termed the Felony Act.'

By this Act of 1811, to be in any way implicated in the slave trade was no longer merely a technical offence or even a misdemeanour; it became a felony. Irby's threat was a terrible one for such a respectable, and even distinguished, gentleman as the Governor-in-chief of the British settlements on the Gold Coast. And Irby had ways of ensuring that his warning was taken seriously. The Admiralty sent a copy of his letter to Earl Bathurst, who was Secretary of State for the Colonies, and the Colonial Office passed it on to Simon Cock. Simon Cock was an important and extremely capable official: he was Secretary of the Africa Committee, the merchant company which controlled all the British settlements in West Africa. Simon Cock replied to the Colonial Office in July, saying that his Committee entirely concurred with Lord Bathurst, and had sent directions to its officers in West Africa 'enjoining them in the most particular manner to carry into effect his Lordship's instructions for discouraging the trade in slaves by Portuguese vessels on the Gold Coast'. The Committee's directions to White and his colleagues are indeed most peremptory. If they have the slightest suspicion that a vessel may be intending to carry on the slave trade, they are to supply it with no canoes and with no provisions of any kind, not even water. And if the Governor hears of any of his officers or colleagues being at all slack or indulgent in this matter, he is to report the case at once to the Committee in London, 'in order that measures may be adopted to prevent a recurrence of proceedings so contrary to law and to the repeated orders of the Committee'. Very plain and definite indeed.

Having issued this blunt warning to Mr White, Irby went on to Whydah, and arrived there on January 5th. There were three Portuguese brigs in Whydah roads, openly trading for slaves; but he could not touch them, for there was a regular Portuguese trading post at Whydah, and as matters then stood, Portuguese ships were entitled to buy slaves at their own ports, but nowhere else. Two days later, at Porto Novo, Captain Irby had better luck. Here there were three more Portuguese brigs; they were all buying slaves, and there was no Portuguese post at Porto Novo, so all three were sent off to Freetown.

At Porto Novo, the *Amelia* was joined by the brig HMS *Protector*. She brought the news that there were no fewer than six ships lying at Lagos; so thither the *Amelia* and the *Protector* went hopefully; surely among six ships there must be one or two guilty ones! They arrived at Lagos on January 10th, and found three of the ships with nearly a full cargo of slaves, so they were duly sent off to Freetown. The other three ships were empty, and 'in a very sickly state', says Irby; so he confined himself to warning them that they were not to load slaves at Lagos or any other non-Portuguese port, or they would find themselves in trouble.

From Lagos, Captain Irby went on to the eastward limit of his beat, the Portuguese island of St Thomas. This part of his cruise was quite fruitless, though he had been told that there were no fewer than forty-five slave ships loading cargoes for Brazil, scattered along the stretch of coast from Cape Palmas to Calabar. Had he found a Portuguese ship loading slaves at St Thomas itself, he could not have interfered with her; but he might have been lucky enough to find slaves being ferried across from the mainland to make up her cargo. But he found nothing at all, so he returned to Freetown, arriving on February 21st. Nearly two months of hard work, and a total of seven prizes, all taken on three days.

Before leaving Freetown in December, Irby had left orders for Captain Lloyd, of the sloop *Kangaroo*, to follow him and if possible to rendezvous at St Thomas, if not earlier. Lloyd had even less good fortune. He left Freetown on January 8th and arrived at Cape Coast on the 24th; he missed Irby there, and went straight on to St Thomas. Arriving at his rendezvous on February 16th, he found that the *Amelia* had already left for Freetown. This left him free to act on his own.

There was a Portuguese brig in harbour, with her hold empty. On February 21st, Lloyd had the first break in the monotony. The island of St Thomas is about thirty miles by twenty, and the *Kangaroo* was at anchor on the north-east side. The morning was cloudy and calm, and at seven o'clock, Lloyd saw a cutter in the offing under full sail. For an hour and a half, lying becalmed in the lee of the land, he watched her helplessly; then at 8.30 there came a westerly breeze, and the *Kangaroo* immediately weighed anchor and made sail in chase. In an hour, Lloyd had brought his ship within range, and at 9.40 he fired a gun ordering the cutter to heave to. Her only reply was to lower her square sail[1] and set a foresail, carrying all sail possible in the attempt to cross the *Kangaroo*'s bows and get to windward and into shoal water. At 9.50 Lloyd fired a second gun, but the cutter took no notice. So the chase continued for another half hour, the two vessels approaching one another at a fine angle on the same tack. At 10.10 they were within musket-shot; and Lloyd fired a musket at the cutter and also sent a round-shot to sing over her and plunge into the sea. Then at last the cutter admitted defeat and hove to. Lloyd sent the jolly-boat to board her. She proved to be a Portuguese vessel from Princes island, with sixty-three slaves on board. The master said she had loaded her slaves at Princes and was sailing direct to Brazil. This seemed to Lloyd an unlikely story. He suspected that she had loaded her slaves wherever convenient, and was bringing them to St Thomas to be transferred to the waiting brig. It was a doubtful case; but he took her crew prisoner, put his master's

---

[1] We do not think nowadays of cutters carrying a square sail, but this one did. No doubt, replacing the big square sail by a fore-and-aft sail would help her to sail closer to the wind and increase her chances of crossing the *Kangaroo*'s bows.

mate and ten men on board as a prize crew, and sent her into Freetown for adjudication.

From St Thomas, Lloyd went on to the Gaboon river, and when he arrived there on Friday, February 28th, he heard the welcome news that there was a brig in the river loading slaves. At 9.40 on a breezy squally morning, he made sail to cross the bar and enter the river. An hour later, the stern of the ship grounded on the tail of a sandbank, and she swung round on her heel. Luckily there was plenty of wind; Lloyd braced the yards full, and she cleared off. By 11.30 he was safely at anchor in thirty-eight feet of water. There was no sign of the slaver, and having grounded once, Lloyd dared not take his ship further up the river; so he ordered away the boats. The jolly-boat's crew had had their outing a week earlier, so this time it was the turn of the pinnace and the cutter. They went off in the afternoon, and Lloyd and the rest of his crew settled down to wait. On Saturday the men scrubbed hammocks and washed clothing, and during the morning they had the mild excitement of seeing a schooner come down the river and anchor near them with some of the *Kangaroo*'s men on board as a prize crew. It was not until 7.30 on Sunday morning that the pinnace and the cutter returned empty-handed, having seen and heard nothing of the slaving brig. 'I therefore presume,' says Lloyd, 'she must either have made her escape in the night or have concealed herself in some of the impenetrable creeks of the Gaboon.' The river mouth is several miles wide; a ship familiar with the river and its shoals might easily slip out past the *Kangaroo* under cover of darkness.

Another blank: the captain and a skeleton crew, only too thankful to have got the ship safely off the sandbank, rocking at anchor and wondering why the boats were so long away: the seamen sailing and rowing hour after hour, expecting at every bend in the river to find their prey awaiting them at anchor in the next reach.

Lloyd had now been at sea for fifty-two days, with only the one doubtful cutter from St Thomas to show for his cruise. He makes no further mention of the Gaboon schooner, so he must have let her go. He turned back towards his base at Freetown,

A CUTTER AND A BRIG. The brig has royals set above her topgallant sails.

and on March 28th he was off Cape Coast. Here he thought that at last he had found something. There was a schooner under sail, and when challenged she refused to heave to, but picked up her skirts and ran for it. Lloyd gleefully gave chase and overhauled her. She turned out to be a British privateer, very appropriately named the *Quiz*. She was a London ship, and her captain had a letter of marque from the Governor of Sierra Leone, authorizing him to hunt for slave ships. Lloyd was furious, especially as he had lost an anchor over her; he dropped his best bower anchor in thirty-five fathoms while his boat was away, and the cable parted. But there was nothing he could do; so, he says, 'I treated her with more lenity than her conduct otherwise merited.' I take this to mean that he told the skipper what he thought of him; and no doubt the skipper retorted with some views of his own about the Royal Navy.

Not only had the *Quiz* made a fool of him, but it was probable that she had skimmed the cream of the prizes on that part of the coast; so, although he managed to recover his lost anchor next morning, Captain Lloyd was not in a good temper as he put the *Kangaroo* about and made sail for Little Popo. But at Little Popo on April 4th he heard more promising news: there had been fighting at Whydah between some Portuguese vessels and a schooner showing British colours. So to Whydah he must go, and he arrived there the next morning, to find six Portuguese brigs at anchor. Lloyd sent his boats to board the nearest, the *Urania*. He found that the *Quiz* had stopped her a few days earlier and taken possession of her, putting five men on board as a prize crew. The ship's company had over-powered the five Englishmen and recaptured their ship; all five of them were still on board, one still in irons and the other four only just released from their irons. The *Urania*'s crew had taken to their boats and fled ashore when they saw the *Kangaroo*'s boats approaching; so Lloyd took possession of this ship, and then turned to examine the others. Four out of the five had no papers or log books. The crews said that a few days earlier a schooner had come into the roads under British colours, but presently hauled down her colours and hoisted the black flag. They fired at her and drove her off; but not, it seems, until she had taken possession of their papers. From their description, Lloyd had no doubt that the schooner was his recent acquaintance the *Quiz*. One of these brigs had 130 slaves on board, so Lloyd took this vessel and the *Urania* with him as prizes, leaving Whydah on April 7th and arriving back in Freetown without further incident on May 16th. No doubt if the Portuguese captain could prove that his slaves had been loaded at Whydah, which was a Portuguese port, the court at Freetown would release his ship. It was bad luck for him that he had no papers to prove it.

Captain Lloyd's cruise from Freetown to the Gaboon river and back had lasted more than four months. His prizes, if the court at Freetown confirmed his claim, would total one cutter and two brigs, with a total of just under 200 slaves.

These typical cruises of Irby and Lloyd were made in the early days of abolition. All ships from the continent of Europe, except those of our ally Portugal, were driven from the sea by the maritime war. Nearly all the British slavers had been frightened out of the trade by the Act of May 1811 which made slave-dealing a felony under English law. The United States Congress prohibited the import of slaves into America from the beginning of 1808, and within a short time there were no slavers flying the Stars and Stripes. In 1812 almost the whole trade was being carried on under the Portuguese flag. It was regulated by a treaty of 1810, under which Portugal abandoned any right to trade in slaves on the African coast except from ports 'within the African dominions of the Crown of Portugal'. But a special reservation was made of Portuguese rights in Whydah and the region of the Gold Coast; here Portugal no longer had any dominions, but she still had traditional commercial interests. Thus, in 1812 when Irby and Lloyd made these cruises, their problem was fairly simple. Any Portuguese slaver or suspected slaver was fair game, unless she was loading at a Portuguese port, in which case she was immune. Any British slaver – if there still were any – could be arrested. Ships of other countries were not to be touched; but in any case there would be very few of them.

The whole position was changed when peace came in 1815

and all kinds of foreign flags appeared once more. The problem of finding and catching the slave ships became much more difficult; and the problem of getting the prizes condemned became complicated with all the delays and frustrations of mixed tribunals.

Let us consider first the problem of catching the slave ships. The slave trade was still a very big thing indeed. It is reckoned that more than two million slaves had been delivered to the West Indian market alone between 1688 and 1789; and if we add to these figures the deliveries to Latin America and the United States, we can imagine the size of the trade and the number of ships engaged in it. In December 1816, after eight years of prohibition, the African Society of London told the Foreign Secretary, Lord Castlereagh, that according to its estimates, some 60,000 slaves were still being shipped from West Africa every year, though none of them under the British flag. The shipowners had some excuse for protesting that abolition would deal a severe blow to the whole shipping industry. It was as if the Government today were to prohibit the trade in oil, and throw the whole oil tanker fleet out of business.

Not only were slaves by far the most profitable commodity in the West African trade, but when it came to a matter of stowage in the ship's hold, they were by far the bulkiest cargo. This was particularly so before abolition. When the trade was lawful, the dealer could reckon that, save for the risks of the sea, he would bring every cargo safely to port; and it was worth his while to try and keep his slaves in good condition during the voyage. In later times, when the net was tightening on the trade, the dealer might expect to have many of his cargoes snapped up by a cruiser and lost altogether. The price of slaves rose accordingly; and the dealer then used all his cruel ingenuity to stow his living cargo as tightly as possible so that his profit on the successful voyage could compensate for his loss on the failures. In 1816, Captain Fisher in HMS *Bann* captured the Portuguese brig *San Antonio* of 120 tons. By the Portuguese regulations, a vessel of her size was not allowed to carry more than 300 slaves; the *San Antonio* carried 600. 'In a passage of eighty leagues', says the official report,

'more than thirty died, and as many more appeared irrecoverably gone; in the midst of the sick lay a putrid corpse, and such a horrid stench, that Captain Fisher was apprehensive of a plague, and was obliged to take not only the crew, but 150 slaves on board the *Bann*, and make the best of his way to Sierra Leone.'

In the same year, Captain Sir James Yeo of HMS *Inconstant* reports that he himself had taken a Portuguese ship whose master had made twenty-two successful voyages before being captured:

'The profits they make are enormous. One of the schooners captured by the *Inconstant* off the river Lagos, having arrived but a few days on the coast, had only purchased ten slaves, for which the master gave ninety-two rolls of tobacco, each roll worth in the Brazils 2,000 milreis, about twelve shillings sterling, making the cost of each slave to the Portuguese merchant £5 10s 0d, for which he would receive 400 dollars.'

When profits like these were to be had from an illicit trade, it is no wonder that all kinds of strong-arm men and unscrupulous adventurers moved into the business. The *Venus Havannera* loaded 530 slaves at Bonny in the Niger delta; 120 of them had died before she was captured. The *La Manuella* loaded 642 slaves, also at Bonny; 140 of them died. The *Gertrudes* lost 200 out of 600.

We may tend to assume that when a naval officer had brought his ship within gunshot of a slaver, he was fairly sure of his prey. It was so in 1812, but not for very long afterwards. The Navy faced a difficult problem even from the point of view of fighting. Soon after abolition, law-abiding ship-owners ceased to send their heavy unarmed ships to carry on the trade. But they were replaced by a very different class of vessel, and of man. Unscrupulous British and American owners began using fast and heavily armed vessels, many of them originally built as privateers in the Anglo-American war of 1812. They dispatched their ship to Teneriffe or Havana. There a nominal sale was effected. Ship and cargo became ostensibly Spanish property; a Spanish captain came on board, the real captain becoming nominally supercargo or even simply a passenger; the ship hoisted the Spanish flag and set out with impunity on her real business of slaving. These ships were beginning to sail in company, and they had orders to fight their way through whenever they could. They made enormous profits and paid their men enormous wages, £7 or £10 a month per man; and a large part of their crews was made up of tough and determined British or American seamen. In May 1817, Sir James Yeo reported on this new development. These Spanish ships, he says, carry about twenty guns and a crew of about eighty men, and usually have an 'active and enterprising commander. One large Spanish ship of twenty-six guns had called in at the British port of Cape Coast; 'the captain made most particular inquiries where the *Inconstant* (Yeo's ship) was to be found, adding that he had come to blow her out of the water.' This sort of service was no child's play. The anti-slavery squadron in July 1819 consisted of six vessels only: the sloops *Pheasant* of twenty-two guns, *Erne* and *Myrmidon* of twenty guns each, and *Morgiana* of eighteen guns, with the brigs *Thistle* of twelve guns and *Snapper* of nine. Yeo's successor in command of the station, Sir George Collier, wrote home in January 1820 begging for more ships, especially for brigs and schooners, for they had the best chances of taking the slavers by surprise. As usual, when peace had come, the cry at home was for economy and disarmament.

Slavery, as Burke said, was a weed that grew in every soil, and in theory, every mile of the long West African coast-line might provide slaves for export. But 300 years of experience had taught the slave dealers that in practice, some stretches of coast were more profitable than others. It was better business to go direct to the places where slaves could be had in shiploads than to gather them in twos and threes all

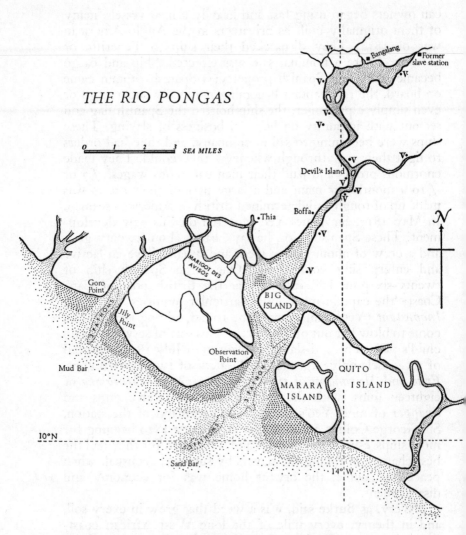

THE RIO PONGAS

0   1   2   3   **SEA MILES**

Bangalang

Former
slave station

Devil's Island

Thia

Boffa

MARIGOT DES
AVISOS

Goro
Point

Jily
Point

BIG
ISLAND

Observation
Point

Mud Bar

QUITO
ISLAND

MARARA
ISLAND

10°N

Sand Bar

14°W

N

NOTES ON THE RIO PONGAS

This labyrinth of creeks, islands and mudbanks makes it understandable that
Curtis, Ormond and their friends should feel themselves pretty safe. The
heavily shaded areas are mudbanks which dry out at low tide. The water
areas enclosed by a dotted line are pools over three fathoms deep, three
fathoms being the depth which a sloop could manage and in which a brig

62

along the coast. There were three such places. One was the Gold Coast (the modern Ghana), where the inland kingdom of Ashanti had set up in business as a large-scale purveyor of slaves. The second was the coast of modern Togo and Dahomey, long named the Slave Coast, where slaves were available from the great markets of the king of Dahomey. The third such place was the Niger delta, which was fed with a steady supply of slaves from the wars between the Yoruba and the Egba. In fact, the slave trade, like any other trade, flourished most where powerful enterpreneurs moved in to control it.

This tendency to concentrate the trade along three special sections of the coast helped the Navy. If these main sources of supply could be blocked, the back of the business would be broken. The Gold Coast was not difficult to manage, for it was thickly set with British, Dutch and Danish castles. But constant attention was given to Whydah and Porto Novo, and to Lagos and other villages in the Nigerian creeks.

---

would feel comfortable. Much of the main river, near Boffa and above Devil's Island, also has three fathoms of water. The river appears to have two mouths; but the west mouth, between Goro and Jily Points, is deceptive. It has good anchorages, but is connected with the main river only by narrow creeks. One of these however, the creek named Marigot des Avisos, has three fathoms of water throughout, so that a ship could be warped or towed through it. That is why the *Tartar* and the *Thistle* had to separate, one blocking each estuary. The Yangouya creek on the east is impassable.

Ormond's town of Bangalang is still there, and nearby is a 'former slave station', his or another's. So far we are on safe ground. But when we try to fit the Curtis affair to the map, we are reduced to conjecture, for the despatches mention no villages by name. Villages are marked V on the map. Where was Inman's landing-stage, and where was Curtis's battery of guns? The village of Thia is described as a 'king's residence' and has a landing-stage, which seems the nearest mainland landing-place to the sea. The channel up the river passes to the west of Big Island, which is hilly and commands the river mouth. If I wished to protect myself from interference by meddlesome naval men, it is on Big Island that I would plant my guns. There is another landing-stage higher up the river at Boffa, and here the shore is higher and suitable for a battery position. But with a favourable tide, the two brigs could have reached Boffa and covered the landing with their gunfire, which it is clear from the story they were not able to do. Big Island seems the likeliest place, with Proctor's ship lying in the pool below, so that Inman's boat would pass it on the way up to Thia.

THE 'THISTLE'S' BOAT, 1820

We have seen that after 1815, powerful entrepreneurs were moving into the slaving business in Europe and America, and they needed to have their contacts or agents on the Coast. The officials there, the employees of the British, Dutch and Danish companies who held the castles, sometimes grumbled at losing the most lucrative part of their trade; but they could not afford to risk a charge of felony.

But some of the free merchants on the coast were less disposed to submit. It was easy enough to settle in some remote place, well away from the company's officials and out of gunshot of His Majesty's sloops. It meant coming to terms with the local chiefs, and of course there was always the risk of having a cargo snapped up by a British ship. But what of that? The fewer the slaves, the higher the price they would fetch, and the loss of a few cargoes might make little difference to a dealer's profits.

Lieutenant Robert Hagan, in command of His Majesty's brig *Thistle,* had dealings with one of these obstinate and enterprising men. We shall hear more of Lieutenant Hagan. He entered the Navy in 1807 and spent his first six years on Captain Sir George Collier's frigate *Surveillante.* He came to West Africa in 1815 as an acting lieutenant in command of an armed brig belonging to the Sierra Leone Government, and was confirmed in his rank next year. He commanded the *Thistle* on the West African station from 1819 to 1823, capturing forty slave ships and freeing 4,000 slaves. But he had to wait until 1843 for his captaincy.

In May 1820, Hagan touched at the Isles de Los, and a British merchant there named Proctor complained to him that shortly before, a ship of his had been piratically seized in the Rio Pongas by a man named Curtis. This man Curtis was a mulatto, born near Boston, Massachusetts, in 1774: that is to say, when Massachusetts was a British colony. Being a British subject by birth, he came to Sierra Leone about 1815, and took the oath of allegiance, thus confirming his British nationality. Lieutenant Hagan and Proctor both knew the Rio Pongas

well. They agreed that the people there were friendly and
well-behaved, and there were some respectable traders living
there, both white and mulatto. The *Thistle* went straight to
the mouth of the river, and Hagan sent a midshipman, Robert
Inman, with a boat's crew to deliver a letter to Curtis, calling
on him to restore Proctor's ship. The boat pulled steadily upstream to the landing-place. Nobody was in sight; but without
warning, the boat suddenly came under musketry fire from
men hidden in the mangrove bushes. Inman and several of the
men were killed, some were wounded; and the boat, with the
wounded and four unwounded seamen, was captured. Hagan
was helpless. He dared not attempt to take his brig over the
bar into the river without a pilot. There was nothing to be
gained by firing cannon-balls at random into the bush against
an unseen enemy. Luckily, he was not far from Freetown;
the best thing to do was to crowd on all sail and report to the
authorities there.

The commodore on the station was Hagan's old Captain,
Sir George Collier. He was away, and the senior naval officer
in port was Captain Leeke of HMS *Myrmidon*. Leeke was only
four years senior in the service to Hagan, but six years senior
as a lieutenant. He was promoted Captain to command the
Myrmidon in 1819; he commanded her on the West African
station for three years, during which he surveyed 600 miles
of coast. He shot far ahead of Hagan; he rose to command a
first-rate, and was knighted in 1835.

Hagan made his report, and Leeke went at once to the
Governor, Lt-Col Charles MacCarthy. Things had come to
a pretty pass when a pirate and slave dealer dared to insult the
Royal Navy in this way. There was only one thing to do:
they must send a strong expedition as quickly as possible to
rescue the prisoners and teach Curtis a lesson. The Governor
felt a little uneasy at taking large-scale action while the commodore was away; but Leeke was prepared to take the responsibility, and the Governor agreed that speed was essential.
Leeke organized a squadron of four ships, the sloops
Myrmidon and *Morgiana*, and the brigs *Thistle* and *Snapper*.
The Governor provided a military force of 'four officers and

about 150 bayonets' from the 2nd West India regiment, under the command of Captain Chisholm, and Leeke placed his marines under Chisholm's command. Chisholm's orders from the Governor impressed on him that in such an amphibious expedition it was essential that he and Leeke should work well together. The landing would be covered by gunfire from the ships; on no account must Chisholm allow his men to indulge in random musketry fire from the boats, though if the enemy showed himself, he might allow a few picked marksmen to do some sniping. Once ashore, the troops must advance with all military precautions, covering themselves with a line of skirmishers. The object of the expedition was to recover the prisoners and to take Curtis. There was to be no plundering of African villages; but if chiefs and people showed themselves hostile, the troops might burn the houses and take some senior chiefs prisoner.

Chisholm and the troops embarked on May 10th, and just at that moment the commodore sailed in. The Governor's anxiety was relieved; the commodore entirely approved of Leeke's arrangements, and the expedition sailed on the morning of the 12th.

On the 15th, the squadron arrived off the mouth of the Rio Pongas. The two sloops could not cross the bar; but all the troops were transferred to the two brigs, and they passed a crowded and uncomfortable night anchored outside the bar, awaiting the morning tide and daylight. At dawn on the 16th the brigs entered the river – the tide must have been higher than when the Thistle had been there ten days before—and the two commanders, not risking another naval boat, sent in a native canoe with a letter. The letter, addressed in the first place to a British trader named Wilson, invited the merchants and the African chiefs to come on board the brigs, under the promise of a safe conduct, 'for the purpose of bringing to a speedy conclusion the misunderstanding between His Majesty the King of Great Britain, and the persons concerned in the late atrocious attack upon the boat of HM brig *Thistle*'.

No one came. In the course of the day a canoe came from the shore with a letter from a certain John Ormond, living at a village called Bangalang. He wrote that he dared not leave his house; for he had the four unwounded naval seamen under his protection, and if he left them alone, Curtis would grab them. He enclosed a copy of the menacing letter that Curtis had written to him, demanding that he hand the men over. 'I have no animosity,' he ended, 'against the British Government, and do assure you that there is no person or persons in my quarters that is ill disposed towards you. . . . The four men that is now under my protection is at your command whenever you please. Remain, Gentlemen, Yours friendly, John Ormond.'

The two commanders were not sure what to make of this letter. Wilson they knew, but there was no reply from him; Ormond they did not know, and his letter might be a trap. They decided to wait until next morning for a reply from Wilson. No reply came, and they decided to go into action.

In the cool of the morning the troops got into the boats. Leeke brought the two brigs as near Curtis's village as he could, and armed the boats with carronades to cover the landing of the soldiers and marines. He wanted to go with the landing party himself, but he found that Curtis had built a mud fort on a hill, and had armed it with several big guns to command the landing-place; so Leeke decided that he must forego the pleasure of joining the landing party, and must stay on board to direct the ships' gunfire against the fort.

The boats moved in under the white flag, hoping that such a strong force would overawe Curtis and his allies, and the matter might be settled without fighting. Curtis too hoisted a white flag on his fort; but 'the signal and our forbearance were totally disregarded'. The moment the boats reached the landing, they came under heavy musketry fire from men posted in the mangroves, and under gunfire from the fort. The troops returned the fire and jumped ashore, the enemy retiring to a stockade built in front of the village. While the ships' guns thundered against the fort, the troops attacked the stockade and dislodged the enemy; whereupon the enemy abandoned both fort and village and retired into the bush. Chisholm more than once invited them to palaver, but no reply came;

so he had the stockade and the houses burnt, and the seamen dismounted the guns from Curtis's fort and took them off in triumph to the ships. Again Chisholm hoped for a palaver, but no one appeared; so he destroyed a few neighbouring hamlets and returned to the ships for the night. There was no sense in keeping the men on shore without shelter, and risking a night action in the bush against superior forces, with the certainty of casualties from fever.

This action took place on May 17th. That evening, Wilson the merchant came on board, and told Leeke and Chisholm that there was a powerful chief called Mungo Braima living about four miles beyond the villages they had already burnt. It was he, rather than Curtis, who was mainly responsible for the attack on the *Thistle*'s boat, and the surviving British seamen were in his town. Leeke and Chisholm determined to land again next morning and march to Mungo Braima's town to demand these men. They did so; but they had an unpleasant day. They had no guides for the forest paths, and had to depend on what directions Wilson had given them. It poured with rain all day, and for several hours they were lost in the bush, unable to find the town they were aiming at. Eventually they did find it, and met with some resistance from what Chisholm took to be a light rearguard screen depending on a much stronger body of troops deeper in the forest. Again, no one appeared to palaver with them; so they fired the town, destroying a good deal of merchandise, most of it (as Chisholm reports with satisfaction) belonging to Curtis. As before, they returned to the ships for the night; and shortly after they got back, a canoe came off to them from the shore bringing two wounded men who had been in the *Thistle*'s boat. These men had been released by a sub-chief named Yando Conny, and they brought the good news that the enemy were ready to hand over the remaining four men also. So early on the morning of the 19th, Leeke sent a boat for them, and brought all four safely on board.

The expedition set sail for Freetown on the 19th, and reached port on the 23rd. They had rescued the prisoners, but they had had not retaken Proctor's ship; nor had they captured 'that infamous villain Curtis', though they had burnt some of his property and brought away his big guns. The casualties were light: two men wounded and one corporal dead 'of excessive fatigue'. Chisholm and Leeke would have been much happier if they had been able to bring Curtis to Freetown for trial. But at any rate they had shown Mungo Braima and his people that it was dangerous to give Curtis and his like too much open support.

It would have been more satisfying if Leeke and Hagan had been able to round off the operation by capturing Curtis and bringing him to Freetown to stand his trial. And as we read the story we perhaps feel it to be somewhat one-sided. What happened to Proctor's ship, which Curtis was said to have seized? Had Curtis in fact seized it? What impelled Curtis to the desperate act of opening fire on the *Thistle*'s boat, which he must have known would bring serious trouble on his river? There is no record that Curtis ever showed himself in Freetown again, and all we know of his fate is that the African chiefs on the riverside turned on him and drove him out.

But Curtis was not without friends, and some of them later made representations on his behalf. According to them, Proctor owed Curtis a large sum of money and showed no disposition to pay his debt. Curtis admitted seizing Proctor's ship, but he did so only with the intention of holding her as security for the unpaid debt, and with no idea of keeping her. What else could he do? The Isles de Los and the Rio Pongas were under no European control, and Curtis had no means of enforcing his claim by any legal process.

Curtis moreover contested Hagan's account of what happened on that unhappy day in the river. According to him, the midshipman Inman was a hot-tempered man, and Curtis admitted that he himself was another. Inman's orders were simply to deliver Hagan's letter. But on his way up the river, Inman saw Proctor's ship lying at anchor, and he decided to take possession of her before delivering his letter. Curtis at once lost his temper, and he told Inman to leave his property alone and to get back to the *Thistle*; he would receive no letter

from Hagan. Inman stubbornly insisted that his orders were to
deliver the letter, and he was going to deliver it; whereupon
Curtis in a fury ordered his men to open fire. His friends
added that Curtis was very sorry for the loss of life, but Inman
had really provoked him beyond endurance.

This story, as far as we know, was never tested in the courts.
It is not on the face of it improbable, and Leeke was inclined
to think there might be something in it. He told the commodore that if an inquiry were to be held, Mr Inman's conduct
might perhaps be held reprehensible. But Inman was dead, the
expedition was over, and no inquiry was held. Even if Curtis's
story of the provocation he had received were entirely accepted it would not justify him in levying open war against the
King.

We have said that Leeke and Chisholm did not know John
Ormond of Bangalang. He was unknown in the sense that they
did not know how far he was to be trusted. But he was far
from being obscure. John Ormond's father was an Englishman, a slave dealer from Liverpool, who settled on the Rio
Pongas and married a wife from the family of an important
African chief there. John Ormond was the son of this mar-
riage. In that tribe, as in many other African tribes, inheritance
passes through the mother, and John Ormond inherited a good
deal of his mother's family influence and position. Three
months before this expedition, Sir George Collier in the *Tartar*
had visited the Rio Pongas, taking Lieutenant Hagan and the
Thistle with him. On this occasion they knew that there were
two slave ships in the river; so the *Tartar* stayed outside the
channel in the sand bar to block that as an escape route, while
the *Thistle* sailed in across the mud bar, ten miles further
north, to cover the attack by the boats of both ships. The boats
captured a Spanish schooner and a Dutch brig, both partly
loaded with slaves; and then they went up the river, says
Collier, 'as high up as Bangalang, where the celebrated
Ormond has his town and factory'. Ormond in fact was a slave
dealer in a big way of business; but unlike the Curtises, he
knew when to be bold and when to lie low. He had no intention of standing up against the Royal Navy; but it did not

necessarily follow that he would mourn if the Navy came to grief through other people.

The Rio Pongas was a wide shallow estuary, something like the estuaries at Falmouth and Plymouth on a large scale. It had many side creeks fed by moderate-sized streams. As it happens, we have a description of the place from an unnamed civilian who visited it two years later and reported on his visit to the Governor of Freetown. He says that the first settlement he came to after entering the river belonged to a man named William Lawrence, who admitted that he used to be a slave dealer but had given up the business, finding it more and more unprofitable and dangerous. Going up-stream from Lawrence's place, the visitor passed two or three ruined factories or warehouses.

'One of these had belonged to a gentleman of the medical profession, who made a considerable fortune by the slave trade and by his professional services to slave traders. He is now living in affluence in one of the foreign West India islands.'

Another of these 'factories' had belonged to Curtis and his brothers; but after Chisholm and Leeke had made themselves so objectionable, the other African chiefs had made all the Curtises leave the district and go much higher up the river.

Ormond's place at Bangalang was in its way very impressive. It was poorly sited; the water was shallow, and at low tide it was surrounded with vast mud banks and mangrove swamps. But it was very large, and was entirely surrounded with a very high wall. At regular intervals there were towers, two stories high, each mounting two brass guns; there were thirty-three guns in all. But the visitor thought these defences intended for use only against the loyal village people or against turbulent slaves, who did sometimes break into disorder while being stored in the sheds to await disposal. Mr Ormond gently lamented the decay of the times. He said it was really not worth while buying slaves at the moment, for since the recent naval expeditions, the traders at Havana were becoming quite shy of sending their ships into his river. What was the good of buying slaves and keeping them in the sheds for weeks or months before you could hope to sell them? If matters improved, he would certainly start dealing in slaves once more.

Seven miles higher up the river was the establishment of one Mr Lightburn, who greeted the visitor genially: 'Well, Sir, you are here among slave traders; so you may make yourself easy.' But he went on to explain that as far as he was concerned, the good old days were gone; he had quite given up the trade. He was confining himself to gold, ivory, horses and cattle, and

A SCHOONER. This is a staysail schooner; she carries two staysails between her masts. Some schooners replaced the staysails by a leg-of-mutton sail carried on the foremast, as shown in the drawing of the topsail schooner on page 142; see also page 237.

was thinking of starting a coffee plantation (in fact, he did import a big consignment of coffee bushes the following year). Both Ormond and Lightburn were reported to have enormous establishments of their own slaves engaged in running their farms and offices and houses: five to six thousand each, people said, but the visitor thought the figure exaggerated.

Away on the other side of Freetown there was another large-scale slave dealer named John Ouseley Kearney, who lived on the Gallinas river and carried on his trade openly under the British flag. Governor MacCarthy badly wanted to lay hands on him. 'I have employed some trusty persons,' he says,

'in order to apprehend if possible the ruffian Kearney, and should I succeed, I will send him for trial to England. I cannot but regret that a commission is not established here for the trial of such British subjects as are found in slave vessels or may hereafter be taken in the adjoining rivers. I am sorry to say that I have the most positive evidence that three British subjects were actively engaged in that manner very lately in the Rio Pongas, two in the Rio Nunez, and J. O. Kearney in the Gallinas.'

The Government responded to this hint, and sent the Governor a commission authorizing him to try pirates and similar offenders. Piracy and slave dealing were often combined; in 1820 the United States made a law equating the two professions, and in 1824 a similar law was passed in Britain.

The proprietors of these establishments, conscious that they were beginning to be called ruffian and villain by Governors and naval commanders in the world outside their rivers, saw nothing ruffianly in their business. It had been regarded as respectable for 300 years, and the supply of slaves and the demand for them were still almost as high as ever. Why should they give up their lucrative business for the sake of this modern sentimentalism? Of course, it would not do to think too much about conditions on the slave ships; but then, factory owners in England – many of them pious churchgoers and supporters of Wilberforce in his abolition campaign – turned a blind eye to the conditions in which women and little children toiled in their factories and in the

coal mines. The slave dealers aspired to live the life of aristo-
cratic Southern planters on their huge estates with their huge
slave households. They lacked, it is true, some of the refine-
ments. The visitor to the Rio Pongas was disappointed to find
that none of his hosts could offer him wine to drink; they all
drank rum and water. When Mr Lightburn invited him to
make himself easy among the slave traders, he 'considered this
somewhat extraordinary', but he did make himself easy –
Lightburn no doubt watching him quizzically. It reads comic-
ally like the embarrassment of an active member of the League
Against Cruel Sports at finding himself invited to dine with
the Master of the local hunt.

Even Mr Kearney further down the coast appears quite
human when interviewed. One naval commander captured a
Spanish schooner and sent her into the Gallinas river to get
information. Two of his petty officers went ashore and met
Kearney. Nothing was more natural than for a Spanish slave
ship to have a partly British crew, so Kearney had no suspicion
of them. They inquired whether he could let them have any
slaves. He said, No, not just at the moment; he must have a
little notice. He had just put 150 slaves on board a French
schooner and for the moment was out of stock. He reckoned
himself the biggest slave dealer on that part of the coast; almost
every slave exported between Cape Ann and the Gallinas river
passed through his hands. Not that he bought them all himself;
he had an African buying agent working for him. He had a
little schooner in the river, and he took the two men on board.
'I buy nothing but slaves,' he said. 'My object is to make a
little more money, and then I'll embark 300 or 400 slaves on
board a large schooner I have (not this one) and go in her
myself to the Havannah.' Meanwhile, he had agents in Sierra
Leone who let him know all the movements of the naval patrol
ships, and he passed the warnings on to all his friends. But he
and his skipper shook their heads sadly. Things were getting
difficult, they said; there was this new ship on the coast, the
Myrmidon, which had scared all the slave captains by her
turn of speed. The skipper added, with a strong Irish brogue,
'By Jasus, the *Myrmidon* gave the slaves a breakfast one morn-

ing, and returned the evening of the next day to give them a ball and a supper.' The two petty officers asked Kearney whether he was not afraid of the risk he ran in this business? Not a bit, he said; no one ever suspected him, for he had a commission from the Governor of Sierra Leone authorizing him to seize anyone whom he found carrying on the slave trade! (In this matter, however, Mr Kearney's intelligence service in Freetown was imperfectly informed; the Governor there knew all about him.)

He makes it sound almost respectable: the successful merchant laying plans for his retirement in Havana. He called himself Captain Kearney. He had in fact been a subaltern in the New South Wales regiment, and exchanged from that into the Royal African Corps. In 1814 he resigned his commission and went to Senegal. Three years later he returned to Freetown and took a Government job; and when he was discharged from that he went to the Gallinas river to make his fortune by slave dealing, which he seemed to be in a fair way of doing. But fear, or shame – what was there to be afraid or ashamed of?

Chapter Four

FOREIGN GOVERNMENTS
AND FOREIGN LAWYERS

Safe, as they hoped, within their rivers, the Ormonds and the Kearneys kept on their business of buying and selling slaves, although no vessel flying the British flag came any longer to trade with them. There was point in Mr Hughan's rhetorical question in Parliament: 'The proposed Act only abolishes the British slave trade. Will the French, the Dutch, the Spaniards, the Portuguese or the Americans abandon it?' The slave trade continued merrily under foreign flags, and the Navy could not set slaves free from foreign ships without raising the sensitive question of the freedom of the seas. If the trade was to be stopped, it was essential that other nations should agree to co-operate by prohibiting the trade to their own people and by allowing their ships to be searched. It became one of the main objects of British foreign policy to negotiate treaties to this effect with other nations. As Foreign Secretary, Lord Castlereagh was tireless in keeping up the pressure on this subject; so was Canning after him.

As early as 1792, fifteen years before Wilberforce's victory, Denmark had passed a law prohibiting the slave trade; it was to come into effect in 1802. The United States made the trade illegal from the beginning of 1808, and sent a small naval squadron to enforce the prohibition. In 1821 Sir George Collier reports with satisfaction the happy co-operation between the British and American squadrons:

'America has enacted very severe laws against her subjects convicted of being engaged in the slave trade. . . . The

76

American officers in command of the vessels of war employed by their Government have on all occasions acted with the greatest zeal in the object; and it is extremely gratifying to me to observe that the most perfect unanimity prevailed between the officers of His Majesty's squadron and those of the American vessels of war engaged in the same view.'

The American law of 1818 went so far as to require an American skipper accused of slaving to prove his innocence, instead of requiring the captor to prove him guilty; in 1820 slaving was made equivalent to piracy and punishable by death.

This close co-operation however did not last very long. The American naval squadron was withdrawn after a few years, and in spite of the Federal prohibition, the slave-owning States were active in smuggling slaves into their territory. British and American ideas of the freedom of the seas were always at variance. Britain held that the seas must be free only to those using them on their lawful occasions; the United States held that its flag protected all its citizens from foreign interference in all circumstances. In spite of all British appeals, the United States Government would never allow British officers to board American vessels. On the African coast, this was not of great importance, for as a matter of prudence, American slavers usually sailed under French or Spanish colours. It was wiser not to make it too flagrantly obvious that the United States was responsible for such a large share of the slave trade. It would be much easier for that Government to maintain its attitude as long as it could decently maintain that American culprits were rare.

With some other countries it was an uphill battle. Portugal was the first country to enter into a treaty on the slave trade. As we have seen, the Anglo-Portuguese treaty of 1810 reserved to Portuguese vessels the right to load slaves at Portuguese ports, but not elsewhere. This meant that they could load in Portuguese Guinea, in the two islands of Princes and St. Thomas, in Angola and Mozambique, and at recognized Portuguese stations in the general region of the Gold

Coast; this last clause meant, for practical purposes, Whydah and nowhere else.

An arrangement of this sort was very difficult to administer, and in January 1815 Portugal made a concession which eased matters a good deal: she took the equator as a boundary line and exchanged her rights of slave dealing in her own ports north of the equator for an unrestricted right along the whole African coast south of it. Two years later she forbade Portuguese authorities to allow Spanish slavers to refit in Portuguese ports. A royal decree of 1813 laid down most salutary regulations to limit the inhumanity of the traffic. The number of slaves carried was to be limited: five slaves could be carried for every two tons of a ship's tonnage up to the first 201 tons, and thereafter, one extra slave per ton. Minimum rations were prescribed. Every slave ship was to carry a doctor. The captain and the doctor were each to receive a bonus if they brought their cargo to port with a mortality of not more than two per cent; if the mortality exceeded this, the bonus was halved; and if it was severe, the authorities were to hold a strict inquiry and punish them. These regulations were admirable, but they were systematically ignored.

Between 1813 and 1820, Britain succeeded in making treaties with Sweden, Denmark, Holland and Spain. Castlereagh tried to get the Congress of Vienna to include in the 1815 treaty a comprehensive set of regulations for suppressing the slave trade. But the Congress would go no further than a general statement that the slave trade was inhuman; all the Continental Governments declared that a series of bilateral treaties would be needed to work out the details of how to stop it.

Holland prohibited the slave trade completely in 1814. In 1817, Spain prohibited the trade north of the equator, and undertook to prohibit it south of the equator as well from May 1820. In a third Anglo-Portuguese treaty of 1817 however, Portugal insisted on retaining her right to trade in slaves south of the equator. The general lines of these treaties were that ships were not to be detained and sent for trial unless they were found with slaves actually on board; even the clearest evidence that the ship had previously carried slaves or was intending to take on a slave cargo was not to justify her capture. Mixed courts were set up to try ships accused of slaving; as far as West Africa was concerned, Anglo-Dutch, Anglo-Spanish and Anglo-Portuguese courts all sat at Free-town. Ships found guilty were confiscated and sold by auction; the proceeds were divided equally between the two Governments concerned, the Government whose Navy cap-tured the ship and the Government of the country to which the ship belonged. The slaves on board were set free in Sierra Leone. Similar courts were set up in Rio de Janeiro, Havana, and Surinam. Britain paid £300,000 to Portugal and £400,000 to Spain, nominally in compensation for ship-owners who might feel hardly used, really as an inducement to the Government to sign the treaty. Further large sums were paid from time to time to induce the two Governments to make further concessions and make the Navy's task easier.

With France, newly admitted to the comity of nations after the long wars, Castlereagh and Canning had no success whatever. The French Government readily admitted that the slave trade was inhuman, and passed a law declaring it a crime; but France did not take the step which Britain took in 1811, of attaching really heavy penalties to a breach of the law. Britain tried again and again to induce France to join in the system of reciprocal rights of search, and of mixed courts to try delinquents. The French Government replied with eloquent despatches. No nation, it said, could be more con-scious than the French of the rights of man and consequently of the inhumanity of a trade which violated those rights. The nobility of the British action in sacrificing the profits of such a trade was beyond all praise. Nothing could be fairer than the system which Britain proposed, that British warships should have the right to stop and search French vessels, and that in return French warships should have the right to stop and search British vessels. The assurance that any French vessel taken into Sierra Leone would be fairly tried by an Anglo-French tribunal ought to satisfy everyone that justice would be done. And yet, and yet. . . . Could anyone be sure that a tactless junior officer in command of a boarding party might not cause an international incident? Of all rights dear to the heart of man, the right of being tried by a judge of his own people was the dearest. Was it not likely that French and British commissioners, with different temperaments and different legal backgrounds, should find themselves often in disagreement? The British proposals were admirable in principle, but France saw the possibility of grave inconvenience occurring in practice; and so, with infinite regret. . . .

These streams of delightful French eloquence merely expressed the hard fact that in declaring the slave trade illegal, the French Government had run ahead of public opinion in France, and dared for the moment go no further. The Duke of Wellington, who was British Ambassador in Paris in 1822, put the case bluntly to Canning. The French Foreign Minister told him,

'that the French Government were sincerely anxious to put an end to this traffic; but that they could devise no measures to produce that effect which they could hope would be adopted; that the measure so often recommended to their attention by the British Ambassador to this Court – that of attaching a *peine infamante* to the conviction of this crime – would be inefficient, even if passed into a law. He said he could not conceal from me the fact that the abolition of the slave trade was unpopular in France; and he begged me to observe, that the existing law for the abolition of the slave trade was the only law that had ever passed the legislature without discussion.'

Presumably because all the members knew that it was merely an empty gesture. Canning's reply expresses his disappointment:

'As to France, I fear that so far from any advantage being likely to be obtained by the separate urgency of the British Government with that of His Most Christian Majesty, every fresh representation does but irritate and confirm the spirit of

III. THE 'NETUNO' BEATING OFF THE 'CAROLINA'

The action has not been long in progress. The *Carolina* is in the foreground, flying Spanish colours, and is about to haul up her jolly-boat at the stern. She is hove-to; her mainmast sails are in the light and her foremast sails in shadow, the yards at different angles. The *Netuno* is under sail, her trysail dangling useless from the foremast with its broken gaff.

IV. THE 'PRIMROSE' AND THE 'VELOZ PASAGERA'

The *Veloz* on the left is under full sail; the *Primrose* has shortened sail to hook on to her prey, and her men are boarding. The *Veloz* has put musketeers in her maintop to pick off the British officers. She is so much longer than the *Primrose* that her rearmost gun will not bear. The waterlogged boat in the foreground probably belongs to the *Veloz*, which has ropes trailing useless from her stern, and had six men drowned.

resistance, and tend to convert more and more a question of moral duty and political obligation into one of national pride.'

France in fact was determined not to be nagged at by Britain. She would abolish the slave trade in her own way and in her own time. For the moment, she must be left outside the system.

There was still plenty to do in getting the system to work. The French Government was but one of several which had outrun public opinion in decreeing the abolition of the slave trade. The mixed courts at Freetown were slow in getting started. Castlereagh appointed the British members promptly, but there were long delays in getting their Portuguese colleagues to join them. Remonstrances went from the British to the Portuguese Government. The Portuguese pleaded that it was very hard to find qualified men who were willing to serve in such a dreary occupation in such an unhealthy climate. The Dutch commissioners arrived to take up their posts in good time, but the British felt that some of them thought it their duty to protect the interests of the slave ship at all costs. One of the Dutch commissioners, Mr Van Sirtema, was so ingenious and assiduous in this that a protest was actually sent to The Hague.

One of Mr Van Sirtema's exploits concerned the Dutch vessel *Eliza*, which was taken in October 1819 off the Grain Coast, the modern Liberia, by HMS *Thistle*. When the crew of the *Eliza* saw the *Thistle*'s boats approaching, they hastily unloaded all the slaves they had on board and took them ashore. They relied of course on the clause of the treaty which provided that a ship was not to be detained unless slaves were actually found on board; and they thought themselves safe. But they had somehow overlooked one man; and when the British boarding party entered the ship, there was this one slave still on board. Lieutenant Hagan, having seen with his own eyes that the ship was carrying slaves, and having watched all the slaves, bar one, being rowed ashore in the boats, very naturally arrested the *Eliza* and sent her to Freetown for adjudication.

He had reckoned without Mr Van Sirtema. Mr Van Sirtema refused to condemn the *Eliza*. He admitted the facts: he admitted that she had been carrying slaves, and was still carrying one slave at the time of her arrest. But, he said, there was nothing in the treaty which permitted the Navy to detain a ship which was carrying one slave only. The treaty-makers might have drafted the treaty to read, 'a slave or slaves'. But they did not; the treaty mentioned only 'slaves' in the plural. His conclusion was that a ship carrying one slave only could not be condemned under the treaty, and that the *Eliza* therefore had been unjustly detained.

A few months later, in January 1820, the *Myrmidon* detained a Portuguese vessel, the *San Salvador*. She had only one slave on board, and when the *Myrmidon* stopped her, this man was put in a boat and sent off to the shore. But the *Myrmidon's* boats were quick enough to intercept this boat; and the man was examined, and swore that he had been bought and put on board the *San Salvador* as a slave. But the Portuguese judge in the mixed court delivered a most learned judgment. Even if it were true, he said, that the man was a slave, the question remained whether carrying one slave was sufficient to condemn the vessel. Even if it were sufficient, was carrying one slave in the ship's boat the equivalent of carrying him in the ship herself? Even if this were held to be equivalent, it would not apply to the case of the *San Salvador*; for the man was not being taken ashore in the ship's own boat, but in a boat belonging to the slave-dealer, one Gomez, who had put him aboard and was now (for reasons the court was not called on to inquire into) taking him ashore again. So the court held that the *San Salvador* was wrongfully detained, and released her.

Other devices were tried. It was suggested that the mixed court ought not to sit if one of the judges was unable to attend. This seemed reasonable; but it was then noticed that foreign judges seemed more susceptible than British judges to fever and other indisposition. In 1821, the Spanish judge in Freetown went to Europe on indefinite leave for his health; and before going, he issued a formal protest against any proceedings being taken against Spanish vessels while he was away. So the Foreign Office got to work, and persuaded the other Governments that if one judge was unavoidably absent, the court might sit with one judge only instead of two. This decision was of great benefit to the health of the Spanish and Portuguese judges.

Spain was fertile in excuses. When she first signed a treaty, there was a special provision in favour of Spanish ships which were already at sea, and must be allowed a reasonable time, several months long, to dispose of cargoes which they had already loaded or contracted to load. But as May 1820 approached, the date from which Spaniards were to be prohibited from slaving in any part of the world, the Spanish Government tried to renew this plea of special hardship. Ships might have left port without realizing that their voyage would become illegal after May 30th; could not Britain order her naval captains to allow them another period of grace of nine months or a year?

Apart from the obvious flaw in the treaties whereby a ship must not be detained unless she had slaves actually on board at the time, the chief worry of the naval officers was in the procedure of the mixed courts. To the British judge, a case might be quite plain: he would condemn the ship. But his Dutch or Spanish colleague was not satisfied, and wanted further evidence; and to obtain this further evidence might delay the trial. The British judge felt it his duty to agree to this delay. But legally speaking, the plaintiff in the court was the naval officer who had taken the ship; and he did not want to hang around on shore awaiting the court's convenience; he wanted to put to sea again. Could he not be allowed to leave his case in the hands of a legal representative? The Dutch judges in particular would not hear of such a thing; the plaintiff must plead his case in person whenever called upon; and here again the British judges reluctantly concurred. This decision opened the way to an abuse of the court procedure. It was possible for a case to be so drawn out that the plaintiff, either through sheer impatience or in obedience to peremptory orders, could wait no longer and put out again to sea. Then, when he was well out of the way, the case might be resumed, and judgment given against him by default.

Sir George Collier complained of these difficulties to the Admiralty in more than one letter:

'It is only by great cunning (or great accident) that they can be surprised with slaves on board. In some instances, while the boats have been rowing to the slave vessel, the relanding of the slaves has been affected, and then paraded upon the beach, compelled to dance and make every sign of contempt for the boats' crews which the ignorance and brutality of the slave factors or masters could suggest.'

A month later, Collier writes of 'the difficulties and delays we meet with in the courts of the mixed commission'; he complains especially that a naval officer is not allowed to appoint a proctor to appear in his interests in the court, and yet if he loses the case, he is liable for severe costs.

THE CASE OF THE 'GAVIAO'

The case of the *Gaviao* illustrates these difficulties. The *Gaviao* was a Portuguese vessel, taken in the Calabar river by the boats of the *Thistle* and the *Tartar* on April 9, 1821. The master said that he had loaded a cargo of slaves at Benguela, which was south of the equator and therefore legal, and had sold them at Princes island. He admitted that he was now loading a fresh cargo at Calabar, which was illegal, and was bound for Brazil. When the boats were rowing to the *Gaviao* she had eight slaves on board, three of whom were newly bought at Calabar. By this time the boats reached the ship, two of these three had been put ashore, and the boarding party found the third still in the hold, where the Portuguese were hastily dressing him in jacket and trousers so that he could pass as a member of the crew. The man could not speak a word either of Portuguese or of the local African language, so the British concluded that he must come from further inland. They consulted one of the local chiefs, called Duke Ephraim. He said, Yes, this man was one of three whom he sold to the Portuguese. He had not yet been paid for them, but he had found the other two men wandering in the bush and had reclaimed them. If the British wanted this man they could have him, but he thought they should pay him the agreed price.

In this, it need hardly be said, Duke Ephraim was disappointed. But the evidence against the *Gaviao* seemed conclusive. Collier put a prize crew on board and sent her to Freetown for adjudication; her captain and officers went with her, and he took the crew on board the *Tartar*.

And then his troubles began. The *Tartar* reached port on June 5th, the *Gaviao* not till June 17th. Collier was under orders to sail for England, and could not wait for his prize; he filed his plea and asked the court to take evidence from his officers and himself, and from the *Gaviao*'s crew. The court refused: the case must wait until the *Gaviao* herself arrived and evidence was available from her officers as well. Collier's orders did not allow him to wait, so he sailed for England, leaving an agent named Walsh in charge of his interests. Walsh applied to be allowed to cross-question the witnesses, but this the court would not permit. Not until the case was complete was he allowed to see the depositions; and then, he says he found such a mass of perjury that there was nothing he could do to help his client. Nevertheless, Walsh was not uneasy, for the court ordered all the vessel's slaving gear (irons, cooking stoves, gratings and so forth) to be sold so that she could not resume slaving, and Walsh assumed from this that condemnation must follow as a matter of course. He was far from well, and was anxious to go on leave to the healthier climate of Gambia, and on June 29th he retired from the case and left. On July 5th the court gave judgment: it held that the case against the *Gaviao* was not proved, and released the ship to her owners. On July 10th, her master filed a claim for compensation; on August 14th, long after Collier had arrived in England, the court gave notice that it would hear the claim three days hence. Judgment was given against Collier by default, and he was condemned to pay the enormous sum of £1,520 13s 9d. On September 13th Walsh came back to Freetown, and was horrified at the news. He again applied to be allowed to study the proceedings and to enter a plea in mitigation of damages; but the court registrar was very short with him and refused.

All this was in respect of a vessel which was admittedly slaving north of the equator, in a place forbidden by treaty; the court even went to the length of compensating the owners for the cost of feeding their illegally acquired slaves. If the courts continued this practice of refusing to take evidence when available and of giving judgment by default when it was no longer available, the Navy's efforts would be quite frustrated. Students of the case of *Bardell v. Pickwick* will realize that even at Westminster, legal procedure was strict. It was likely to be still stricter where foreign judges trained in Roman law were sitting on the bench with their British colleagues.

With these procedural devices in the courts, and the proviso in the treaties that only the actual presence of slaves on board could justify a ship's detention, the slave-dealers were now in a position to drive a coach-and-four through the anti-slavery legislation. They made it a regular practice to claim that male slaves were free men hired as part of the crew, though this, of course, would carry credence only in small vessels carrying a dozen or so slaves. 'The contempt,' says Collier,

'in which the slave masters now hold the treaty is such as to induce them to boast of their evasions, and confess themselves waiting for the number of slaves they have agreed for; and in some instances they have carried this so far as to point out their live cargo upon the beach, waiting only the absence of the ship of war to load.'

The trade began to revive on a large scale. In July and August 1822, the *Myrmidon* examined sixteen slave ships, only one of them coming within the terms of the treaty. The *Pheasant* found six Portuguese slavers at Whydah and Badagry, all equipped with the fittings for a cargo of slaves; but none had slaves on board, and so none could be detained. On her next cruise, the *Myrmidon* found the port of Bonny swarming with

86

slave ships under different flags. Captain Leeke was told there
that in four months, 190 cargoes of slaves had been exported
from Bonny, and 162 from Calabar. If we take the low estimate of an average of 200 slaves to a cargo, this means a total
of over 70,000 slaves in four months from these two rivers
alone. Even on the windward coast, from Cape Verde down
to the Rio Pongas, the trade was beginning to revive; our
friend John Ormond was beginning to think that the good old
times were returning.

And, of course, ordinary lying was being used to cover up
breaches of the treaty. The *Morgiana* captured the Portuguese
slaver *Emilia*, with 396 slaves on board. When taken, she was
in three degrees north latitude, and the master said that he had
loaded his cargo at Cabinda, which is a Portuguese possession
nearly six degrees south of the line. If this were true, he would
be immune under the treaty. But was it true? The slaves themselves said that they had been on board only a day or two.
The British officer inspected the ship's water casks. They were
so nearly full that he was sure the ship could not possibly have
brought her slaves all the way from Cabinda, a voyage of forty
to fifty days. Moreover, all the slaves, both men and women,
had been branded on the breast with a hot iron. The
Morgiana's doctor looked at the burns, and said that they were
not more than a day or two old. Slaves were branded before
being loaded, not afterwards. Clearly the master of the *Emilia*
was lying; the slaves were (as they themselves said) newly
brought on board. Slave captains usually kept two logs: one
a genuine log for their owners and for navigational purposes,
the other faked to display to a British officer who boarded
them.

There were good reasons for branding slaves before loading,
not afterwards. To carry more slaves, the hold was fitted with
extra tiers, with only three feet of head-room; the slaves

'were all fettered in pairs, jammed (for so only can I speak
when I describe their situation) one within the feet of the
other. Fever, dysentery, and all the train of horrible diseases
common to the African climate (increased by filth so foul and

87

stench so offensive as not to be imagined) has attacked many of them.'

One common disease was a form of ophthalmia, very contagious, which caused temporary and sometimes permanent blindness. Sanitation there was none, and ophthalmia and the other diseases often spread from the slaves to the ship's crew. The man detailed to brand the slaves might in the course of his duty have been prepared to endure the filth, the stench, and the risk of contagion; but he could not possibly have moved about in the hold.

THE 'ROSALIA' AND THE 'DICHOSA ESTRELLA'

The path of the naval officer in the anti-slavery patrol was beset with legal pitfalls. Our enterprising friend Lieutenant Hagan of the *Thistle* fell into one in January 1822. It was still the law at that time that a vessel could not be condemned as a slaver, no matter how plainly she was equipped for slaving and how plainly she admitted her intention of slaving, no matter how notorious she might be in the trade, unless she was captured with slaves actually on board.

Hagan visited the Rio Pongas, and found the Spanish schooner *Rosalia* at anchor near John Ormond's establishment at Bangalang. He inspected her on January 7th, and found her empty; but he was told that Ormond had a cargo of sixty slaves all ready to put on board. Two days later, Hagan put a few of his men on board the *Rosalia*. They were invalids; he meant to go further up the river, and he thought they would be better left in the sea air near the river's mouth. He gave them strict instructions that they were not to interfere with the vessel in any way: 'Lieutenant Hagan told us,' said one of them later in evidence, 'that we were not to touch a single rope yarn belonging to her.'

Hagan then went off up the river. Ormond and the African chiefs hesitated to put the slaves on board; but something that Hagan had said – exactly what he said, we do not know – apparently led them to believe that they might safely do so.

On January 11th, Ormond marched all the sixty slaves out of his warehouse and tried to put them into one large canoe for ferrying out to the schooner. The canoe was overloaded; so Hagan, who had now returned from his expedition up the river, kindly helped him by providing one of the *Thistle*'s boats to take the surplus. All the slaves were put on board the *Rosalia*, whereupon Hagan boarded the vessel and put her under arrest.

When the case came before the mixed court at Freetown, the Spanish owners of the *Rosalia* put in no defence. The slaves, of course, were set free. But the court took an unfavourable view of Hagan's action. The *Rosalia* was plainly intending to break the law, but when Hagan put his men on board, she had not yet done so. Although he had told his invalids not to interfere in any way with the ship, as soon as they came on board, she was, the court held, to some extent under his control. By encouraging her to load her cargo two days later, and actually helping her by lending the use of one of his own boats, Hagan had in fact acted as an *agent provocateur*. Had the owners of the *Rosalia* put in a claim to have their vessel restored to them, the court would have granted it. As no such claim was made, the court condemned the vessel; she was to be sold, but the proceeds, instead of being shared between the British and Spanish Governments, were to be held in trust for the owners until they should claim the money.

The court sent home an abstract of the case with its judgment, and received a rebuke from Canning at the Foreign Office. He agreed that the *Rosalia* had been unjustly detained; that being so, he could not understand why the court had condemned her. Condemnation was for guilty ships; the *Rosalia* was, legally speaking, innocent. She should have been held and her owners notified so that they could come and claim her.

Poor Hagan fared much worse.

'Their Lordships have directed the officer commanding His Majesty's squadron on the coast of Africa to convey to Lieutenant Hagan their decided disapprobation of his conduct on the occasion alluded to; and to issue such instructions to the commanders of the naval vessels under his orders as may prevent the repetition of such a proceeding. And my Lords have stated the circumstances of the case to the Lords Commissioners of His Majesty's Treasury, with a suggestion, whether there are not means to prevent Lieutenant Hagan's enjoying any advantage by his irregularity.'

The Treasury is seldom at a loss to suggest means for saving public money. H.M. ships at that time were normally paid a bounty of £60 for every man slave they set free. We do not know what proportion of the *Rosalia's* sixty slaves were men. If the cargo was equally divided between men, women and children, she would have been worth £2,000 to Hagan and his crew; the Treasury simply said that they should have nothing. Hagan had jumped the gun; a year later, he would have been entitled to detain the *Rosalia* on proof that her cargo of slaves was awaiting her on shore. But in that case there would have been no head money : only a share of the proceeds when the vessel was condemned.

Two months after Lieutenant Hagan's arrest of the *Rosalia*, Captain Knight of the *Morgiana* arrested the Spanish schooner *Dichosa Estrella* off Trade Town in what is now Liberia. Like the *Rosalia*, she was empty when arrested. Like the *Rosalia*, she had a cargo of slaves awaiting her on shore. But Knight found clear evidence that the *Dichosa Estrella* had been cruising along the coast and picking up a few slaves here and there. The bulk of her cargo was waiting at Trade Town; and for her own convenience, she had put ashore the slaves she had already gathered, to be kept with the others until the vessel was ready to load her complete cargo and leave the coast. No doubt the master was thinking of the slaves' health; from that point of view, the shorter voyage, the better. Captain Knight arranged with the dealers ashore to load the ship; and like Hagan, he at once arrested her.

The court at Freetown drew a distinction between this case and the case of the *Rosalia*. It was proved that the *Dichosa Estrella* had already loaded slaves at various places, and some of the liberated slaves pointed out one member of the crew as the man who had been on shore and had bought them. Consequently, the court held, although all the slaves had been embarked on Captain Knight's requisition, many of them were being re-embarked on a vessel which had already embarked them once. Having held the *Rosalia* innocent, the court held the *Dichosa Estrella* guilty, and condemned her. But in this case, too, the Government in London held that Knight had exceeded his powers, and they withheld his bounty.

THE CASE OF THE 'AURORA'

Captain Grace, commanding the twenty-gun sloop *Cyrene*, also had his bounty withheld. His case seems a hard one. On October 23, 1822, he was just north of the Gallinas river, running down the coast with the south-westerly wind almost directly abeam on his starboard side. The general trend of the coast here is south-easterly, and a few miles ahead of him was the conspicuous promontory of Cape Mount. A little after noon he saw two schooners on his lee bow, between him and the shore. It looked as though he had them; for they were close inshore, and if they ran before him they had the difficult alternatives of crossing the bar into the Gallinas river, or keeping unpleasantly close to the reefs at the foot of Cape Mount. For five hours he chased them, and they ran straight ahead.

At 5.30 they separated; the more easterly of the two schooners, apparently feeling herself uncomfortably close to Cape Mount, put about and stood out across the *Cyrene*'s bows to gain more sea-room. Her consort held on her course. Half an hour later they were seven miles apart, with the *Cyrene* nearly midway between them. Grace had to choose which of the two to attack, and he chose the one which had stood across his bows; she was now about four miles ahead of him and slightly to windward. It was a cloudy afternoon, and it was getting dark; at 6.30 the schooner tacked again and crossed his bows for the second time, perhaps hoping to slip away in the darkness and get safely round Cape Mount. But she was now within range, and Grace fired some musket shots to bring her to. She gave up the attempt, and Grace took possession of her. She proved to be the Dutch vessel *Aurora* of 144 tons and four guns, coming from St Thomas; she was empty, but was clearly fitted for the slave trade.

This chase had lasted some thirty miles, and having secured the *Aurora*, the *Cyrene* put about and made sail again to the north-west in chase of her consort. Soon after midnight, Grace had brought her also within range, and after a warning shot she hove to and allowed the *Cyrene* to put a prize crew on board. She was the French schooner *Hypolite* of 95 tons and two guns; like the *Aurora*, she was empty, but clearly fitted for the slave trade. Both vessels had been on the coast for two months, and had cargoes of slaves awaiting them in the Gallinas river. Both captains and part of both crews were ashore there with the cargo.

Grace escorted his prizes to the Gallinas river and anchored there after dark on the 24th. At dawn on the 25th he sent his boats into the river to ask the principal African chief there, King Siaka, to release the slaves he was holding for the *Aurora* and the *Hypolite*. He ran no risks: the three boats, under the command of Lieutenant Courtenay, were 'armed and prepared for any event'. The boats crossed the bar through a tremendous surf; the cutter was struck by a sea and nearly filled, losing some of her gear and arms and ammunition. As soon as they entered the river, which was less than 200 yards wide, they were received with a heavy fire of musketry from the jungle banks. Luckily the fire, though heavy, was badly aimed; and the boats pushed on upstream until they came within sight of what was called Factory Island. Here they came under a severe raking fire from two long 18-pounder guns and an 8-inch howitzer on the island, protected by about a hundred men with muskets. The tide was ebbing and the navigation was most intricate; no fewer than seven times the boats grounded on shoals, always under a heavy fire of musketry and grape-shot. Courtenay and his men landed on the island, took the guns, and turned them against the enemy on the banks of the river, quickly silencing the fire for the time being. Then they turned their attention to another island, on which stood some houses and a big slave warehouse. Fire was being directed at them from this island, and they returned it; but while doing so they had the mortification of seeing the slaves being hustled out of the warehouse into canoes and taken up the river.

Lieutenant Courtenay and his men were in an uncomfortable situation. Their island was low and flat, with little shelter; their ammunition was running low; the tide was still ebbing. Courtenay decided to withdraw while there was still a chance of crossing the bar safely. He spiked the three enemy guns, set the warehouse and the other buildings alight, and went downstream, the enemy musketry being renewed on both banks of the river as he left. The bar was recrossed safely, and by 4.0 in the afternoon all three boats were again alongside the ship. One man, Alexander Crozier, had been mortally wounded, and three others slightly. The enemy had several killed, including four Europeans. There were eight or ten Europeans living on the Gallinas river (including our old friend Kearney), 'the dregs of France, Spain and America', says Captain Grace. In this action against the *Cyrene*'s boats they had been aided by the two masters, Benjamin Liebray of the *Aurora* and Louis Gallon of the *Hypolite*. Liebray had formerly commanded a corvette in the French navy; he had indeed come down in the world.

Next morning the body of Alexander Crozier was committed to the deep; and a few days later, Grace logged another unpleasant sequel to the action: three men were flogged 'for getting drunk when boarding a vessel at sea and getting their boat stove'.

Lieutenant Courtenay had been unsuccessful in his mission of holding a palaver with King Siaka; but a few days later, King Siaka sent a message to say that he had been away from the river at the time of the action. He put all the blame for the bloodshed on the two European ship captains, who had given his people rum and arms, and had told them not to let a single Englishman get away alive. He sent on board 43 men slaves, 21 women, and 116 boys and girls; these people were sent in the *Aurora* to Freetown and liberated there.

One would have thought that Lieutenant Courtenay and

his men had done their duty nobly and had earned the bounty. But Their Lordships in Whitehall did not agree. Capturing the battery and silencing the enemy's fire was all very well. But the bounty was not given for this sort of action; it was given for liberating slaves who were taken from a slave ship condemned in accordance with the treaties. The *Aurora* and her consort, like the *Rosalia*, had certainly been intending to slave, but they had not yet begun to slave. As the law then stood, Captain Grace had no right to detain them, and he could claim no bounty for slaves sent on board the *Aurora* at his own request.

THE CASE OF THE 'SYLPHE'

The *Aurora*'s consort was French, and British officers had to be very careful of interfering with French vessels. In February 1819, Captain Hunn of the sloop *Redwing* fell in with the French schooner *La Sylphe*, a little south of Freetown and two or three hundred miles out at sea. She was on her way from Bonny to Guadeloupe with a cargo of 368 slaves. He detained her, landed the slaves at Freetown, and sent the ship to Cape Town for adjudication.

This was just the sort of international incident that the French Government feared, The British ambassador in Paris had to apologize; the French Government graciously accepted his apology, and assured him that the captain of the *Sylphe* would certainly be tried when handed over to French jurisdiction. Meanwhile, Captain Hunn had to be offered up as a sacrifice. The Admiralty wrote to the Rear-Admiral at the Cape in the correct tone of pained surprise:

'I am commanded by Their Lordships to express to you their surprise that Captain Hunn should without orders and of his own authority have violated the flag of a friendly Power....'

The *Sylphe* must be handed over immediately to the nearest French authority, and meanwhile, Their Lordships are awaiting Captain Hunn's reasons for detaining the vessel at all, and

for sending her all the way to the Cape instead of to Freetown.
Captain Hunn explained. He had been told that there were
many piratical schooners in those waters. On February 9th at
1 a.m.,

'a sail was seen in the south-west, which was almost immediately tacked and made sail for H.M. sloop under my command,
as if with an intention to make her out; upon which I took in
topgallant sails and hauled up to meet him. In a very short time,
being broad moonlight, he made us out and hauled his wind,
which encouraged me to hope I had met one of those lawless
plunderers. Consequently I made every exertion to bring him
to, which he as earnestly wished apparently to avoid.

Towards daylight he hoisted a flag at his foretopgallant masthead which from the haze I could not make out distinctly but
took it for that of the American nation, and of which I have
now no doubt, having found the flag on board of him afterwards. Shortly after daylight, having hauled down the flag
from forward, he hoisted that of His Most Christian Majesty
at his main gaff, and shortened sail at 6.45 or thereabouts, the
colours and pendant of H.M. sloop under my command being
up during the whole chase. At 7.0 I sent on board a boat with a
commissioned officer to examine him, and if at all suspicious of
being the vessel I had hoped, he was to send the master with
his papers for my examination. On going on board, the officer
found the master with his crew, amounting to about 38 persons, with their clothes and bedding packed up, the master
surrendering the vessel and cargo; of which no further notice
was taken than by sending him and his papers on board this
vessel.

Upon examination of the latter I found he was a French
schooner cleared from Guadeloupe for St Thomas; but instead
of going to St Thomas he had been to Bonny and other places
of the continent of Africa, and had on board a cargo originally
of near 400 slaves, in direct violation of the *Ordonnance* of
His Most Christian Majesty, endorsed by the French authorities upon his *Rôle d'Equipage*, by which he was most strictly
and positively forbidden to take on board a native African

black, either as passenger or crew, upon any pretence whatever. . . .'

So Hunn took the vessel to Freetown, 'where I believed', he says, 'a French Commissioner was resident to take cognisance of this breach of the laws of their country'. But, of course, France had signed no treaty, and there was no Anglo-French mixed court at Freetown; so Hunn sent the *Sylphe* all the way to the Cape, where he felt sure there must be a French consul or other authority, if not indeed a mixed court. But why, we may ask, did he not send her into a French port in Senegal?

Hunn was certainly injudicious. If he had read his orders more carefully, he would have realized that he was authorized to detain vessels belonging to Britain, Denmark, Sweden, Holland, Spain, and Portugal: but not to the United States or France. He was censured by Their Lordships, and the *Sylphe* was handed over to the French authorities at the island of Bourbon in the Indian Ocean, the modern Réunion, this being the nearest French port to Cape Town.

These cases of the *Rosalia*, *Dichosa Estrella*, *Aurora*, and *Sylphe* all occurred at a period when a suspected vessel could not be convicted of slaving unless she was taken with slaves actually on board. (The *Sylphe* would have been fair game for Captain Hunn had she been Spanish or Dutch or Portuguese; it was bad luck that she was French.) This was a plain weakness in the anti-slavery treaties; another was that (according to the *Eliza* judgment) she must be carrying at least two slaves; one was insufficient for conviction. Castlereagh and Canning set themselves to negotiate the supplementary treaties needed to stop these loopholes. In September 1822, Spain agreed that a vessel might be condemned on proof that she had been carrying slaves, even if none were on board at the time of capture; Holland made the same concession on the last day of that year, and Portugal a few weeks later, in March 1823. Other countries would not accept this for many years; and there were horrible cases in which the captains of slave ships, finding themselves loaded with slaves and unable to escape from a

British cruiser, hastily jettisoned their living cargo, flinging the slaves, fetters and all, into the sea. The Navy could see it happening; sometimes the last slave splashed into the water only a few minutes before the naval officer came up over the ship's side. The skipper was able to laugh in his face. Yes, he had been carrying slaves; he would again be carrying slaves; but he was not just then carrying slaves, and so the Navy could not touch him.

Like every other kind of commerce, the slave trade depended on a delicate balancing of risks against profits. It is noticeable how much the trade fluctuated from time to time and from place to place. A daring naval raid, the condemnation of a big cargo, an extension of the treaties, and the word quickly went round. 'Too risky in the Rio Pongas; better go elsewhere Spanish colours not much protection; better hoist French. Nothing to be gained now by putting the slaves overboard when you are caught – unless you can prove you are Brazilian.' On the other hand, news encouraging to the slavers spread just as quickly. The slave ships left one pitch, but they went elsewhere; and naval officers reporting one stretch of the coast clear of the trade found that the trade had sprung up in full force in another.

But apart from these minor fluctuations, the main facts remained. The naval squadron was not strong enough to blockade the whole of the coast. As a rule (though there were exceptions to this) the slavers could outsail the warships. On the whole, Spanish and Portuguese judges showed little inclination to condemn slave ships. French and American ships could not be touched, and American skippers (often under Spanish colours) were among the most daring of slavers. A naval officer had to be very sure of his ground in capturing a slaver; the financial risks of failure in the mixed courts (as we have seen in the case of the *Gaviao*) were very heavy. What Commodore Sir Robert Mends wrote in 1822 remained largely true for many years afterwards:

'The traffic in slaves has not decreased; nor do I see how it can whilst it is supported by European protection in the most

G   97

open and avowed manner, and defended by force of arms. Were the British ships, employed on this coast for its suppression, allowed to act with freedom, it would in a short time be so cut up and harassed, as not to make it worth the risk, trouble and disappointment which would inevitably follow. But till then, we must submit to the mortification of seeing the anxious hopes of our country on this subject disappointed, and the efforts of the Navy rendered ineffectual.'

Chapter Five

FIGHTING AGAINST ODDS

Apart from the heat, the fever, and the strenuous monotony of handling a sailing ship in tropical light airs and calms, the men on the naval patrol had another hardship: trivial at first, but growing more severe as the weeks and months of the cruise wore by. This was the sameness of the landscape. Freetown itself, with its Lion Mountain, is vividly picturesque, and far away to the east there are the twin volcanoes of Mount Cameroon and Santa Isabel. But the 1,500-odd miles of coast in between are dull. There is plenty of attractive country in West Africa, but it does not show itself from the sea. The coast is generally flat, a ribbon of dull green scrub or forest, with no natural harbours and few conspicuous landmarks. There is Cape Mount, with its single bold hill; there is Cape Three Points, a flat platform with three little knolls on top – the very names show how thankful mariners were to find something they could recognize and tag with a name. One river mouth is much like another; most of them are muffled in mangroves. We, who pass so quickly, even in a sailing yacht, from Dover cliffs to Romney marsh, to the red sandy cliffs of Hastings, and back to chalk again at Beachy Head, find the enormous sameness of the West African coast oppressive.

The monotony deepens as one enters the mangrove creeks. Mangrove country is interesting to the naturalist, but twenty men rowing a ship's boat will see little animal and bird life. There are several species of mangrove, some of them mere bushes, others tall trees. They all prefer the brackish water where river meets sea. They grow in the soft alluvial mud, and they stride out into the water, casting down from above

99

aerial roots, each tipped with a pointed cap to strike deep into the mud and take up its duty. The water laps softly; and as the tide falls, scores of little semi-amphibious fish called mud-skippers lie out on the wet mud, looking rather like frogs. Each keeps his fishy tail in the water, and as the boat passes they hurry back into safety with a skip and a plop. From the military point of view, a mangrove swamp is ideal for defence. The innumerable trunks and roots make an impenetrable obstacle; nothing can be more slippery than the soft wet mud; a dark-skinned enemy on the bank is quite invisible to the men in the boat. One mangrove creek is just like any other. They are all formidable; one has the feeling of being constantly watched by hundreds of invisible eyes, and one longs to get clear, either on to solid ground or out to the open sea.

As Sir Robert Mends said, the Navy was working under great difficulties. Quite apart from the difficulty of getting their prizes condemned and the mortification of seeing slavers protected by flags which rendered them immune, the Navy had its own professional problems.

The West Africa station was not popular at the Admiralty; constant service in tropical waters was hard on the ships, and the crews suffered much from malaria and dysentery. From the point of view of the Admiralty officials, the maintenance of the anti-slavery patrol was a hard and expensive service, carried out at the request of the Foreign Office; on the other hand, the Foreign Office seemed unable to bring about the conditions (notably of course certain and speedy condemnation of captured slavers) which would enable the Navy to put a complete stop to the trade. There seemed no end to the operation, and there never would be an end until the Navy was given freedom to act, freedom which the Foreign Office seemed unable to give.

The facts of the trade were making it plain how right Wilberforce and his friends were when they said that merely prohibiting the slave trade would be insufficient; the status of slavery itself must be abolished. As Sir James Yeo had written as early as 1816:

'Neither mountains, rivers nor deserts will prove barriers to the slave trade, as the black chiefs will bring their slaves from every extremity of Africa as long as there is a nation that will afford them a slave market.'

As long as the New World needed slaves and was prepared to pay for them, as long as the Navy was hampered by shortage of ships and legal obstruction, so long would human cupidity ensure that the demand for slaves would be supplied.

The ships which the Admiralty provided were detailed from the general list of vessels in commission, built primarily for hard service in northern waters. Designers and builders were thinking mainly of the need for a ship to keep station in the winter blockade of Ushant, or to run with despatches from Gibraltar to Portsmouth through an Atlantic gale. Many of the slave ships, on the other hand, were specially built Baltimore clippers, designed for service in the light airs of the tropics. We have seen that the *Myrmidon* alarmed the coast by her unusual turn of speed; but normally, the naval ships on the West Coast must expect to find themselves outsailed by their quarry. The naval commanders met this problem in two ways: by intensifying the close inshore blockade, and by using surprise whenever they could.

Inshore patrolling came to mean more and more the use of boats in a cutting-out expedition: sometimes successful, sometimes not. In August 1821, Captain Kelly of HMS *Pheasant* had to report a failure. While running from the Gaboon to Corisco island, he saw a small schooner anchored close inshore. One of the *Pheasant*'s boats was taking soundings along the coast, and when she came near the schooner, a party of Africans fired on her. Captain Kelly at once stood in towards the shore, and sent the rest of his boats, under his first lieutenant, Lieutenant Jellicoe, with orders to bring the schooner off or to destroy her. Lieutenant Jellicoe found that the schooner was securely anchored to the beach by two anchors, so it would be a difficult business to bring her off. He tried to board her, but a large party of Africans rushed out of the bush and opened a heavy musketry fire, by which one seaman was killed and six wounded. Lieutenant Jellicoe himself was badly wounded in the throat, and decided that the attempt was hopeless; he withdrew under fire and returned to the ship. Captain Kelly determined to try what he could do with gunfire, and stood in towards the shore. The water was shallow, and having gone in as close as he dared he anchored in three fathoms, and even then was only within long range of the schooner. The tide was ebbing; he saw reefs appearing both ahead and astern of his ship, and he feared that she might ground as the tide fell. He fired at long range as long as he dared; and then he gave it up and stood out to sea again as the sun was setting.

In reporting this failure, Captain Kelly adds two recommendations which throw light on another problem. Lieutenant Jellicoe, he says, had already lost a hand in action some years before, but had received no compensation of any sort. Now he has a severe throat wound, which will certainly mean a long spell of hospital in England, and probably invaliding out of the service, his windpipe being damaged and the throat muscles partly shot away. Kelly hopes that the authorities will be able to pay him something for this disability.

One of the wounded seamen was a Kroo, a member of that solid and dependable race living on the coast of what is now Liberia. Even in those days, the Navy was enlisting them for short service; and today the first officer of a modern liner will tell you that he finds Kroo men better than Europeans at handling the ship's derricks. Captain Kelly suggests that if this Kroo seaman could be given some kind of a wound gratuity, it would make it easier to recruit his fellow-tribesmen for the naval service.

Naval pensions and prize-money were always a difficulty. By the Abolition Act of 1807, the officers and crew of a ship capturing a slaver were to share between them a bounty of £60 for every man slave set free, £30 for every woman, and £10 for every child. These rates were far too generous to be maintained indefinitely. No doubt it was assumed that in a few years the trade would be completely extinguished. In 1824 the bounty was cut to a flat rate of £10 a head, and in 1830 to £5; but in addition to this, the Crown ceded to the Navy men half its share of the proceeds of the condemned ship when sold – that is, one-quarter of the whole. But it was one thing to become entitled to bounties, another thing to receive the money. In practice, naval officers usually employed agents to act for them in the dreary business of besieging the Admiralty paymasters for payment of their dues; and the agents charged a heavy commission.

This short action by Captain Kelly was unsuccessful; but in that same year, Sir George Collier and Lieutenant Hagan had better luck. Theirs was one of the first actions in which the Navy was able to surprise the enemy. The *Tartar* and the *Thistle* were approaching the east entrance of the Bonny river, intending to explore it with the boats. The *Tartar* was a large frigate of forty-two guns; her tall masts would be as conspicuous to the enemy as the tripod masts of Admiral Sturdee's battle-cruisers were to Admiral von Spee when he was approaching the Falkland Islands in 1914. Collier therefore kept the *Tartar* out of sight, and sent in the brig *Thistle* under Spanish colours. The *Thistle* entered the channel, and found a schooner at anchor; so Hagan signalled for the boats of the *Tartar*, and they were launched. Long before they reached him, a large canoe came alongside; she had just piloted the schooner down the river, and seeing the Spanish colours, asked Hagan if he was a Spanish slaver and wanted a pilot upstream to the anchorage.

This was the critical moment. With the best will in the world, Hagan could not act the part of a Spanish slave captain; the canoemen saw that something was wrong, and turned in alarm to push off. But Lieutenant Hagan, 'with that presence of mind and activity I have so long known him to possess', says Collier, jumped down into the canoe, followed by a sailor and one Kroo man, and swore that the canoe should stay where it was.

It was nearly sunset, and the *Tartar*'s boats had not yet come up, so Hagan determined to make use of the Bonny canoe. It was big enough to carry a good many extra men, so he put in her a boarding party of thirty men under the command of a midshipman, Charles Lyons, and told them to see what they could do. All this by-play must have taken a minute or two. Presumably the canoe had drawn up on the far side of the *Thistle* and was hidden from those on board the schooner.

Lyons and his men lay down flat in the bottom of the canoe so as to be hidden behind the canoemen as they sat paddling on the gunwale. Lyons gave the order to push off and to make for the schooner. The schooner's look-outs saw their pilot canoe, instead of piloting the incoming brig upstream, come paddling across the river back to them. They hailed it to ask what ship was that which had just come in? The canoe's headman, terrified at the menace of Lyons's pistol, shouted back what he had been told to say: that she was a Spanish slaver, and that there was a British ship a little outside the river, coming in for palm oil. The schooner's men were satisfied; they had been manning their guns, but they now left them, and the supercargo and his officers retired to the cabin for another drink; it seems they had already had several. Nothing more was said. A few more strokes of the paddles brought the canoe alongside the schooner, and Lyons and his men scrambled aboard. Then the schooner's crew realized what was happening, and the officers at once opened fire from the cabin; Lyons himself and two of his men were slightly wounded. The boarding party returned the fire and stormed the cabin. Amid the shouting and the firing, the Bonny canoemen took the opportunity of escaping; they fled up the river and warned all the other ships there of what was happening. Some of the women slaves in the schooner were so terrified that they leaped overboard. Whether they jumped in blind terror, or whether they hoped to be able to swim ashore, we do not know. None of them reached the shore; the sharks took them all.

The supercargo was in such a drunken fury that he had to be put in irons. He, like the master, says Collier, was 'American, English and Spanish by turns'. The captured vessel was the Spanish schooner *Anna Maria* of 172 tons, armed with six

18-pounders. She had over 450 slaves on board, and Collier sent her into Freetown for adjudication. She had already once been taken by the *Myrmidon*. On that occasion she was empty, and the court released her; she was refitted and took on a full cargo of slaves at the Gallinas river (no doubt supplied by 'Captain' Kearney), which she delivered safely at her home port of Havana. This time, however, the *Anna Maria*'s luck was out; on June 16th she was condemned by the court.

The capture of this schooner ended the action. All the ships further up the river were warned, and no doubt they made haste to put their slaves ashore, which at that time (March 1821) would make them safe under the treaties. The horrible episode of the sharks swarming round the *Anna Maria* and taking the unfortunate women as they leaped into the sea reminds us that this was a regular feature of the slave ships. Every few days some of the slaves would die and be flung overboard, and slave ships were regularly followed by expectant sharks, just as a ship nowadays is followed by gulls.

This smart little action took place in March 1821. It was followed by others in the same river in August and April. In August, Captain Leeke in the *Myrmidon* had a bright idea for springing a surprise on the slavers in the Bonny river. Instead of sending his boats up the Bonny river itself by the way that large ships used, he discovered a sort of back entrance called the Antony river, which was navigable by small boats and led directly to the anchorage off Bonny town. He spent the night anchored at sea off the entrance to this creek, and sent off Lieutenant Bingham and the boats next morning, as soon as it was light enough for them to see their way. At sunrise, Bingham's little flotilla suddenly emerged into the Bonny anchorage, and found six French vessels busily loading slaves. Bingham was not authorized to interfere with French vessels, but he boarded one of them to ask for information. The French captain told him that a little higher upstream there were two Spanish vessels, a brig and a schooner; both were fully loaded with slaves, and their crews were mutinous and had gone ashore.

If this news was true, it sounded most promising; and Bing-ham went with the gig and the pinnace to search the Spanish vessels, whose officers at any rate, he thought, must still be aboard. He fired a musket shot or two to make them hoist their colours. He seems also to have hoped that the noise would dis-suade the slaves from jumping overboard as the slaves from the *Anna Maria* had done; presumably he thought that the slaves would conclude that their liberation was near.

The Spaniards took no notice of the British shots. They allowed the boats to row close up, and when they were within pistol-shot they suddenly opened all their ports and began a heavy fire of musketry and of grape-shot. The first round of grape hit the stern-sheets of the gig. Bingham himself was knocked out by a shot which went through his chest and into his elbow; the midshipman, Deschamps, was severely wounded in the head, but remained conscious; two other men were wounded. Bingham appeared to be dying, so Deschamps took command and ordered a retirement. In spite of his wound he stayed at the tiller, and steered the boat down the river under heavy fire.

Leeke sent up reinforcements, and the boats returned to the attack. This time, in defiance of the enemy fire, they reached the vessels and tried to board. But the Spaniards were prepared for this. They had lashed hundreds of iron bars all round the bulwarks to form a sort of *chevaux de frise*, and had arranged a system of planks and tightly nailed awnings so that only one man could enter the vessel at a time. So for the second time the boats withdrew, and returned to the ship with the news of their failure.

When Leeke heard this, he felt there was only one thing to be done. Hazardous though it was, he must take his ship into the river without a pilot, as Lieutenant Hagan had wished but had not dared to do in the Rio Pongas. It was an operation that could not be hurried; fortunately, there was no need to hurry, for the Spaniards were bottled up in the river and dared not come out. He had two bars to cross. He sent his boats to take soundings; and when they had charted and buoyed the channel, he waited until weather, wind and tide were right and then put leadsmen in the chains[1] and felt his way in foot by foot. By sunset on August 31st, three whole weeks after Bingham's first unsuccessful attack, Leeke had the *Myrmidon* safely at anchor inside the river.

The Spaniards did not wait for him to come up the river and open fire. They all fled on shore, and the two captains sent him a joint letter, admitting that they had done wrong in firing on the *Myrmidon*'s boats, and begging him to be content with taking their ships as prizes, and not to insist on having them hanged for piracy. The Spanish brig was found to contain 154 slaves, the schooner 130; both were sent to Freetown, Lieutenant Bingham recovered from his wound, but had to go home to convalesce.

The two Spanish captains were justified in fearing for their lives. It was a weakness in the mixed court at that time that no criminal penalty was imposed on the owner or master of a vessel condemned for slaving. He lost his ship, it is true; but he was free to set up in business again as soon as he could find another. But piracy was a very different matter. To fire on a vessel doing her lawful duty was piracy, and to kill her men was murder. The end of that voyage was Execution Dock.

Piracy and slaving in fact often went together. Slave dealers often behaved like pirates in firing on peaceful vessels, as well as in using unnecessary force in resisting arrest. The Sierra Leone Government owned a few armed patrol vessels, largely manned by liberated slaves. The slaving brig *Camperdown* of sixteen guns destroyed two of these vessels and carried off their black crews into slavery afresh. In 1820, slave dealing was made equivalent to piracy in American law, and liable to the same penalty; a similar law was passed in Britain four years later.

The Bonny river continued to be a happy hunting ground for French and Spanish slavers, and in April 1822 the new commodore, Sir Robert Mends, visited it in his flagship the

---

[1] Leeke's narrative does not mention this detail of the leadsmen in the chains. But we may take it for granted that he would not hazard his ship by neglecting to take confirmatory soundings as she crept over the bar.

A BRIGANTINE. Compare this drawing with the plate of the brigantine *Netuno* in action. The *Netuno* carries one trysail; this vessel carries two.

Iphigenia, with the very experienced Captain Leeke and the *Myrmidon* in company.

Soon after sunrise on April 15th, the boats of both ships, under Lieutenant Mildmay of the *Iphigenia*, crossed the Bonny bar, and found seven ships at anchor in the river: two schooners, four brigs, and a brigantine. He hoisted his colours, and began his long row of four miles. The boats had some distance to go before they would be within range of the slavers' guns. As they pulled up the river wondering what reception they would receive, Mildmay saw the two schooners slowly turn so that instead of lying stern towards him, they lay across the river presenting their broadsides. They had anchored with springs on their cables in case they had to face an attack. This manoeuvre could have but one meaning; they meant to fight. The moment the boats came within range, the two schooners opened fire with their full broadside, not troubling to hoist any colours. Very soon afterwards the fire was joined by two of the brigs and by the brigantine, and the boats finished their journey under a heavy fire of grape and musketry from all five vessels. The remaining two brigs took no part in it.

The boats contained between them only a few light guns; not all of them were armed in this way. As soon as he was able to do so, Mildmay returned the enemy fire with his guns; but the sooner he came to close quarters, the better. In twenty minutes or so the boats were alongside, and all five vessels were speedily boarded and taken. They were the Spanish schooner *Ycanam*, 306 tons, armed with eight long 18-pounders and two long nines, with 55 men and 380 slaves; the Spanish schooner *Vecua*, 180 tons, armed with eight long 18-pounders and one long nine, with 45 men and 300 slaves; the French brig *Vigilant*, 240 tons, with four 12-pounder carronades, all of which had been brought over to face the boats, with a crew of 30 men and a cargo of 343 slaves; the French brig *Petite Betsy*, 184 tons, armed with four 9-pounder carronades, with 25 men and 218 slaves; and the French brigantine *Ursula* of 100 tons, with four 9-pounder carronades, a crew of 27 and with 247 slaves. Altogether a formidable opposition. Mildmay and his men were lucky to escape so lightly; they had two killed and seven wounded. The *Ycanam* alone lost sixteen killed from the British fire. The crew of the small schooner the *Vecua* left her and escaped on shore; before going they left a lighted fuse over the magazine, caring nothing for the 300 slaves they had in the hold, nearly all of them fettered. They hoped that the British boarding party would be blown sky-high with the ship and the slaves.

What can you do with people like this, asks the commodore. He had given Mildmay written orders to be very careful not to interfere with American or French vessels, and if he inadvertently boarded one of them he was to apologize and explain.

'These people on the contrary hold no terms with us; but making quite sure of being able to defeat the boats, we are informed that they had determined to put every one of our people to death who fell into their hands, nor do I the least doubt it.'

The two Spanish schooners were sent to Freetown on a charge of slaving, and the two French vessels who aided them were sent there on a charge of piracy: 'this wanton act of hostility and murder,' says the commodore. Indeed, the French captains had no reason to expect that they would be interfered with, and they had no justification for opening fire in support of the Spaniards before Mildmay and his men had fired a shot.

In that period of the anti-slavery patrol, the slavers were desperate and were still hopeful of victory; and they showed a good deal of unnecessary brutality. At daylight, a few days before Christmas 1819, Captain Leeke in the *Myrmidon* detained a Spanish schooner, the *Virgen*, on a charge of piracy, and put Lieutenant Belcher and a prize crew on board. 'At this moment,' says Leeke,

'a fleet of schooners hove in sight, when I made her signal to chase, doing the same with the ship I have the honour to command. At eleven, I had brought to and boarded three schooners, one of them with 140 slaves; but being under French colours I could not detain her. . . .
A short time after this, Lieutenant Belcher in the schooner made sail in chase of a large brig, the ship (i.e. the *Myrmidon*) being at this time out of sight. The moment he got within gunshot of her she hoisted Spanish colours and fired her broadside into the schooner, hove up, and run on shore. The slaves immediately jumped overboard; the vessel, I am happy to say, has been totally destroyed, having her back broken and three shot holes through her bottom.'

That was a desperate fellow; one wonders what happened to him when he reached land, with his slaves all free around him.

Lieutenant Belcher seems to have been an enterprising officer. Finding himself thus in a Spanish schooner and out of sight of his own ship, he decided to make use of this disguise to gain information. It was he who put two of his petty officers ashore; coming from the *Virgen* they were received without suspicion, and they paid the very interesting visit to Kearney's establishment, which we have reported on page 74.

Within a few days of this action, another lieutenant from the *Myrmidon* had his chance of glory. Leeke heard that the Gallinas river was full of slavers, and at sunset one evening he sent his first lieutenant, Lieutenant Nash,

'with the pinnace and cutter, properly armed, and furnished with a copy of the late slave treaties, to examine any vessels he might find there. I am happy to say that the next evening he succeeded in getting alongside the largest schooner, and the only one that had slaves on board at the time (the others having landed theirs on discovering the *Myrmidon* in the morning) and after a slight resistance took possession of her. She proved to be the *Bella Dora*, a Spanish schooner of 150 tons, two guns, a complement of twenty-five men, and part of her cargo, consisting of 122 slaves bound to the Havannah.'

So far, Lieutenant Nash had had nothing to worry about. But Leeke continues:

'As soon as the other schooners observed her to be taken possession of, they fired their broadsides into her, and at the moment of her slipping her cable they did the same, and to the number of five hove up in a line, and each gave the *Bella Dora* three or four broadsides. I am happy to say, we lost no men in this little affair, and but one wounded, a musket ball having gone through his arm.'

An unpleasant twenty minutes, to which Nash with his two guns could make but little reply. There must have been casualties among the slaves. On this occasion and others, it is strange that in spite of what Leeke calls 'the determined conduct of the renegadoes' – many of them British and American

— their fire caused so few casualties. We have seen how Lieutenant Courtenay survived eight hours of heavy musketry and gun fire in the Gallinas river with only four casualties. We can only conclude that the 'renegadoes' must have found it easier to recruit skilled seamen than trained gunners, and that while at sea they spent too little time in practising their gunnery.

The Navy's superior gunnery enabled it to take many heavily-armed vessels with surprising ease. Sir James Yeo was perhaps not unduly alarmed when he heard that a Spanish slave captain with a heavier broadside than that of the *Inconstant* was promising himself the pleasure of blowing her out of the water. Captain Fisher in the 20-gun sloop HMS *Bann* fought two actions in 1816 which ought to have given him more trouble than they did.

On January 18th, off the Manna river, Fisher saw a sail away to the NNW. at eleven in the morning. He made all sail, but the day was calm and he could make no headway, so he cleared away his boats under the command of Lieutenant Tweed. From noon till sunset the *Bann* was becalmed and stationary, her head swinging slowly backwards and forwards. The other ship too was becalmed; her sail was visible all day long on the horizon, though by 3.30 the *Bann*'s boats were out of sight. About sunset, a light breeze sprang up, and in the last of the daylight Fisher saw a schooner approaching. His boats rejoined him at eight, bringing with them their prize. She was the Spanish schooner *Rosa*, with eight guns and twenty men. (We learn from the court at Freetown that her crew was largely American, and that she was suspected of being British-owned, her Spanish owners being mere dummies.) The *Rosa* had fought the boats for twenty minutes, but had succeeded in wounding only one man, Mr Keith the assistant surgeon. There were several casualties among the schooner's crew. Had the action been fought between the two ships, the *Rosa* would have stood no chance at all against the *Bann*, which carried twenty guns to her eight, and probably threw five times the weight of metal. But against the boats, which had four or five miles to row in a dead calm, and cannot have carried anything heavier than a light carronade, the *Rosa* should have been easily able to hold her own. Admittedly, once the boats came close, the schooner's gunners may have been unable to depress the guns sufficiently. But her broadside of four guns, if well served, ought to have kept the boats at a distance and caused heavy casualties among the men toiling at the oars.

Two months later, the *Bann* was off Whydah, and at 9.30 in the morning Captain Fisher saw a sail in the NNE. He gave chase, and after three hours had brought his ship within long range. The other vessel was flying the Stars and Stripes, but Fisher did not believe that tale; so at 12.40 he opened fire with his bow-chasers. The enemy's guns were evidently outranged, for she stood this fire for twenty minutes without returning it. At one o'clock, she hauled down the American colours and hoisted Portuguese, and opened fire with her stern guns. Fisher cleared his ship for action, and began firing grape-shot at the enemy's rigging in the hope of disabling her. Half an hour later he came alongside, and was able to fire a broadside; this carried away most of the enemy's running rigging, and she struck. She was a Portuguese brig of eighteen guns and seventy men, with a cargo of slaves awaiting her on shore at Whydah. The *Bann* had no casualties, and very little damage apart from shot-holes in her sails; had the Portuguese guns been well handled, Fisher would not have taken his prize so easily. We do not know the brig's tonnage. She carried a surprising number of guns for a brig; the *Thistle* carried only twelve guns and the *Snapper* only nine. Probably her guns were small, mostly 9-pounders with one or two twelves: no match for the *Bann*'s thirty-twos. However, the Portuguese wasted their shot on the *Bann*'s sails; the *Bann* shot the Portuguese rigging to pieces. The British vessels had probably profited by the sharp lesson taught them by the Americans in the war of 1812; not only were the American ships in that war more heavily gunned, but their gunnery was far better.

So the eighteen-twenties drew to a close, the Navy battling on against enemy gunfire and legal chicanery. In the thirteen years 1814 to 1826, British captains landed 15,900 slaves to be set free in Sierra Leone. But this was a small proportion of the total number being handled. In the single year 1825, 25,769 slaves were delivered to the market in Rio de Janeiro alone. Cuba too was insatiable. In April 1825, Canning instructed the British Ambassador in Madrid to protest to Spain about the flagrant way in which the Spanish authorities in Cuba were conniving at the trade, which had been illegal to Spanish subjects for five years. His information was that 16,000 slaves had been imported into Cuba in the previous year. Slave ships were constantly clearing from Havana for the African coast, loading their black cargo, and arriving back in Cuba. But they did not put in to their home port until they had landed their cargo 'at the back of the island'; then they came home to Havana in ballast, and were allowed to enter with no questions asked. The British representative in Havana was constantly making representations:

'he is either answered that it does not lie within his sphere to demand an inquiry, or he is referred from one authority to another, and each authority declares that it does not feel itself called upon to interfere in the matter, in any way that can be effectual; when all these evasions and excuses are exhausted, His Majesty's commissary judge is told that the question has been referred to Madrid –'

and so the merry game went on.

In these circumstances, the Navy could not hope to extinguish the trade; it could be no more than a nuisance to the Ormonds, the Kearneys, and their wholesale suppliers. A nuisance it certainly was: during 1825 and 1826 it took sixteen prizes in nine months. But this merely added slightly to the risk of the business and put up the price of slaves. In 1821, Collier had sent home a description of a certain Senhor da Souza, who ran the slave trade at Whydah;

'where he is the agent or slave factor to the Brazilian nation, and lives in prodigious splendour; assumes the rights and privileges of a person in authority, granting papers and licences to the slave traders, in all the form and confidence of one empowered to do so by the Portuguese Government.'

Five years later, we find this gentleman ordering his own ship from an American shipyard. She was the *Principe de Guinea* of 260 tons,

'a fine brig pierced for sixteen guns, carrying a long 24-pounder on a pivot and six smaller guns at the side; she was supposed to be better constructed for sailing than any vessel out of America, and entirely new. The master of her stated that Da Souza had given him a very considerable sum of money to build her, fit her out, and load her. Her cargo was loading at Whydah when HMS *Brazen* left. . . . Captain Willes (of the *Brazen*) observed that he did not suppose any ship of war on the coast could come up with her, and that there would therefore be but little chance of taking her when she commenced slaving (for which purpose she is declared to have been purchased and fitted) unless during a calm, with boats.'

However, this fine vessel had but a short life. With 609 slaves on board, she was taken by Lieutenant Tucker of HMS *Maidstone* after a sharp action. Thirty of the slaves were lost, but the remainder were set free in Sierra Leone, and the vessel was condemned by the court in September 1826, only six months after loading her first cargo.

It would not be quite true to say that the Royal Navy carried on the struggle single-handed. We do hear occasionally of a Dutch or a French naval vessel being sent to cruise on the coast, and a respectable number of French vessels (including the *Vigilant* and the *Petite Betsy*, taken by HMS *Iphigenia* at Bonny) were condemned by the French courts. The American naval squadron was withdrawn in 1824; not only was American national sentiment (as opposed to that of the American naval commanders themselves) strongly hostile to the idea of any cordial co-operation with British naval men, but some federal officials had strong Southern feelings in favour of the South's 'peculiar institution' of slavery.

For most of the time, the Navy was left alone to fight against slavers and pirates. In 1826, HMS *Redwing* detained the Spanish schooner *Invincival* and sent her to Freetown with a prize crew on board. A few days later, the *Invincival* met the Brazilian schooner *Disunion* with slaves from the Cameroons, and took her. The British prize-master, Jackson, sent half his men on board the *Disunion*, and the two vessels continued the voyage in company. But they were met by a large Spanish pirate of thirteen guns, who captured them both; he took the slaves with him to Havana, and after looting and slaughter turned both vessels adrift. The *Disunion* eventually reached Rio with but five men on board, emaciated and mutilated; all were Brazilians. Nothing more was heard of the *Invincival* or of Jackson and his British crew.

THE STORY OF THE 'NETUNO'

We may end this chapter of battles against odds with the story of the Brazilian brigantine *Netuno*, which was detained in the Benin river on March 4, 1826, by the boats of HMS *Esk*. She was a small vessel of 75 tons only, armed with two 6-pounder carronades. She had a cargo of 150 slaves, and as usual made haste to put them ashore when she saw the boats of the *Esk* approaching. She was too late; fifty-eight reached the shore, one boat-load of twenty was intercepted by the naval boats, and seventy-two were still on board. It was a clear case; and Captain Purchas put on board a prize crew of six men under a warrant officer named Crawford. Two days later the *Netuno* set sail for Freetown, in company with another prize, a sloop, also taken by the *Esk*.

The sloop was faster, and during the night the two vessels parted company; in the morning, Crawford and his men found themselves alone. The wind was contrary, and the *Netuno* sailed like a haystack. In fourteen days she covered less than 300 miles, in a general south-westerly direction; no doubt Crawford was hoping to get into the direct sea-lane from St Thomas island to Freetown and pick up the south-easterly breeze. On March 20th, the *Netuno* was roughly south of the modern port of Lome in Togo, and nearly 300 miles out to sea. At three in the afternoon, Crawford saw a vessel to the south-east, coming towards him under full sail. The rest of the story is best told in his own words. When he refers to the prize, he means of course his ship, the *Netuno.*

'Three-fifty, stranger fired two guns, prize hoisted an English ensign; 4.00, brig south-east two miles, thought she was a man of war. At 4.50, stranger one mile; tacked, stood towards her and shortened sail; at 5.00 observed stranger shorten sail, and that she was not an English man of war.

At 5.10 filled, and in hoisting foretopmast studding sail, stranger fired at us, then no colours flying, but immediately after, hoisted French ensign and pendant, beat retreat with drum and lowered five ports a side, hove to (used a boatswain's call), hailed prize in English and lowered a boat.

At 5.20 p.m. boat came alongside with the captain and four men, who asked whether we had slaves? Also several other questions in Spanish and broken English. The captain could not speak French, and on my remarking it to an English interpreter, one of his boat's crew, at the same time observing that brig was not a French man of war, he replied that she was, but that the captain was a Spaniard; and on my further interrogating him, the captain, who had previously used threatening language, both Spanish and English, repeatedly ordered me into his boat, with papers, etc., etc. I as often, pointing to the English ensign, told him, vessel was prize to an English man of war, that I had no papers for him, neither would I go into his boat, adding again that she was not a French man of war, and that he himself was a Spaniard. He in a menacing manner and tone said, "I am a Spaniard from the Havannah brig *Carolina*; into the boat immediately, prunto, prunto, etc., etc.", and concluded by ordering me to be silent and his men to board. I dared them at their peril, told them to remain, and that the papers should be produced.

Now seeing the necessity of acting promptly, knowing with whom I had to deal, and resolving not tamely to give up my charge, I brought a brace of pistols (the only small arms in prize, and supplied by the *Esk*), and three distinct times asked the captain and interpreter whether he still remained determined to have me in his boat with my papers, etc. Finding him increase in abuse and threatening language, I shot the

captain and bow man,[1] and made the remainder of boat's crew
jump overboard; holding by the gunwale they regained their
boat, and pulled to their vessel.

The pirate commenced firing five guns in the broadside,
round and grape, returning by the prize from thirty to fifty
yards, with one 6-pounder carronade, round-shot and canister,
from 5.30 till 7.15 p.m., when observed pirate's crew leave
their guns and retreat forward. Fired amongst them; pirate
ceased firing and hauled her wind; her gangway ports in one
and part of forecastle bulwark knocked down. We had at this
time only four cartridges left.

The *Netuno*'s crew are six in number; she is armed with two
six-pounder carronades, one brace of ship's pistols, and six
slave cutlasses; she has sustained considerable damage in sails
and rigging, main gaff wounded, trysail gaff shot away; also
tack of foretopsail, one shot between wind and water.

The slaves, ninety-two in number, were below during the
contest, and fortunately escaped with only one woman killed
and one girl wounded. . . . .'

He concludes with a detailed description of the pirate brig
so that all His Majesty's ships may be on the look-out for her;
and he signs his report:

R. B. Crawford, *Prize Master*
Admiralty mate, HMS *Esk*

Mr Richard Borough Crawford had passed his examinations
for lieutenant, and for his gallant conduct in this action he
was immediately commissioned. He was promoted commander in 1842 and captain in 1856. Mr Crawford did not
stay very long in the West African squadron, but this action
of his was being talked of long after he had been transferred
to other stations. And may the Navy never lack men like him.

[1] Because he would be holding on to the *Netuno* with his boathook and
keeping alive the danger that the boat's crew might come aboard. It was
lucky for Crawford that the action was fought at such close range, so that
his single carronade could take full effect.

Chapter Six

THE EQUIPMENT CLAUSE

It was now plain to the British Government that the major slave-using countries – the United States, Cuba, and Brazil – had no intention of doing anything effective to hinder the slave trade. The Government in Madrid was prepared to issue decrees, but the Spanish authorities in Cuba saw to it that they should not be enforced in the island.

On the other hand, there was progress with Holland and France, and even to some extent with Brazil. As we have seen, Portugal, Spain and Holland agreed that a vessel could be condemned if it were proved that she had been carrying slaves, even if she had no slaves on board at the time of capture. The Dutch treaty of 1822 contained the additional provision that a vessel might be condemned if she was plainly equipped for slaving, even though she was a new ship, newly arrived on the coast, and had not yet purchased a single slave.

There were certain signs which showed a vessel to be intended for the slave trade. Instead of solid hatches to cover her hold, she had gratings to allow for ventilation. She had extra bulkheads and spare planks for fitting extra tiers – like gigantic book-shelves – in the walls of the hold to increase her carrying capacity. She carried iron shackles for fettering the men slaves. She had supplies of food and water adequate for feeding the slaves and far in excess of the quantity needed for the crew; and she carried cooking boilers and mess tubs to correspond. It was common for a vessel with a crew of thirty to carry a cargo of 300 to 400, so there could be no concealing this extra provisioning. The treaty-makers foresaw the possibility that a vessel might be carrying extra water casks without yet having filled them; in this case, the onus was laid on the master of the vessel of proving that his empty casks were intended for the innocent purpose of carrying palm oil. Again, it was highly suspicious, though not conclusive, if a ship carried one or two native canoes in addition to her ordinary boats. Slavers always carried them, legitimate traders seldom. Much hasty surreptitious trading for slaves had to be carried on from open sandy beaches constantly pounded by heavy surf. The native canoe was broad-beamed and round-bottomed to suit these conditions; she was admirable for flying up the beach on the crest of a wave and taking the ground upright, whereas the ordinary keeled ship's boat with her deeper draught would turn on her side and fill with water. The legitimate trader, buying gold or ivory or palm kernels, would not need to carry his own canoes. He was in no hurry; he could spare the time to wait for the African traders to load their own canoes and come out to his ship.

This clause in the Anglo-Dutch treaty of 1822, whereby a vessel's being equipped for slaving became sufficient to secure her condemnation, is known for convenience as the 'equipment clause'. In 1825 and 1826 a whole string of Dutch vessels was condemned by the court at Freetown under the equipment clause; none of them had slaves on board when taken, but all were equipped for slaving. The Dutch flag disappeared from the slave trade as rapidly and completely as the British flag had done.

It now became the object of British diplomacy to persuade other slave-trading countries to accept the equipment clause as an amendment to their existing slavery treaties. Spain accepted the clause in 1835, Portugal (after heavy pressure from Palmerston) acquiesced in the clause from 1839 onwards, and accepted it formally in 1842.

Brazil signed a treaty in 1826 which abolished the slave trade, and prohibited the import of slaves into the country after 1829. The treaty contained no equipment clause; but from 1827 onwards, batches of Brazilian vessels were condemned because they were loitering empty at Whydah, Badagry, Lagos and other ports, having already unloaded their cargo of trade goods. The Navy's conclusion was that they were waiting to receive the slave cargo which they had already paid for: and the court upheld it. Importing slaves into Brazil was illegal after 1820, but large-scale smuggling continued. The Brazilian authorities connived at it, and the treaty seems to have made very little difference to the numbers of slaves landed.

France too agreed at last to a treaty. In 1822, reciprocal rights of search were granted over French and British vessels between the geographical limits of fifteen degrees north and ten degrees south, and the Greenwich meridian and thirty degrees west. These geographical limits excluded from the treaty Whydah and the big eastern slave markets. This meant that the Navy could not hinder French vessels from loading a cargo there, and must try and intercept them on the high seas once they had passed the Greenwich meridian on their homeward voyage. Seeing that no slaver dared fly British colours, the reciprocity provided by the treaty was merely nominal, and in spite of its geographical limitations, the treaty was a real concession by France. The treaty contained no equipment clause. In 1841, the French plenipotentiaries agreed with their colleagues of Britain, Austria, Prussia and Russia on the terms of a generously-worded treaty which did contain an equipment clause and which widened the geographical area to include the whole of the Atlantic and Indian Oceans between thirty-two degrees north and forty-five degrees south, and from the American coastline to the 80th meridian of east longitude. But the French Government refused to ratify the treaty, and preferred to provide its own naval squadron to deal with French slavers.

Although Canning, 'calling the New World into existence to redress the balance of the Old', had been prompt to recognize Brazil's independence of Portugal in 1825, Brazilian slavers were legally on the same footing as Portuguese until the treaty of 1826. They were allowed to load slaves south of the equator, and they could not be detained south of the equator unless they had been chased across it from the north. As Collier had written in 1821 about the importance of Whydah:

'Vessels from Whydah, if met at sea and boarded by a British cruiser, report themselves bound to Cabinda and Molemba[1]; and if they have left the coast of Benin a day only, they declare themselves to have sailed from the above-mentioned ports, or even from the more southern parts of the coast of Angola. Thus, although a vessel receiving a cargo of slaves at Whydah is subject to seizure, she avoids this by her short run, until she is in security by passing south of the line; and then, if met with and boarded, the master has a ready answer. The ship's log, if fairly kept, will be at variance with his declaration; but the hazard to an officer is so great by a capture, however supported by written documents, and this so easily overturned by the affidavits so readily made by every Portuguese in the vessel before the mixed commission, that against the evidence of plain facts and common sense, prudence and self-defence will generally prevail, and the slaver will escape detention.'

Collier had had bitter experience of Portuguese affidavits and of counterfeit logs.

This rule that no seizure could take place south of the line was a well-known trap. In 1826, Captain Murray of HMS *Atholl* fell into it. He took the Brazilian brig *Activo* with a cargo of slaves. The master said he had loaded the slaves at Molemba, but the court upheld Murray's belief that he had loaded them at Badagry. Nevertheless, the seizure was held to be illegal, for it had taken place more than four degrees south of the equator; the brig was well on her way to Brazil, several hundred miles south of the Liberian coast. The court released the vessel, and the master filed his claim for compensation. It was a heavy one. The 163 surviving slaves became impatient as the ship lay in Freetown harbour to await the court's decision. They saw slaves being set free from other vessels. Sundry free Africans in small boats and canoes encouraged them with shouts and gestures to make a dash for it; and suddenly the whole crowd burst out of the ship and made their way ashore in triumph. There could be no question

[1] Both these places are south of the equator: Cabinda in 5 degrees 40 and Molemba or Molembo about 5 degrees 25.

of recapturing them and handing them back into slavery. The court merely added the value of the cargo, 163 slaves worth £61 5s 0d each, to the bill which poor Captain Murray had to pay for his unwarranted seizure.

After the new treaty came into force, things were easier. In October 1827, Lieutenant Badgley of HMS *Eden* detained the Brazilian *Sao Joao Voador* off Keta on the Gold Coast. She was equipped for slaving, but had no cargo, and he suspected her of having paid for a cargo of slaves and to be awaiting delivery. The court however noted that the vessel held a valid passport from the Brazilian authorities for trading north of the equator in palm oil and other local produce. Lieutenant Badgley brought a British trader to give evidence that there was no palm oil available at Keta, or any other local produce except slaves. But the defendant trumped the trick by bringing another expert witness, also British and with a much longer experience of the coast, to say that though no one would claim Keta as a major source of supply of palm oil, it was sometimes possible to load it there. The court found for the defence and released the vessel. There being no equipment clause in the Brazilian treaty, the vessel could not be condemned; but the court remarked that a vessel trading in palm oil ought not to be carrying slaving equipment, and it rejected the master's claim for demurrage.

In 1828 there was welcome evidence that France was co-operating in putting down the trade. Commodore Collier[1] in HMS *Sybille* took a slaver, *La Fanny*, under French colours. She had loaded her cargo at Calabar only a few days before, and Collier knew that the Calabar river had just been searched by a French man of war. All French slavers in the river had been arrested, so Collier concluded that *La Fanny* must have escaped by showing Dutch or other colours. He sent her to Freetown, but the court there could find no evidence that the vessel had ever claimed any other nationality but French, so she was sent to Senegal to join her sisters in misfortune.

In 1833, the British abolitionists had their greatest triumph:

[1] Commodore F. A. Collier, not Sir George Collier, whom we have met earlier.

the status of slavery was abolished throughout the British empire, and Parliament voted a sum of twenty million pounds to compensate slave owners. This Act made no difference to the traffic in slaves. No fresh slaves had been imported into British colonies for many years past. Slave-owners generally held that it was cheaper to buy slaves than to breed them, but British slave-owners had long been restricted to breeding their slaves.

In the early 'thirties, the illicit smuggling of slaves into Brazil and Cuba was the biggest problem. We have seen that Canning was moved to make a strong protest to the Spanish Government at the way in which its officials in Cuba connived at the slave trade. In 1826 the Spanish Government accepted his protest and issued a new decree. Every vessel arriving in a Cuban port from any part of the African coast must produce its log to the Spanish naval authorities, and every slave smuggled ashore would mean a 200-dollar fine on the purchaser. The British naval men were cynical about this plausible decree. They wondered which of his alternative logs the Spanish skipper would produce for inspection, and how zealous and efficient the authorities in Cuba would be in supervising the unloading of his cargo and preventing the illicit landing of slaves.

A few months later, they found out. In September 1826, two British men of war chased the Spanish schooner *Minerva* right into Havana harbour. The British commander asked permission to send an officer to accompany the port authorities when they visited the ship. Permission was granted, and Lieutenant Smith went on board. As soon as he set foot on the deck it was plain to him that the ship was a slaver, and he said so. The grave Spanish official replied that she could not be, for there was no mention of slaves in the ship's papers. Smith went back to his ship and reported this to his captain, and the captain himself went ashore to interview the authorities. In the classical manner, he was politely referred from one to the other, and was assured that in due course the *Minerva* should be strictly investigated. He guessed what this meant, and posted picket-boats to watch the *Minerva* all night long.

Sure enough, Lieutenant Smith was able from his boat to count
the slaves as they were rowed ashore and landed at the main
wharf. His boat went so close that someone in the *Minerva*'s
boats cursed him and threw a log of wood at his head, which
missed; and when the *Minerva*'s hold was empty and the last
slave was safely ashore, all the boats made a concerted rush
at Smith's picket-boat, and he had to beat a hasty retreat to his
ship. Next morning, his captain reported to the Spanish
governor, the Captain-General, what Smith had seen. The
Captain-General blandly assured him that in a civilized city
like Havana it would be quite impossible to put large numbers
of slaves ashore at the main wharf without the police seeing
them. The police had seen nothing, so there can have been
nothing to see, and it was really quite out of the question for
the Government to take action on hearsay. We are driven to
the conclusion that the Captain-General and some of his
officials must have been making a very good thing out of the
illicit trade.

Not all the slaves landed in Cuba stayed in the island. Then,
as in some more recent times, there was much surreptitious
to-ing and fro-ing between north-west Cuba and the Florida
keys. A good many slaves were re-exported from Cuba and
found their way to the Southern plantations.

In the 'thirties the Navy found its situation changing. In the
first place, the slavery squadron was strengthened in numbers.
Instead of the six vessels that had been the rule in the early
'twenties, it was increased to fifteen or more: one frigate of
forty to fifty guns, four or five sloops of sixteen to twenty
guns, and up to a dozen brigs and schooners. Next, its speed
was increased. Two or three of the captured American-built
clippers were added to the squadron, and the first steamships
made their appearance. The early steamships were not a complete success; their coal bunkers were too small. But, like the
Portuguese galleys 300 years earlier, they were deadly against
sailing vessels that were lying idle in a tropical calm.

The Dutch flag had disappeared from the slave trade.
France was beginning to co-operate in suppressing the trade,
and the French flag was ceasing to be a protection; French

warships made arrests on their own, and British captains were able to detain French slavers and send them to Senegal with some confidence that they would be adequately dealt with. Brazil had not accepted the equipment clause, but the Brazilian Government seemed to acquiesce in the condemnation of Brazilian vessels taken without slaves on board, at all events if they had already discharged their cargo. Brazilian slavers however found an answer to this problem. They shifted their base of operations to the Portuguese territories south of the line, where they were immune from seizure; and in spite of the Brazilian law the illicit trade went merrily on.

To offset these improvements in the Navy's situation, there were two serious changes for the worse. One was that the United States Government, which for three years had actually maintained its own naval patrol on the coast, now gave way to Southern sentiment, and openly and bluntly refused to join in any convention whatever on the subject of the slave trade. The immediate result of this was that more and more slavers were openly fitted out in American ports and cruised along the coast defiantly flying the Stars and Stripes. They were safe from British cruisers, who had orders not to touch them. There were no American cruisers on the coast, so all they had to fear was that they might fall in with one on the high seas before they had landed their cargo. If such a misfortune did befall them, they had a ready way out. They were all provided with Spanish flags and sets of Spanish papers in case they were needed; and if stopped by an American cruiser, they hoisted Spanish colours and took their Spanish papers out of the drawer. The United States Government took the extreme view that no foreign officer had any right to board a vessel flying the American flag, in any circumstances whatever. Admittedly, if this were accepted, a scallywag of any nation could protect himself by simply hoisting American colours. To the United States Government, always abnormally sensitive over the sanctity of its flag on the high seas, this seemed a lesser evil than admitting even the most rigidly controlled right of search by a foreign officer.

The other change for the worse was that public opinion at

home, which had enthusiastically supported the suppression of the slave trade in its early stages, was now beginning to flag. People had hoped that other nations would join Britain in outlawing the traffic, and that by hearty and effective international co-operation it would speedily be killed. This had not happened. For twenty years and more, Britain had slogged on almost alone. The operation was costing a fortune in prize money, legal expenses, and subsidies or bribes to foreign governments and African kings. The Navy was paying a heavy price in killed, wounded and diseased. And yet, more slaves than ever were being shipped, and though a higher proportion of them than before were dying on the voyage – dying from disease or sorrow, or being flung overboard while alive at the sight of a British cruiser – greater numbers than ever were reaching the markets of the New World. Would it not be wiser to admit that the task was beyond Britain's unaided strength, and give it up?

More than this. The old eighteenth-century economic ideas were fading. Britain was now the workshop of the world. She needed an unlimited supply of food and of raw materials from overseas, and she needed the oversea markets for her manufactures. Free trade was the new fashionable theory. Britain was ceasing to care about protecting the economy of her West-Indian colonies. Lancashire needed cheap cotton, Bristol needed cheap tobacco, the sugar refiners needed cheap sugar. To many people, it was beginning to seem merely quixotic to refuse Louisiana cotton, Virginian tobacco or Cuban sugar because they were produced by slave labour.

For these reasons, there came to be, in the years after emancipation, an increasing campaign in favour of calling off the naval patrol, and leaving the fate of the slave trade to be settled by the ordinary commercial considerations of profit and loss. As long as the traffic paid, the theory went, no British efforts would be able to stop it; if it ceased to pay, it would die without Britain's needing to lift a finger. However, this campaign never won a majority in parliament. The old humanitarian sentiment was strong enough to keep the Navy at its task until the end. The Navy carried its bat; the naval patrol on the

African coast was not abandoned until the American slave markets were closed and the last of the slave ships had abandoned the trade.

Steamships appeared during the 'twenties on the Cuban coast; a Spanish coasting steamer was captured with a cargo of slaves in 1826. Next year, the Sierra Leone Government was running its own steamship; but it was not until 1832 that the first naval steamship appeared in the West African squadron. She was the *Pluto* of three guns; after being on the station for two years she was withdrawn, but reappeared in 1841 and 1842. In 1842 she was joined by four other naval steamships.

The Navy evolved its own scheme for strengthening the West African squadron with fast ships. Throughout the 'twenties, condemned slave ships were sold by public auction. The Dutch schooner *Hoop* was condemned in 1826, and was bought privately by Commodore Bullen. She carried a long twelve and four eighteens; Bullen renamed her the *Hope*, manned her with some of his crew, with Lieutenant Tucker in command, and sent her off to cruise as a tender to his flagship the *Maidstone*. Tucker was lucky; he fell in with Da Souza's fine ship the *Principe de Guinea*. He was outgunned and outmanned, but he chased her for twenty-eight hours and fought her for two hours and forty minutes; he carried her by boarding, and she struck. It was a great blow to the slavers, for the *Principe de Guinea* was reckoned one of the fastest ships on the coast.

Other condemned slave ships were bought similarly. The *Black Joke* became a tender to HMS *Sybille*. Commodore Collier bought the *Arsenia* and renamed her the *Paul Pry*. These fast vessels, manned by naval crews, soon began to pick up good prizes and to spread dismay among the slavers.

But there was a weakness in the system. The naval officers bought the vessels as private ventures, in the hope of increasing their ships' prize-money. When they left the coast, they disposed of these private tenders, as a colonial official might dispose of his horses; and it was a matter of chance who bought them. Bullen bought not only the *Hope* but also the *Hope*'s prize, the *Principe de Guinea*. He sold them both. The *Hope*

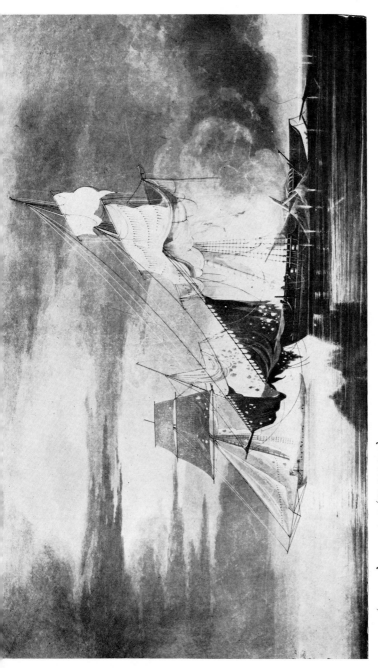

V. THE 'PICKLE' AND THE 'VOLADORA'

Both vessels are topsail schooners. The wreckage of the slaver's mainmast is over the side and her rigging is shot to pieces; the *Pickle's* main topsail is hanging useless. The *Pickle* is shown as wearing her square sails; they were stowed early in the action, but may have been reset when the enemy tried to rake her.

VI. THE 'MONKEY' AND THE 'MIDAS' OFF MIAMI

The *Midas* is anchored; the little *Monkey* has backed her topsails to take off her speed and is trying to avoid the slaver's broadside by remaining astern and raking her. In the distance an American brig of war is at anchor watching the fight.

became the Brazilian *Esperanza* and was again taken and condemned; this time she was bought by a man acting as agent for a slaver, went to the Gallinas to pick up a fresh cargo, and delivered it safely in Brazil. The *Principe de Guinea* became the Brazilian *Vengador*, which was again taken and condemned. Other condemned vessels, not bought by naval officers, were bought cheaply at the auction and re-entered the slave trade. The Admiralty decided that this system lent itself to abuses, and sent orders that a naval officer who bought a condemned vessel must not re-sell her unless into the naval service. This stopped the practice; for an officer could not count on the Navy's buying his tender, and he might find her left on his hands before she had earned her keep in prize money. Shortly afterwards, the Foreign Office went one better; for it gave instructions that all condemned ships (except those of Portugal and Brazil, who refused to accept this modification of the system) were not to be sold, but were immediately to be broken up.

THE 'VELOZ PASAGERA'

We must not assume that all the British warships on the coast were slow old tubs, whose only chance of catching a Baltimore clipper was to wait at the river mouth like a cat sitting outside a mouse's hole. Some of them, like the old *Myrmidon*, were quite fast. The eighteen-gun sloop *Primrose* was another which had a good turn of speed. On September 6, 1830, she was 140 miles out at sea off the Niger delta, and at 4.0 in the afternoon saw a sail on her weather bow. Captain Broughton gave chase. It was thick squally weather, and after a time he lost sight of the stranger, but at 10.30, long after dark, he found her again and soon came up with her. He hoisted the blue ensign and fired a shot across her bows; she hoisted Spanish colours and hove to. Broughton felt himself fortunate, for she was a vessel he had been specially told to watch for, the full-rigged ship *Veloz Pasagera*. Her ports were open, and there was a light showing in each; it was clear that her gunners were ready for action.

The *Primrose* hailed in English to know what ship she was

and whither bound. The answer came back in English: 'Going to St Thomas for wood and water.' Broughton sent Lieutenant Butterfield to board her.

Butterfield found the first mate waiting to receive him as he came on board. The mate apologized civilly for the captain's absence; the captain was sick in his cabin. The ship, he said, had just left Badagry and was bound for Princes. (Not St Thomas, as the ship had previously said.) Butterfield, having strong reason to suspect that the ship was a slaver, said that he would just go round the decks and inspect her. As he spoke, he was standing at the head of the companion-way; at this moment the captain appeared at the foot of it, and replied in broken English, 'No possible.' Butterfield looked around, and saw a man standing near him whom he recognized. The man had been in the crew of a Spanish slave ship that Butterfield had taken when he was in command of the *Black Joke*, and Butterfield remembered that he spoke English. He called on this man to interpret for him. 'My ship,' he said, 'is His Britannic Majesty's ship *Primrose*, and I am come on board to search you. Do you understand me?' The captain said Yes, he understood; and twice he asked again whether it was the *Primrose*, and Butterfield patiently replied yes. All this time, the *Primrose*, which was by far the better sailer, kept drawing slightly ahead and then falling back into place as the men trimmed her sails. From where he stood, Butterfield could look down into the slaver's gun deck; he saw the crews standing to their guns, and as the two ships kept slightly changing position, the men kept the guns steadily trained on the *Primrose*. They evidently had their orders and knew what they had to do. Three more times he asked to be allowed to go below and inspect the ship. 'If you will not allow me,' he said, 'I shall have to go back and report it to my captain; and you know what the consequences of that will be.' It was of no use; treaty or no treaty, they were evidently prepared to resist by force. The mate's civility had vanished, and no one accompanied Butterfield back to the rail. He went over the side again and back to his own ship; he had been away a quarter of an hour.

Captain Broughton was confident in his own mind that the *Veloz Pasagera* knew the position perfectly well, but he wanted to make quite sure that there was no misunderstanding. He had a Spanish interpreter, and he hailed the *Veloz* again more than once, both in English and Spanish, saying that he would send another boat with an officer to inspect the ship. The *Veloz* answered, sometimes in Spanish and sometimes in English, saying that they did not understand what he wanted, and were not sure who he was; he might be a pirate, and they were taking no chances. To be on the safe side, Broughton decided to wait till morning; the weather had cleared, and he knew that the *Veloz* could not get away from him.

At daylight, the *Primrose* ran down towards the slaver ready for battle, the blue ensign flying and the Union Jack hoisted forward. Broughton hailed her again in English and Spanish: 'This is His Britannic Majesty's ship *Primrose*, and I want to send a boat immediately to examine you.' No one answered, so he repeated it; and this time he added, 'If this is not complied with in five minutes, I will fire at you.' This time someone from the *Veloz* answered, both in English and in Spanish: 'I can't help it; you can do as you please. If you fire, I will fire too.'

Broughton gave orders that the *Primrose* should open fire when he gave the signal by taking off his hat. He repeated his hail to the *Veloz* more than once, but she made no further reply. The ships were on the same tack, and were gradually closing. At the end of the five minutes they were almost touching Broughton took off his hat, and immediately the *Primrose*'s broadside crashed out, answered at once from the *Veloz*. The *Primrose* fired a second broadside, and then put up her helm, ran alongside the enemy, and fastened on to her with a lashing round the bowsprit. The *Veloz* stood a good deal higher out of the water, and a boarding party assembled in the *Primrose*'s fore-rigging on the port side. Captain Broughton himself led the boarders on to the enemy's starboard bow. The men of the *Veloz* were drawn up on the forecastle to repel the boarders. As Broughton leaped down, someone thrust at him with a pike; he fell wounded on to the deck and lost consciousness. Butterfield took command, cheered on the men, and in a few minutes had cleared the forecastle. The British swept on down the ship to the quarter-deck; here there was some more resistance, but the Spaniards soon ran below. One of the *Primrose's* men hauled down the Spanish flag, and Butterfield secured the hatches and took possession of the ship. The hand-to-hand fighting had lasted something under a quarter of an hour.

The two ships were fairly matched: the *Veloz Pasagera* had twenty guns and a crew of 150, the *Primrose* had eighteen guns and a crew of 135. The Spaniards had lost forty-six killed, six drowned and many wounded; the British loss was three killed and twelve wounded. The slaver had 555 slaves on board, who were duly set free in Sierra Leone. Butterfield, who had been promoted to lieutenant as recently as 1827, was promoted commander for his conduct in this action, and was a captain by 1841.

In June 1835, Spain signed a new slavery treaty including the equipment clause, and the Spanish flag began to go out of fashion. The slavers now hoisted Portuguese or Brazilian colours; in 1842 Portugal also accepted the equipment clause, though apparently she had in practice acquiesced in its being applied since 1839. Nevertheless, so much of the trade in the late 'thirties was in Spanish hands that Spain's adoption of the equipment clause was a great blow. In Cadiz there was a merchant named Pedro Martinez,

'a notorious slave-merchant, who from very humble origin has become, by means of the slave trade, by repute the wealthiest man in the city, and is said to be the owner of no fewer than thirty vessels engaged in that traffic.'

Captain Kearney's position as the greatest slave-dealer in the Gallinas had passed to the Spaniard Pedro Blanco, and several other Spanish firms had established themselves in the river under his shadow. Pedro Blanco prospered because he improved on Kearney's methods. It was possible, as we have seen, for Kearney to be caught temporarily with no slaves in stock. Pedro Blanco decided that with the increasing efficiency of the naval patrol, it was impossible to do business that way. A ship must be able to find her cargo waiting for her in the river, load in a few hours under cover of darkness, and be away again before daylight. This sure and speedy turn-round had been highly desirable before 1835, when a Spanish vessel was immune from capture until she had loaded her slaves; now that she could be taken while empty, it was essential if any business was to be done at all. Pedro Blanco built extensive barracoons capable of holding several hundreds of slaves, and by arrangement with King Siaka and other local chiefs he saw to it that his barracoons were always kept full.

In 1837, an Englishman named Jennings, whom Pedro Martinez employed to buy ships in England, was heard to boast of the generous payment he received for his services in buying ships and delivering them to Martinez in Cadiz to be fitted out for the slave trade; and he added that as things then were, not one slaver in twenty was taken by the British cruisers, and that the dealers would still make a profit if the rate of capture were to rise to one vessel in three. A slave bought for less than twenty dollars in the Gallinas would fetch 350 dollars in Cuba, so there was still plenty of money to be made at the game as long as the rate of capture could be kept below this danger mark of one in three. In 1837 the courts in Sierra Leone condemned 27 vessels; but in that year, 72 vessels left Havana for the African coast, and 92 vessels, in spite of the law, succeeded in landing a total of 46,000 slaves in Brazil. The Navy was still merely a nuisance; it was not yet within sight of crippling the trade.

THE 'FAMA DE CADIZ' AND THE 'MARIA'

However, no business man will be content with a profit of 200 per cent if he thinks he has a chance of making 300 per cent; and after the Spanish treaty of 1835 there was a good deal of despondency in Cuba.

'The trade is by no means flourishing. Many persons engaged

in it have been considerable losers by the captures on the coast of Africa, and the premiums in insurances have arisen, it is said, to even more than 40 per cent.'

To the risk from British cruisers there were added the risks from piracy and from disease. The *Fama de Cadiz* was one of the most capacious of slave ships; she could carry 1,200 slaves. In 1828 and 1829 she was so long away from her home port of Havana that her owners were anxious; but eventually she arrived back in Havana, having landed about 300 slaves elsewhere in Cuba to avoid tiresome official formalities. She had been stopped and inspected on the African coast before she had embarked any slaves, and since this was before the 1835 treaty, she was, of course, released. After this, however, she found herself so closely watched that she was unable to load any cargo. She hung about for a long time in vain. Then she gave up the attempt and turned pirate; she plundered other vessels and in the end accumulated a cargo of 980 slaves, with which she turned for home. She had hardly got out of sight of land when small-pox broke out among the slaves, and soon spread to the crew. By the time she reached port, her crew of 157 had been reduced to sixty-six, and of her 980 slaves, only 300 remained;

'of whom the greatest part are in so wretched a state that her owners have been selling them as low as a hundred dollars. This expedition has been altogether ruinous, from the exorbitant wages due to the sailors and the length of time she has been out.'

The *Maria* was another slaver which took to piracy. The *Maria* was a Spanish schooner, which was chased off the coast of Cuba by HMS *Skipjack* in November 1827. She fired on the *Skipjack* and ran herself ashore, and in this irregular fashion she managed to land her slaves. All, that is, save one man, who was very sickly. Him the crew left on board; and before leaving the ship, they left a lighted fuse leading to the powder magazine. The poor man survived the explosion, and when the *Skipjack*'s men took him, they found that he was a Congolese. But from papers found on board, they learned that the *Maria* had sold all her cargo of trade goods at Calabar, and Duke Ephraim there had given them a receipt for it. How then did the *Maria* acquire this slave from the Congo, which is some 700 miles from Calabar? Gradually the story was pieced together. After landing her cargo at Calabar, the *Maria* found herself so closely watched that she was unable to load any of the slaves that Duke Ephraim had ready for her; in 1827 she was immune from search while empty, but would have been taken at once with her slaves on board. French ships at that time could not be touched; so the captain arranged with a French ship to load her cargo for her and transfer it at sea out of sight of the British cruisers. The French captain did the *Maria* this service, charging a commission of fifty slaves; and with this cargo of slaves from Calabar the *Maria* turned for home. But she met a pirate, which plundered her of her whole cargo; so the *Maria* in desperation became pirate in her turn, and captured a Brazilian vessel with a cargo of slaves from the Congo.

THE 'VOLADORA'[1] AND THE 'MIDAS'

The Navy's main network was spread off the African coast; but there was a second net off the coasts of Cuba and of Brazil, whither the slavers must come to discharge their living cargo. The Spanish schooner *Voladora* left Havana on October 2, 1828, and during April she was twice boarded and released on the African coast before she had loaded her slaves. In the end she obtained her cargo at Popo and evaded capture, and in June she was nearly home. But Lieutenant MacHardy of HMS *Pickle* was cruising off the coast of Cuba. The *Pickle* was a topsail schooner of three guns, with a crew of thirty-nine men. This is Lieutenant MacHardy's report of what happened on June 5, 1829, off Port Naranjos in Cuba.

[1] Mannix and Cowley in their book *Black Cargoes* call this vessel the *Boladora*. But all the British records call her the *Voladora*; *Voladora*, 'The Flyer', seems a likely name, whereas *Boladora* as far as I know has no meaning. I prefer to 'spell it with a we'.

'On morning of June 5th, 6 a.m., discovered a strange sail to the eastward. She appearing suspicious, every means were used to disguise ourselves, and to prevent her from suspecting us, until 9.30, when HM schooner *Pickle* was tacked in chase — upon which, stranger hauled to the wind on the starboard tack, under all sail. At 4.20 p.m. gaining fast on chase, we showed our colours with a gun. At 6.30 chase having shown no colours, and we having no doubts of our coming up with her in the night, we showed our colours again and fired several shots, that she might not after dark plead ignorance of what we were. At 8.45 we tacked; 8.55 tacked. At 9.15 we tacked again, when chase tacked and edged away. We now set square sail, and kept to leeward of him. At 11.15 closing fast with chase, down square sail, and fired a shot over him.

At 11.30 chase shortened sail, and endeavoured to pass under our stern; hailed him repeatedly, which was answered with musketry and a broadside. We avoided his passing under our stern and commenced firing, aiming principally at his spars: believing him to be a pirate, from the circumstance of his showing no colours, either previous to or during the action. Kept up a continual fire, never out of pistol shot, until 12.50, when enemy's mainmast went, about eight feet from the deck, without a sail standing fore and aft. He then hailed to say he had eight killed, captain and seven men wounded, his mainmast gone, that he could now do nothing; he therefore surrendered, saying that he was unable to send a boat aboard.

I then thought it advisable to wait until daylight before taking possession; which being done, she proved to be the *Voladora* (formerly the notorious *Mulata*, of which memorandum is made on her papers by Commodore Collier) commanded by Bonifacio Echelacu, pierced for sixteen guns but mounting two long twelves and two long eighteens, with a crew of fifty-two exclusive of killed, which I believe to be ten, as two died after she surrendered; and with 335 slaves — measuring 94 feet on deck and about 235 tons English, from Popo, coast of Africa.'

The *Pickle* had one man killed and nine wounded: one

mortally, eight slightly.

Three weeks later, Lieutenant Sherer in HMS *Monkey* met the Spanish brig *Midas*. The schooner *Monkey* was one of the smallest fighting vessels in the Navy; she had five officers and twenty-one men, and carried one gun. The *Midas* left Havana on November 25, 1828, loaded 562 slaves at Bonny, and set sail for home on May 1st. She had a crew of fifty-three, including four British and two Americans, and was armed with four twelves and four eighteens. The *Monkey* met her on June 27th, not far from Miami.

'When within about two miles of her, she anchored with a spring on her cable, and hoisted Spanish colours. On getting within good grape-range she gave us a broadside, which I immediately returned; and after a sharp exchange of fire for about thirty-five minutes, she struck.'

There were no casualties on board the *Monkey*; the *Midas* had one killed and three wounded, and her rigging was 'wholly cut to pieces'. When captured she had 369 slaves surviving, but 78 more died before the *Monkey* could land them at Havana.

Even the Spanish authorities at Havana could not shut their eyes to these two captures. Both the *Voladora* and the *Midas* were condemned and their slaves were set free.

Chapter Seven

THE STARS AND STRIPES

In spite of the Federal laws against the slave trade, American businessmen, in the North as well as in the South, had long been thriving on its profits. The South bought the slaves, the North built and owned the ships and manufactured the slaving equipment. The United States Government on the whole sincerely desired to stop the trade; but the slaving interest was too strong in Congress, and members of the Federal executive sometimes had strong pro-slavery sympathies. American slavers usually carried on their business under Spanish or Portuguese colours; but Spanish colours gave no protection after 1835, and Portuguese after 1839. In the 'forties, American slavers, relying on their Government's extreme sensitivity on the subject of the right of search at sea, began to come out into the open and ply their trade defiantly under the Stars and Stripes. No American slave ship left Havana openly before 1836; in that year, five left the port, next year eleven, in 1838, nineteen and in 1839, twenty-three. Instead of American vessels seeking safety under foreign flags, foreign vessels were beginning to seek safety under the Stars and Stripes. In December 1839, President Van Buren said to Congress,

'Recent experience has shown that the provisions in our existing laws which relate to the sale and transfer of American vessels while abroad are extremely defective. Advantage has been taken of these defects to give to vessels wholly belonging to foreigners and navigating the ocean an apparent American ownership. This character has been so well simulated as to afford them comparative security in prosecuting the slave trade – a trade emphatically denounced in our statutes, regarded with abhorrence by our citizens, and of which the effectual suppression is nowhere more sincerely desired than in the United States.'

And he recommended Congress to tighten up the laws. But Congress would not do so.

The President had misjudged public opinion. A large section of the American business world was far from regarding the trade with abhorrence and sincerely desiring its suppression. The slave trade was good business and extremely lucrative. Nearly twenty years earlier, the United States Government had already refused to join Britain in a treaty allowing reciprocal rights of search. After the Anglo-French treaty of 1833, Britain again tried to induce the United States to come into the international system, but the United States Government refused somewhat brusquely to have anything to do with the scheme.

The British commissioners of the mixed court in Havana seem to have spent a great deal of their time in fruitlessly giving the Captain-General lists of Spanish slavers departing for Africa and returning, after a suitable interval, 'in ballast', having landed their slave cargo at the other end of the island. They now had to go through a similar exercise with the American consul, Mr N. P. Trist. In October 1836 we find them writing to him to draw his attention to the arrival in Havana of four newly built Baltimore topsail schooners. The vessels are unarmed, but carry sweeps for rowing in a calm. They are taking on the usual slaving equipment and are about to sail for Africa. Is there anything that Mr Trist can do to stop them?

Mr Trist thought not. He kept them waiting some time for a reply and then he wrote,

'It has probably escaped your attention that overtures, previously made, for a convention of the character referred to in the closing paragraph of your letter were more recently repeated by His Britannic Majesty's Minister in Washington, and then declined by the Government of the United States in a manner evincing the most decided disinclination to become a party to even any discussion whatever of the project.

Had this been adverted to, you would have been sensible that, besides the general objection to my holding with any agent of a foreign Government any correspondence not warranted by the very limited official character with which I am invested, the occurrence to which I refer has rendered it particularly incumbent upon me to decline receiving any communication of the nature of that which I now beg leave to return.'

There are ways and ways of saying 'No'. The British commissioners thought that Mr Trist had gone out of his way to say it as nastily as he could. His 'very limited official character' gave him the opportunity of issuing passes and certificates of American nationality to vessels applying for them, and it was common knowledge that he used this power generously.

The Foreign Secretary of the day was Palmerston, who was never excessively tender of other nations' susceptibilities. He was prepared to admit that until the United States was disposed to accept a treaty, British naval commanders must not interfere with genuine American slavers. But he would not admit that foreign vessels should be able to protect themselves by a fraudulent use of the American flag. In May 1841, after fortifying himself with legal advice, Palmerston instructed the Admiralty that the mere fact that a vessel hoisted American colours should not protect her from being boarded and having her papers examined. If she was genuinely an American vessel and her papers were in order, she must be immediately released; but if her American papers were irregular or imperfect, or if she carried papers from another country in addition, she was to be detained and sent for trial. The Admiralty sent corresponding orders to the squadron. Every possible courtesy was to be shown when boarding an American vessel; but no one was to be allowed to refuse inspection. Force was to be used if necessary.

Whatever the legal merits of the case, it seemed for a time as though friendly relations between the two Governments, and between British and American officers, might allow this limited right of inspection to be tacitly admitted. A number of American vessels were boarded; in some of them, the master was surly and truculent, but in many, there was no trouble at all. The United States Government sent a commissioner down to Havana to investigate the way in which Mr Consul Trist had been using his powers, and as a result of the investigation he was recalled.

In 1840 the United States sent a warship, the uss *Dolphin*, to cruise on the African coast; she did not stay long, but was relieved by the uss *Grampus*. The British commodore and the commander of the *Grampus* seem to have got on well together. They made a formal written agreement by which British and American warships should detain British, American and other vessels. American vessels were to be handed over to the *Grampus*, others to the British. The arrangement worked smoothly; in March 1840 for example, a British warship found the American slaver *Sarah Anne* in the Rio Pongas and handed her over to the *Grampus*, which sent her to America for trial. If this friendly arrangement could have continued, the slave trade would have come to an end twenty years sooner than it did. But alas, the *Grampus* was soon withdrawn, and the arrangement lapsed.

The commander of the uss *Dolphin*, a newcomer to the coast, reported to his Government on what he found, and was naturally ready with suggestions. He says that there were twenty British cruisers on the station, usually cruising out of sight of land. There were slave barracoons at Gallinas holding 5,000 slaves, and others at New Cess with 1,500. He had asked three British captains why, instead of cruising in the hope of taking loaded slavers at sea, they did not blockade these places and take the empty ships as they went in to load. They had explained to him that there was no money in taking an empty slave ship to Sierra Leone; the legal expenses of getting the ship condemned swallowed up nearly the whole of her value. But if they took in a loaded vessel, they were sure of their £5 a head bounty without deductions. The American officer thought this a mercenary attitude. Would it not be best to land a force and destroy the barracoons? A hundred men

TOPSAIL SCHOONER AND BARQUE. Compare this drawing with the plate of the *Monkey* and the *Midas*.

could do it in the Gallinas, and a third of the number at New Cess. No doubt the barracoons would be rebuilt, but they could be destroyed again and again until the slavers lost heart.

The American Minister in London passed on these comments to the Foreign Office. Palmerston was not disposed to allow a newcomer on the coast to teach the Royal Navy how to do its business, and he made a spirited reply. As for the idea of the blockade, he said, both places mentioned had sometimes been blockaded for months on end But it was only recently that the Navy had been authorized by treaty to detain empty Spanish and Portuguese vessels: Spanish since 1835, Portuguese since 1839. Since 1835, the Navy had sent in eighty-five empty Spanish vessels, detained under the equipment clause, and fourteen Brazilian, against eighteen Spanish and two Brazilian vessels with a cargo of slaves on board. So much for the suggestion that British naval officers were mercenary. And Palmerston added that no foreign warship on the coast had ever detained a slaver; all vessels condemned had been detained by the Royal Navy. In this, Palmerston was going somewhat too far: a few captures had been made by Dutch, French, and even by American warships. But he was not very far from the truth, and the American Minister did not argue the point.

Nevertheless, the commander of the *Dolphin* had made one suggestion which might prove fruitful: why not destroy the barracoons? The operation might perhaps not be as easy as he thought, for since Lieutenant Courtenay's expedition in 1822 the river navigation had not been improved and the defences had been immensely strengthened. But if these large depots could be destroyed, it would be the heaviest blow ever struck against the slave traffic. The idea was worth bearing in mind.

Meanwhile, the new spirit of co-operation between British and Americans allowed the seizure and trial of vessels flying American colours. In 1839 and the first half of 1840, the *Eagle, Laura, Lark, Asp, Octavia* and *Eliza Davidson* were all condemned by the court at Sierra Leone.We have never before met English names like this in the records. All were flying American colours, but in each case the vessel's American nationality was dubious. The *Asp* for example was (like so

143

many more) built at Baltimore; she flew American colours and carried an American pass; her crew consisted of five Americans and eighteen Spaniards. But she was never American-owned; she was built to the order of Pedro Martinez and Co. of Cadiz, and was owned by them. The court held her American nationality to be fraudulent, and condemned her as a Spaniard.

THE 'EAGLE' AND THE 'CLARA'

This sunshine of co-operation was too bright to last, and the sky soon clouded over. The Americans did not take at all the same view of the right of search as the British law officers whom Palmerston consulted. It needed only two or three American slaving captains to return home, with tales of how the haughty British had interfered with American citizens sailing the high seas on their lawful occasions, to produce an outbreak of public indignation. In the autumn of 1841, feeling was heightened by the affair of the *Creole*. The *Creole* was an American vessel taking slaves from Hampton (Virginia) to New Orleans. No British warship came near her; but on the voyage, the slaves mutinied and compelled the crew to sail the vessel to the British port of Nassau in the Bahamas. There the slaves landed and proclaimed themselves free. The United States asked to have them handed back, but no British judge could possibly deliver them back to slavery, and they were allowed to stay in the Bahamas as free men.

The complicated cases of the *Eagle* and the *Clara* added to the tension. The *Eagle* was a brigantine, detained in Lagos on January 14, 1839; the schooner *Clara* was detained in the Rio Nun on March 18th in the same year. Both vessels were flying American colours; both were suspected of being Spanish. They were taken to Sierra Leone. The court there, more cautious than it became a few months later, refused to hear the cases, holding that British captains were not authorized to detain, nor was the court competent to try, vessels claiming American nationality. The court at Freetown was established, under the authority of sundry treaties, for the purpose of trying vessels belonging to nations which were party to those treaties. The United States was party to no treaty, and vessels claiming to be American were, the court held, out of its jurisdiction.

By arrangement with Spain, the Navy had a sort of advanced base in the Spanish island of Fernando Po for its operations in the Bight of Biafra. The *Eagle* and the *Clara* were taken to Fernando Po, and Lieutenant Fitzgerald of HMS *Buzzard* was ordered to escort both vessels to New York and hand them over to the American authorities there. He took them to New York and laid the evidence before the authorities, who observed that the *Eagle* had an American captain, who could be, and was, put on trial for slaving. But on the fundamental question of the vessels' nationality, the American court could give Fitzgerald no relief; it held that they were Spanish, and that he must take them away again. While awaiting the decision, the *Eagle* had been driven ashore in a gale; Fitzgerald had her repaired, and set sail with both ships for Bermuda, where he hoped the British court of Vice-Admiralty might take cognisance of the case and settle it. But the Bermuda court agreed with the court at New York: the vessels were Spanish, and so were properly under the jurisdiction of the court at Sierra Leone, and should be taken back there.

Fitzgerald, who must by now have been thoroughly sick of his charges, made sail again for Sierra Leone. The convoy had not been long at sea when it was struck by another Atlantic gale. The *Eagle* foundered, Fitzgerald managing with difficulty to save the prize crew; he had luckily kept her papers with him on the *Buzzard*. On Christmas Day he reached Freetown without his prize; on January 18, just over a year after she had first been detained, the *Eagle* was posthumously condemned by the court as a Spanish slaver.

The *Clara* parted company in the gale that sank the *Eagle*. Her prize crew managed to get her as far as Antigua. There she was patched up and sent on to Jamaica, the headquarters of the West Indian squadron of the Navy. The dockyard authorities there surveyed her and condemned her as unseaworthy. The *Clara* too was in due course condemned as a Spanish slaver by the Freetown court, though the vessel herself was unfit to appear.

To say the least of it, Fitzgerald and his crew had been put to a great deal of trouble in order to spare American susceptibilities; a whole year of hard work, anxiety and danger had got the two ships condemned at last, as they might have been in the first place if the Americans had not been so touchy. On the other hand, said the Americans, if the British were less high-handed, and would leave honest American seamen alone, two vessels flying the American flag would still be sailing the seas and earning money for their owners, instead of being dead, one rotting in dock and the other at the bottom of the sea.

In the early days of the naval patrol, West Africa had very little to export except slaves. Three or four ships a year could have carried all the gold and ivory there was available; and there was hardly anything else. But by the eighteen-forties, there was a good deal of legitimate trade. In 1808, the first year after abolition, the West African export of palm oil was only 200 tons; in 1827 it had risen to 4,700 tons, in 1834 to 14,000 tons, and in the 'fifties it was running at over 40,000 tons a year. This affected the Navy's problem in two ways. Whereas in the early days, a strange sail was more likely than not to be a slaver, this was no longer the case. A vessel carrying dozens of empty casks was just as likely to be carrying them for palm oil as for drinking water.

On the other hand, the legitimate trade in palm oil and palm kernels fluctuated according to the fortunes of the slavers. The African dealers much preferred the slave trade. It was much more lucrative. The 14,000 tons of oil exported in 1834 fetched £450,000, about £32 a ton. We have seen that eight years earlier, the Freetown court assessed the slaves on the *Activo* at over £60 each. If we take the conventional shippers' equivalent of 40 cubic feet to the ton, slaves were worth two or three times as much as palm oil; if we calculate by weight, they were worth twenty or thirty times. What African chief would trade in palm oil as long as he had a chance of trading in slaves? In 1848, James Hook, the British judge of the court at Freetown, wrote to Palmerston. He had been an abolitionist for more than thirty years, and had lived in Africa for a long time. If the British naval squadron were withdrawn, he was sure the slave trade would start up again everywhere.

'If our merchants entertain a hope that the trade of palm oil, gold, ivory, groundnuts, hides, wax, etc., will continue to exist after the withdrawal of our squadron, I fear that they will be woefully disappointed. The thousands of palm-oil carriers and agricultural labourers would instantly be kidnapped and carried on board slave vessels. After a time the remaining natives would avoid the coast as they would the locality of a plague.'

An increasing proportion of the American vessels on the coast was thus able to pass as legitimate traders, though not always without suspicion. In 1840 the barque *Jones* and the brig *Seamew* were sent to Sierra Leone; but they were released, and compensation was paid. The suspicion was sometimes very strong. In October 1839, Lieutenant Seagram of HMS *Termagant* detained the American brig *Douglass*, bound for Brass and Bonny. The master, Captain Baker, protested, 'with very strong and insulting language', says Seagram; though Baker says he was studiously polite and restrained under severe provocation. The vessel being American through and through, it would be useless to send her to Freetown, as the court there would not touch her. Seagram found what he considered enough to justify him in sending the vessel to America; but his superior officer told him not to send her there until they heard how the United States authorities behaved over the *Eagle* and the *Clara*. So Seagram kept the brig by him for eight days in the open sea; and then, hearing nothing from America and being unable to get in touch again with his superior officer, he took it on himself to let her go.

The cargo of the *Douglass* consisted of rum, cloth, tobacco, and a quantity of casks, planking and timbers. Baker said that all this wood was meant to build a house on shore; Seagram thought it could just as well be used to make a slave deck. Though he did not find them when he inspected the vessel, Seagram afterwards learned that she carried three large boilers of the kind normally used for cooking the slaves' food. There were seven Spanish passengers on board, of whom one was a well-known slave-dealer, and two others were admittedly going to take charge of slave factories in Brass and Bonny. Reading between the lines, I suspect that Seagram's judgment was influenced by Baker's curses and by the ironical politeness of the slave-dealer, Don Pablo Frexas, who 'gave him permission to examine his freight, under the impression that it was well protected by the American flag'. But Seagram was surely going much too far when he said that there was no cargo to be picked up at Brass and Bonny but slaves.

All these cases were sensibly and tactfully handled by the American Minister in London, Mr Stevenson. He admitted that he was not bound to believe that all American skippers were invariably as mild in manner as they claimed to be. On the other hand, one skipper was indignant because his cargo had been thoroughly inspected, and had been damaged by being roughly and carelessly stowed again. The British officer in command of the boarding party protested that his men had taken the greatest possible care to put everything back exactly as they found it. Mr Stevenson commented to Lord Palmerston that this cargo had been carefully stowed at the vessel's home port by professional dockers working under the eye of the ship's officers. It was surely not reasonable to suppose that British bluejackets, who were amateurs, could possibly have re-stowed the cargo to the master's satisfaction. Each side was naturally making the best case it could for itself; the truth must lie between them. As United States Minister, Mr Stevenson seems to have done a very good job in improving Anglo-American relations.

Under Mr Stevenson's persuasive influence, even Palmerston admitted that in the case of the *Douglass*, Britain had not a leg to stand on. The evidence against the brig was slender, and nothing could justify the Navy in detaining her for more than a week on the high seas. Still, for what it is worth, the evidence did suggest that the brig was to some extent involved in the slave trade; and Palmerston suggested (no doubt without any real hope) that the United States Government might consider taking proceedings against her in its own courts.

With Mr Stevenson in the United States embassy, and Palmerston and his much more pacific successor Lord Aberdeen at the Foreign Office, Anglo-American relations were improving. With so many more slavers flying the American flag, the United States Government was finding it harder to reject the principle of the British plea: Either allow us to inspect vessels flying the Stars and Stripes, or else send a squadron of your own to do the job.

In 1842, various points of difference between the two Governments were settled by the Webster-Ashburton Treaty, and relationships became much more friendly. The treaty provided a convenient opportunity for the United States to accept the British invitation and to send an American naval squadron to patrol the West African coast. The treaty provided that for the next five years, each nation should maintain on the West Coast a squadron of at least eighty guns. This minimum figure was low, about a third of the armament carried by the British squadron on the West Coast. American vessels tended to be more heavily gunned than British vessels of the same class; an American sloop carried twenty-eight guns compared with the British sloop's sixteen to twenty. The treaty did not specify a minimum number of ships; only of guns.

In a formal treaty between Governments, it was perhaps too much to hope for arrangements as frank and easy as those between Commodore Tucker and the USS *Grampus*. The United States Government dared not go so far ahead of public opinion as to grant the Royal Navy the right to board and inspect American vessels. But the two Governments hit on an ingenious compromise: the system of joint cruising. The ships would cruise in pairs, a British and an American vessel together. If they stopped a vessel and she hoisted the Stars and Stripes, the British ship would stand aside while the American cruiser inspected her. If she hoisted any other colours, the

British cruiser would do the job. American vessels would be sent to America for trial, others to the mixed courts at Freetown.

The system of joint cruising implied that the two squadrons should be equal in numbers. Loyally worked, it should be able to put down the slave trade quite soon, if indeed it could ever be put down by naval operations at sea. This was an important qualification. Lawyers, diplomatists and other landsmen do not always realize how wide is the ocean, and how great are the difficulties in catching a ship when once she has disappeared over the horizon on a voyage of 4,000 miles. There was a plentiful supply of slaves at one end of the sea-lane, an almost insatiable market at the other. Could even forty ships of war hope to catch two slavers out of three? Would it not be better to destroy the barracoons?

There was certainly no lack of loyalty on the part of the American naval men. When they had seen the slavers at work, they were just as bitterly angry as their British colleagues at the wastefulness and brutality of the business. The American squadron stayed on the coast beyond the five years prescribed by the treaty, and British officers, as they had done twenty years before, spoke highly of the zealous and cordial co-operation they received. In 1849, Commodore Gregory commanded an American squadron consisting of the sloops *Portsmouth*, *John Adams* and *Dale*, and the brigs *Porpoise* and *Perry*; and his relations with Commodore Fanshawe of the Royal Navy were most cordial. But the American commanders worked under difficulties. They did not use the Freetown base, but set up a base of their own at the Cape Verde islands, nearly a thousand miles away to the north-west. Here the squadron was reasonably well placed for cruising on the sea-lane between West Africa and the Caribbean, but 1,000 miles worse off than its British colleagues for patrolling the slaving grounds from the Rio Pongas to the Gaboon. An American vessel's stay on patrol was correspondingly shorter than that of its British partner. Freetown itself was awkwardly placed for a naval base, nearly at one end of the coast; the Cape Verde islands were far worse. If only the United States Government had been able to establish a naval base at Fernando Po or the Gaboon!

Moreover, the American commanders did not always receive much support from the civil authorities at home. Sir Charles Hotham, who was commodore of the Royal Navy squadron on the West Coast from October 1846 to March 1849, was questioned by a parliamentary Select Committee. Did the American squadron, he was asked, interfere in any way in the suppression of the slave trade?

'In one case only, to the best of my recollection; and for so interfering, the officer got into great difficulty with his own government. He watched and captured a ship that evidently intended to take a cargo of negroes across; she was at that time of course under the American flag. He sent her to New York; it was found by the commander that the trial was nearly concluded, and was going entirely against him, when he arrived in the port of New York, made his appearance in court, and obtained a milder sentence, but not more than that.'

Hotham went on to emphasize that there was no possible doubt about the case; the master admitted that he intended to load a cargo of slaves – but he had not yet loaded his cargo. And he emphasized, too, that all the American naval commanders were anxious to take ships to New York for trial; 'but the certainty that they will be convicted in costs naturally deters them'. It sounds as if the American courts were afflicted with the same sort of difficulties through an inflexible procedure as the mixed court at Freetown had been twenty years earlier. No doubt they would overcome these difficulties in time.

Relationships between the British and American squadrons seem to have been good. When the American squadron under Commodore Perry arrived on the station in 1843, the British commodore, Captain Foote, wrote Perry a cordial letter. Perry acknowledged it in warm terms:

'I . . . beg to assure you that it will afford myself and the officers under my command the greatest pleasure to join in mutual acts of courtesy and friendship with those of your squadron; and as evidence of my desire to meet your proposition with frankness and promptitude, I have this day addressed a General Order to all commanders of vessels of the American squadron expressing my wishes in the subject; a copy of which, with the extract from the rules and regulations referred to, you will receive herewith. . . .'

Perry's General Order to his captains copies Foote's letter,

'in which he enjoins upon all captains, commanders and commanding officers under his command to use their best endeavours to create a feeling of courtesy and friendship towards the officers of the American squadron when they may be in company with each other.

In the same spirit and with a like desire to foster a friendly intercourse with the officers of Her Majesty's Navy, as well as with those of other powers serving on the African coast, I have to request the officers of the American squadron studiously to endeavour not to be outdone in those courteous interchanges of civilities which are alike honourable to all parties.'

The rules and regulations, to which Perry goes on to refer his officers, are not specially impressive. They merely lay down in great detail the etiquette of salutes and other courtesies between American ships of war and the naval and civil authorities of foreign powers.

All this is very well; and if we are inclined to demur to the emphasis which is laid on creating feelings of courtesy and friendship, as if such feelings ought to exist naturally, we must remind ourselves that it was scarcely thirty years since British and American warships had been fighting each other broadside to broadside, and a good many British frigates had been captured and recommissioned into the United States Navy.

The arrangements seem to have worked. In October, 1843, Lieutenant Gray commanding HMS *Bonetta* detached his gig with a week's provisions to keep watch on two Liberian ports; and in reporting this to Foote, he takes

'the opportunity of making known to you the very handsome

conduct of Lieutenant Stellwagen of the US brig of war *Porpoise* in volunteering to remain off New Cestos and look after the safety of the boats and render them any assistance they may require; and I have never known more kindly feelings evinced than the officers and crew of the US brig have shown whenever we have been in company.'

But joint cruising was another matter, and it never became fully effective. Like a wise man, Foote had a long talk with Perry about it before putting anything in writing, and he found Perry eager to co-operate. He had already given the American commanding officers orders to cruise in company with British ships when they could:

'I shall consider it highly desirable that a vessel of each nation should as far as possible cruise in company with a vessel of the other, so that each may be in a condition to assert the rights and prevent the abuse of the flag of our country. In this way, all just ground of difference or collision will be removed, while this harmonious co-operation of the two powers will go far to insure the full development of their common object, in the suppression of the slave trade.'

So Perry had instructed his captains. But there was an insuperable difficulty, which he thus explained to Foote:

'In regard to the proposition of joint cruising, you will perceive by reference to the paper herewith enclosed that the commanding officers of vessels under my command have been from their first coming on the coast instructed on that point. But I fear from the small number of vessels composing the American squadron, and considering its various duties and the great extent of their cruising ground, that the co-operation by joint cruising has been and will continue to be less effective than might be desired. I shall however continue so to arrange the movements of the vessels under my command as to enable them to act in concert, whenever it can be done, with those of Her Britannic Majesty.'

There we have it. However keen the two commodores

might be to work a system of joint cruising, it is unworkable unless the two squadrons are equal in numbers. Six or eight American ships based on the Cape Verde islands could not possibly cruise often in company with eighteen or twenty British ships based on Freetown. The United States Government never raised its African squadron to anything approaching the strength of the British West African squadron.

However, the system had its successes: some American slavers were taken, whether or not they were subsequently condemned in the American courts. Even American vessels could sometimes be caught unawares. Captain Broadhead, RN, was lucky enough to catch the American slaver *My Boy*, which had eluded the whole squadron very often. He heard that she was going to Accra (a British port) to replenish her stores. He took care to be well away from Accra when she arrived; but he left one of his boats there, lurking behind one of the merchant ships at anchor in the roadstead. The *My Boy* arrived and found the coast apparently clear; and the instant she went in and dropped her anchor, Broadhead's boat went alongside and took her. She was tried and condemned in a British Admiralty court for being equipped for the slave trade and at anchor in British waters.

In spite of the inflexible attitude of the United States Government on the inviolability of its flag, American ships often submitted to a British boarding party without trouble. The Navy logs record the event in the most matter-of-fact way in four words: 'Boarded American schooner *Kathleen*', or whatever the vessel's name and rig might be. In 1843, for example, HMS *Ferret* boarded the schooner *Providence* on January 16th, the schooner *Kathleen* on February 14th, the barque *Reaper* on March 8th, the brig *Mary Pauline* on April 1st. Two years later, HMS *Cygnet* boarded nine American vessels in eight months.

It may be thought dangerous to infer that a matter-of-fact log entry means that there was no trouble. But trouble seems to be duly recorded. On August 27, 1845, HMS *Cygnet* found the American schooner *Merchant* with other ships in Cabinda bay. The *Merchant* was boarded, and next day Commander Layton sent

'Mr Will Davidson (Acting Gunner) and a party of seven men to take charge of and navigate to Sierra Leone the *Merchant* flying American colours, which schooner is detained on suspicion of flying false colours. . . . .'

But twenty-four hours later the schooner was still there, and Layton had to take stronger measures:

'At 5.15 sent marines (armed) to assist in getting under weigh the schooner *Merchant* in consequence of the mutinous conduct of her mate and crew. Found it necessary to put one Spaniard, who appeared to be the ringleader, both legs in irons. Sent one marine and one seaman to increase her crew. 6.30 sailed the schooner *Merchant*. . . .'

If Commander Layton records this sort of trouble in such detail, it is probably safe to infer that when he merely says 'Boarded American brig *Margaret Ann*', the boarding officer met with little or no difficulty.

One of the nine American vessels which the *Cygnet* met on this cruise was the schooner *Tellus*, which seems to have aroused suspicion by being always in the *Cygnet*'s way, and yet to have been very easy-going. The *Cygnet* boarded her three times in ten days towards the end of March near Whydah. After this the *Tellus* ambled easily along westwards, and a week later the *Cygnet* saw her again on April 10th and 12th near Popo, without boarding. On the 13th, having covered eighty miles in a week, she was off Keta, and was boarded for the fourth time. No doubt this sort of loitering on the coast was suspicious. Slavers, having put their equipment ashore, often loitered about until their cargo was ready. But why behave in this way if you are coming for ivory or palm oil or hides; why not drop anchor and wait for it?

On this cruise, the *Cygnet* also spoke two American warships, the ship *Yorktown* and an unnamed corvette. She met them within two days of each other, but there was no question of cruising in company.

When a British cruiser had to act on her own, a delicate situation could easily arise. In February 1844, Commander Bosanquet, of HM sloop *Alert*, met the American brigantine *Uncas* at sea some distance south-west of Sherbro island. The wind was light, and he sent a lieutenant in the gig to board her. The master allowed the British officer to go on board, and when he returned to his ship he reported that 'there were several suspicious circumstances' about the vessel. The master said that she was coming from Havana, but refused to show him his clearance certificate from Havana, or from any other port. He was not at all co-operative. Bosanquet decided to press the matter further. The *Uncas* had made sail again and got well ahead of the *Alert*, so Bosanquet had to chase her. He caught her up without difficulty, and fired a blank shot to make her heave to once more. This time, Bosanquet went on board himself, taking the same lieutenant with him. The master saw that he would have to be more communicative, and he produced his log. According to this document, his ship had left the West African coast the previous September for Havana; she called at Key West in Florida for a bill of health and duly arrived at Havana in ballast. There she loaded half a cargo of trade goods – only half a cargo – and sailed for the Gallinas. She was on her way there now, and should arrive in a few days. 'And what then?' asked Bosanquet. Then, said the master blandly, he expected to return to Havana in ballast, as he did before.

Bosanquet felt he could do nothing with a man who was so sure of his position that he did not even take the trouble to tell a plausible lie. He and his lieutenant turned to inspect the ship. The crew were all foreign; the ship was equipped with the usual type of gratings that slavers all carried for ventilating the hold; she had some very large casks, which were not water-tight but which the ship's cooper could easily make so. He says nothing about food boilers or mess tubs or shackles. But the master's story was as leaky as his water-casks. What ship-owner will run his ship outwards with a cargo, or even half a cargo, and homewards with nothing? Was the skipper proposing to distribute his half cargo in free gifts to the African chiefs? Nothing was more likely than that he should arrive empty in Havana harbour. That was a well-known trick among slaving captains; they put their slaves ashore in some minor port at the other end of Cuba, and came home to Havana to bewail the bad state of trade which had brought them home with an empty ship. The two British officers were convinced they were dealing with a rogue. 'I have no doubt in my own mind,' says Bosanquet in his report to the commodore, 'that this vessel carried slaves to Cuba last voyage.' But he adds regretfully, 'I considered it advisable to let her proceed, fearing it might cause an unpleasant correspondence between Her Majesty's Government and that of the United States.' There are many such vessels, says the commodore, Foote; let us hope that the United States squadron will be able to deal with them. As for the *Uncas*, Commodore Foote soon had satisfactory news of her. Shortly after being released by HMS *Alert*, the *Uncas* had the misfortune to fall in with the USS *Porpoise*, which arrested her and sent her with a prize crew to New York for adjudication.

Nevertheless, with American as well as British warships on patrol, the slavers' position in the 'forties was becoming insecure, and their captains often showed their nervousness. On August 10, 1845, the *Cygnet* boarded the American ship *Calhoun* at Cabinda. When the *Cygnet* returned to Cabinda on August 27th, the *Calhoun* was still there. The *Cygnet* stayed a day or two and then sailed again for the south; and in the next few weeks she met the *Calhoun* hanging around aimlessly more than once. On September 24th, the *Cygnet*, acting on information received, decided to sail up the Congo, and she saw a strange ship in the river ahead of her. From two in the afternoon till 3.30, the *Cygnet* chased her up the broad estuary, and then the officer of the watch saw that the stranger was on fire, but was still standing steadily up the river. At 4.30 the stranger, still blazing, turned sharply and ran herself full on shore, and three boatloads of men left her. The *Cygnet's* boats went off to inspect the ship and see if they could find out anything about her, but they could not get near because of the heat. Next morning the fire had burnt itself out, and the boats went off again to search the ship, but she was burnt down to the water's edge; they could find nothing, and there was nothing left to salve but her anchor and its cable.

It was a mystery. One thing was certain: no captain with a clear conscience would destroy his ship thus. The sequel came a month later, when Commander Layton took on board the *Cygnet* two distressed British subjects from Cabinda:

'they having been landed from the American ship *Calhoun* from Baltimore, E. C. Fales master and owner, previous to her shipping slaves and being run ashore in the river Congo by this brig[1] on September 24th'.

So it was our old friend the *Calhoun*. Mr Fales had been boarded once by this Limey brig. For weeks she had been hanging around on his tail as if she suspected him of being up to no good; and now, just when he thought he had shaken her off and was running up the river to load his cargo, here she was after him again. The game was up; better scuttle the ship than be sent back to New York for trial.

This suicidal tendency was not uncommon. In April 1846 the *Cygnet* was near Quicombo in Angola, and saw a sail ahead. There was very little wind, so Layton sent his boats after her. She promptly turned towards the land and ran herself ashore under full sail, her crew landing in the boats. The two boats from the *Cygnet* reached her after a two-hour row, and the men boarded her. They found her to be on fire in both holds. The fire had got such a grip that they could do nothing with it; the master had taken her papers ashore with him and they could find out very little about her. They did find that she was fully equipped for slaving, with the slave deck laid

---

[1] The *Cygnet* was rated as a sloop. The early volumes of her log are headed 'Log of HM brig *Cygnet*'; but after she had been refitted and recommissioned, all the later volumes are headed 'Log of HM sloop *Cygnet*'. There is at least one other similar case, that of HMS *Ferret*. By 1845 the word *sloop*, which had been used to mean the smallest kind of full-rigged ship in the Navy, was being used more loosely to cover other kinds of smallish vessels.

and the shackles all ready. But who she was, and of what nation, it was impossible to discover. As for salvage, all the *Cygnet* could get from this wreck was floating timber for firewood, which as it happened she did need. The boats spent all the afternoon rowing about picking it up; and there was an end of that anonymous slaving brig.

Off Little Popo, just before four in the morning on January 4, 1845, Layton saw a sail on his starboard bow. He made all sail ahead in chase, and rapidly overhauled her. Both vessels were standing WNW., reaching with the breeze full on the port beam. When the chase began, the *Cygnet* was eight miles from the shore; but the coast here trends slightly south of west, and before long, Layton saw the land on his lee beam. It the stranger went on much longer at this rate, she would pile herself up on the beach; surely she must soon put about and try to duck past him? As soon as it was daylight, Layton hoisted his colours and fired a gun to tell the chase to heave to. She took no notice but carried on her course for another quarter of an hour; and then she fired a gun, put up her helm and turned sharply to starboard, and ran herself ashore under full sail, the crew escaping to land in the boats. Layton brought the Cygnet to anchor in six fathoms and sent his boats to board the vessel. They found her to be a heavily armed brig, fully equipped for slaving; she was rapidly settling in the heavy surf, and the crew had set her on fire in two places. Layton's men were at work searching the wreck from early morning until nearly midnight, and again for some hours the next day, Layton meanwhile firing an occasional gun to keep the local African villagers from coming on board to loot her. He took her papers and went off to report and to set the legal machinery moving.

From the log of only one of HM ships, here are three slaving captains within a few months – one of them certainly an American – who deliberately destroyed their vessels at the mere sight of the naval patrol, without the least attempt to fight or to bluff their way out. The slavers must have felt by this time that the game was going very much against them. They must have been greatly afraid of the consequences of capture if they preferred to destroy their ship and risk the hardship of spending some weeks ashore as the guests of their disappointed African clients. Sir Charles Hotham thought that American skippers ran but little risk. Still, by American law, the master of a slave ship was guilty of piracy and liable to the death penalty. Many an American captain may well have had insufficient confidence in his legal advisers and a New York jury, and thought it safer to destroy all evidence of his slaving – even including his ship – than to risk being escorted home by an American warship to stand his trial.

As far as it went, the system of joint cruising was infallible. Once cornered by a pair of cruisers, no slaving captain had a chance of escape. If he hoisted American colours, the American ship boarded him and sent him home for trial. If he hoisted Spanish or Brazilian or any other colours, the British ship boarded him and sent him to Sierra Leone.

But as the American squadron never became strong enough to make joint cruising the rule, the British ships were usually alone, and a British ship without American support was always at a disadvantage in dealing with an American merchant captain. The American might be co-operative and allow his papers to be inspected; but if he chose to be truculent and stand on his rights as a free citizen of the United States, there was very little that the British officer could do for fear of provoking an international incident.

After the Brazilian market was closed in the early 'fifties, nearly all the remaining Atlantic slave trade was carried on in American vessels. For the American owners and skippers, it became a sport; and not the less a sport because there was big money in it. They built themselves the fastest possible clippers and embarked with glee on the game of outwitting and out-sailing the British cruisers. The game was not ended until the abolitionist movement in the North became strong enough to control the actions of the Federal Government. In 1854 the Republican party was established on an anti-slavery platform; and the cause of slavery and the slave trade was doomed when the Confederate guns opened fire on Fort Sumter.

It is not easy to sum up fairly the American attitude to the slave trade. The American laws against it were severe, and the Federal Government seems on the whole to have wished to enforce them. But extremely powerful business interests, even in the North, were deeply involved in the trade, and when American citizens were charged with slave dealing it was difficult to get them convicted by a jury. The death penalty, laid down in 1820, was not exacted until 1862.

Mr N. P. Trist and many other Americans did not believe in the British humanitarian motive. They thought the humanitarian plea a piece of typical British hypocrisy. They knew that a great part of the trade goods which were used to buy the slaves came from British factories, and they suspected that the British Government's real motive in maintaining the African squadron was to chivy American vessels off the coast and secure a monopoly of the trade there for Britain. Most of the American naval men who saw the slave trade in operation were as convinced as their British colleagues that it was a devilish business which ought to be stopped. But their Government never gave them very much support. The American ambassador John Quincy Adams was asked in England whether there could possibly be a worse evil than the slave trade. He replied tartly that there could: it would be a much worse evil if the United States Government should allow any vessel flying the Stars and Stripes to be stopped and examined by a British cruiser, for that would be to make slaves of the whole American people. That American attitude persisted fairly widely until the last days of the Atlantic slave trade.

The crux of the matter is that if the Government and people of the United States had sincerely wished to end the slave trade, they could easily have done so at any time by making full use of the Freetown naval base (which they were invited to do) and by providing a naval squadron strong enough to carry out the system of joint cruising. Stationing a squadron of five or six ships at the Cape Verde islands was merely playing with the problem.

Chapter Eight

TRIUMPH, DISAPPOINTMENT REVIVAL

During the 1840s, both the Foreign Office and the Admiralty could congratulate themselves. The Navy had great success with a new type of offensive action against the slavers. The Foreign Office had succeeded in making effective treaties with all possible slaving nations, both in Europe and in America. Lord Aberdeen even 'remembered the Alamo' and included in this diplomatic network the infant republic of Texas; but here he overreached himself, for Americans were already looking on Texas as a future State – or maybe a group of States – in the Union, and they did not approve of its having independent diplomatic links with the Old World. In 1841, the five Great Powers of Europe agreed to a treaty with the equipment clause, and with reciprocal rights of search over the whole area of ocean between 32 degrees North and 45 degrees South, and from the American coast to 80 degrees East. France, which signed the treaty, afterwards refused to ratify it; but her refusal was of no great importance, because by then there was an adequate French squadron at work patrolling the coasts and sending suspected French vessels for trial at Senegal or Cayenne. In 1839, with little regard for the niceties of international law, Palmerston brought pressure to bear on Portugal by obtaining an Act of Parliament which provided that Portuguese and stateless 'pirates' might be treated as if they were British. This induced Portugal to acquiesce in the operation of the equipment clause, and in 1842 she accepted it formally by treaty. As for the United States, it seemed for the time as if the system of joint cruising which was established by the Webster-

Ashburton treaty had sufficiently tightened the control over American vessels.

Brazil was still a weak spot. The slave trade had been illegal for Brazilians since 1829, but nothing was done to enforce the law. There was one case in the 'thirties where a captain in the Brazilian Navy dared to capture a vessel engaged in the illicit slave traffic. *Pour encourager les autres,* that captain was dismissed his ship. Slaves continued to pour into Brazil, and the Government would listen to no British representations on the subject from the commissioners of the mixed court at Rio or from the British Minister. In 1835, British and Brazilian delegates agreed on supplementary articles to the treaty, but the Brazilian Government refused to ratify them. The Bill for ratifying the articles was defeated in the Brazilian parliament, and the Government had some difficulty in staving off a counter-motion in favour of resuming the unrestricted importation of slaves in defiance of the treaty with Britain. In 1841 and 1842 Britain made fresh proposals, but Brazil refused to consider them:

'The Imperial Government not only consider that other dispositions besides those which already exist are now unnecessary in order to the total extinction of the traffic, but they regard it as prudent not to adopt any others.'

Lord Aberdeen replied that the two nations were bound by a treaty, and that if Brazil would not fulfil her side of the treaty, Britain might have to act alone.

Brazil was still defiant. In 1845 she closed the mixed court at Rio and told Britain that the treaty of November 1826 must now lapse, as the traffic had now been illegal for all Brazilian citizens for more than fifteen years.

Even the pacific Lord Aberdeen was ready to call this sort of bluff. He replied that the trade had certainly been illegal for fifteen years, and as it still flourished, it must be assumed that the Brazilian Government was powerless to do its share in suppressing it:

'This being the case, Her Majesty's Government have no

longer any course open to them under the convention of November 23, 1826, than that of giving full effect to the stipulations of the First Article of that convention, under which Her Majesty has acquired the right to order the seizure of all Brazilian subjects found upon the high seas engaged in the slave trade, of punishing them as pirates, and of disposing of the vessels in which they may be captured, together with the goods belonging to them, as *bona piratarum.*'

Unless the Brazilian Government had any useful counter-proposals, he was prepared to introduce a Bill into Parliament to give the necessary authority to the officers of the Royal Navy. In fact, the bill was introduced, and passed, in 1845.

The wealthy slave-dealers in Brazil, many of them Portuguese, were too influential for the Brazilian Government to make any useful counter-proposals. Brazil was under-populated and needed the slaves; it was merely a question of playing for time while the enormous illegal importation of slaves went on. Brazil played for time from 1845 till 1849, during which time Aberdeen as Foreign Secretary was replaced by Palmerston. In 1849 Palmerston lost patience and sent Admiral Reynolds with a squadron to capture the slave ships on the Brazilian coast. It was, of course, contrary to international law to take such action in Brazilian waters. But there was an abolitionist movement growing up among the younger generation of Brazilians, who resented the influence of the corrupt and wealthy Portuguese in their country's affairs. Palmerston knew this, and knew that there was a section of public opinion in Brazil that would respond when he blandly explained that he was merely assisting the Brazilian Government to enforce its own laws. Admiral Reynolds was very successful. The British Minister in Rio reported that in the last half of 1850, only eleven ships had managed to land slaves in Brazil, and every one of the eleven had later been seized, burnt, or sunk. The slaves landed totalled 5,108, whereas the average import during the second half of the three previous years had been over 24,000.

The agitation in Brazil was intense, and the air was thick

with protests, appeals, and denunciations. Brazil promised that if only the British warships would cease their violence, she would herself take effective steps to put an end to the traffic. The British squadron did hold its hand for six months, and nothing effective was done; so Admiral Reynolds became active once more. The Brazilian Minister in London made a vehement protest. 'You assert,' said Palmerston in his reply,

'that the measures adopted by Her Majesty's Government on the coast of Brazil tend to retard instead of accelerating the suppression of the slave trade, and that if Her Majesty's Government would confine their measures to the coast of Africa, and cause them entirely to cease upon the coast of Brazil, the Brazilian slave trade would at once and for ever cease.'

But from 1826 to 1850, said Palmerston, there were no British naval operations on the Brazilian coast; and what happened? 'During the whole of that time, an enormous number of Africans were annually imported into Brazil with the full knowledge of the Brazilian Government and with the undisguised connivance of its officers, high and low.' Brazil had never lifted a finger to enforce her own laws against the slave trade, except during the last few months, when the Royal Navy had been active.

The Brazilian rejoinder was honest, if somewhat lame. It is not true, says the Brazilian Minister, that from 1826 to 1850 the Brazilian Government has done nothing. It has done a great deal. It has laboured to calm the irritation in Brazil over the seizure of Brazilian vessels off the African coast. It has tried to educate public opinion to disapprove the slave trade. And (this is most significant) it has worked hard at the difficult task of persuading its people that Britain's motives were genuinely philanthropic; the general opinion was that Britain was merely trying to cripple Brazilian agriculture in the interests of British colonies.

But this was the end of an old song. The Brazilian importation of slaves during the 1840s was running at about 50,000 a year. It dropped to 3,000 in 1851, to 700 in 1852, and to nil in 1853. Many of the Portuguese slave dealers took their profits and returned to Portugal, and the Brazilian slave market was closed.

POLITICAL DEVELOPMENTS IN WEST AFRICA

On the West African coast itself, the Navy's task was being somewhat eased by political developments. British influence was becoming stronger on the Gold Coast, which had formerly been one of the chief seats of the slave trade. The Gold Coast was dotted with British, Dutch and Danish 'castles', fortified trading stations maintained by the big commercial companies. Denmark had effectively abolished her slave trade before Britain. The British company men dared not encourage the trade after the British Act of 1811 declared it a felony. The Dutch officers were slower to come into line; in the 1820s at least one British naval officer received a very tart answer when he protested to a Dutch commandant for allowing slave vessels to be supplied with water and with canoes from under the guns of his fort. This was all cleared up by 1830. But the Europeans did not control the whole coast. They were tenants of the local African tribes, paying rent for the land they occupied, and they had no political authority. The castles stood fairly thickly along the coast, but slaves could be, and occasionally were, exported in small boatloads from villages out of gunshot of any European post.

From 1831 to 1843, the British stations on the Gold Coast were ruled by an outstanding man, Captain George Maclean. So great was his personal reputation among the Africans that they came to him from all quarters to submit their disputes to his judgment. Over a hundred miles of coast and to a depth of thirty to forty miles inland, Maclean's word was law. After Maclean's time we may take it that over this stretch of coast, between the Volta and Pra rivers, and even for a short distance west of the Pra, slave trading was extinct.

Further east, British missionaries and African traders from Sierra Leone were beginning to settle and work in the Yoruba country of Western Nigeria, the hinterland of Badagry and Lagos, whence so many slaves were exported.

There was political development, too, on what the naval men called the Windward Coast. With the constant landing of freed slaves taken from captured slave ships, the British colony of Sierra Leone was growing and consolidating its position. In 1825 the Governor, Charles Turner, took the opportunity of an inter-tribal war to persuade the chiefs of Sherbro island to cede political authority to the British; but the Government in London disowned his action. Sherbro was almost as important a centre of the slave trade as the Gallinas. The channel between the island and the mainland was called Shebar, spelt by the naval men Seabar; it was a great haunt of slavers. In 1818 the American Colonization Society, which was formed to imitate the British example at Sierra Leone, made a settlement on Sherbro island. They soon found it too unhealthy, and in 1821 they moved their settlement of liberated Negroes to a new site further east, which they named Monrovia in honour of President Monroe. In 1847 the Society gave its settlements at Monrovia and elsewhere their independence, and they formed the republic of Liberia. It was only a matter of time before the slave trade in Sherbro, Shebar and the Gallinas would be suppressed either by the Sierra Leone or by the Liberian Government.

THE GALLINAS BARRACOONS

The Sierra Leone authorities had been disturbed more than once by the kidnapping of free citizens of Sierra Leone who had gone on business to the Gallinas or the Rio Pongas. In 1840, the combination of a determined Governor, Richard Doherty, and a determined naval officer, Commander Joseph Denman, decided to put a stop to this nuisance.

There lived in Sierra Leone a poor woman, Mrs Fry Norman, who earned her living as a washerwoman. One of her customers was a Mr Lewis; he owed her money, and one day in October 1840 Mrs Norman heard an alarming report that he was going to the West Indies, and had already left Freetown on his way to the Gallinas, where he hoped to find a ship. The loss of Mr Lewis's washing money was a serious matter for Mrs Norman, so she tucked her baby on her back and went off to the Gallinas to catch him before he could escape. She saw Mr Lewis and she got her money, but then she fell into terrible trouble. She was recognized by an African chief named Manna, the son of King Siaka; he had seen her some time before at Freetown, when she had been employed as an apprentice by a Freetown lady, Mrs John Grey. Mrs Grey owed him money, and he announced that he would keep Mrs Norman and her baby as security for the debt. Poor Mrs Norman pleaded that she no longer had any connection with Mrs Grey. That was immaterial to Prince Manna; he was sure that Mrs Grey would rather pay the money she owed him than see Mrs Norman and her baby held indefinitely in the Gallinas, with the horrible possibility of being passed into the slave barracoons.

So Mrs Norman wrote to her husband and to Mrs Grey, begging them to do what they could to get her out of this trouble. Her pathetic letters are still extant. 'Respected Mother, Rosamia Grey,' she wrote,

'I hope when you receive this letter it may find you and family well. I have to inform you that Mr Manna has catched me on your account, and is determined to detain me till you come yourself; you may try to come as quick as possible, and if you cannot get a passage direct here you may get to Sherbro, and Mr François will see that you get a passage here. I am now equal to a slave, because I do not know what may happen to me. Between now and night all depends on the good or evil heart of Mr Manna. Therefore you will lose no time in coming to my assistance on your account. I hope to see you in a short time after you receive this letter.'

Her letters came to the hands of the Governor, Richard Doherty. He was not the man to submit to this blackmail. Fry Norman was a British subject and entitled to British protection. He passed the case to Commander Joseph Denman of

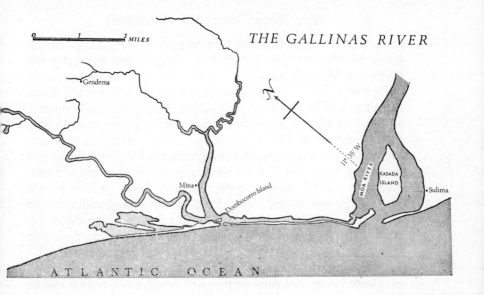

NOTES ON THE GALLINAS RIVER

The name Gallinas has disappeared from the modern ordnance map. The river is now called Kerefe. Modern aerial photography shows that the description given by the naval officers is not quite accurate in detail; but Denman and Hotham had no opportunity to do any proper surveying, and their broad outlines are true enough. Much of the coastline here consists of a narrow sandspit with creeks and lagoons behind it. A large-scale map shows the entrance to the river to be narrow and twisty, in the shape of an S-bend. Immediately on emerging into the lagoons you come to an island of solid land (not merely sand-dunes) on the left; this, though un-named on the map, must be Dombocorro. No other islands are marked, and the three-mile basin does not now exist. There may have been some silting in 130 years. But the three creeks are there: one running north and somewhat west, one running north-east, and the third running south-east. King Siaka's town of Ghindamar is no doubt the modern Gendema. The south-easterly creek runs parallel to the coast, only the sandspit separating it from the Atlantic surf; and it communicates with the Moa river, up which your boat will turn north-east, as Denman describes it. On the Moa river stands the town of Sulima, which is no doubt the Solyman of the narrative. Hotham, we are told, proclaimed a blockade of the coast between Solyman and Cazee. There is a tiny hamlet, its name now spelt Kasi, on the coast about ten miles north-west of the Gallinas mouth. The whole counryside is as flat as your hand: much of it swamp, some of it scrub; round Gendema there is a tongue of forest country. The mangroves thrive still as they did in Denman's day. The hamlet of Tinch seems to have vanished, unless this name was a mishearing of the name Mina.

HMS *Wanderer*, and asked him to go to the Gallinas and to stand no nonsense, but to get Fry Norman and her baby out of Prince Manna's hands.

Denman was an energetic commander. He had already maintained a close blockade of the Gallinas for eight months on end, and out of twenty-one slave ships that used the river in that period, sixteen had been taken. Not only was this a privation to the slavers, but it made things difficult for King Siaka and his chiefs. Since the Spanish slavers, Pedro Blanco and the rest, made their headquarters in the Gallinas, Siaka and his people had specialized in the slave trade. They had abandoned not only their former trade in ivory and other local produce, but even the growing of their own food; they imported their rice from Sherbro island. They had powerful rivals inland who were jealous of their wealth and privilege, and Denman's blockade hampered their imports of rice from Sherbro and of consumer goods and firearms from America. Denman knew them of old. His first visit to the coast was in 1834, when he came there as prize master of a vessel captured near Rio; he had commanded HMS *Curlew* on the Coast in 1835; and for some months now he had been senior naval officer from Cape Verde to Cape Palmas. He had old scores to settle with the Gallinas chiefs, and he welcomed the chance of taking more drastic action against them.

The Gallinas bar was still as formidable as ever, and the Spaniards had greatly developed the estuary. Within the bar there was a sheet of water about three miles across in every direction, studded with islands, many of them occupied by warehouses or slave barracoons. Beyond this basin, the estuary divided into three creeks. One turned north-west and provided water communication with Sierra Leone; the second turned north-east, and on its bank, nine miles from the sea, stood King Siaka's town of Ghindamar; the third turned first south-east and then north-east. The water was shallow; the attack must be made by boats.

Denman collected a squadron, and on November 19th at daylight he entered the river with the flotilla of ship's boats. He was prepared for stiff resistance, but there was none. He saw the Spaniards, as Lieutenant Courtenay had seen them in 1822, hustling the slaves into canoes and taking them further up the river. He chased those canoes, and rescued about ninety slaves. Then he landed on the island of Dombocorro, the island nearest the bar, and awaited the arrival of King Siaka to palaver.

The Governor had given Denman a letter for King Siaka, but Denman did not give it to a messenger. He sent instead a letter of his own, saying that he expected King Siaka to come to Dombocorro and meet him. Moreover, he had come to demand the surrender of Fry Norman and her child; and after they were given up to him he had other matters to discuss.

Denman had enough African experience not to expect a speedy reply. None came that day. Next day Denman again waited at Dombocorro, and at 12.45 he had the first result of his firmness: one of Siaka's brothers appeared bringing Fry Norman and her child. This was a promising beginning, but for more than an hour nothing else happened. At two o'clock, Denman sent off another note, saying that he still had the Governor's letter to deliver, and that he intended to deliver it to King Siaka and to no one else. This message produced results. Prince Manna came, attended with crowds of chiefs, who all assured Denman that King Siaka was old and bed-ridden, and that his son Prince Manna was fully empowered to act for him.

Very well, said Denman, then we will talk. And there ensued a long palaver, in which Denman recounted a whole string of unfriendly acts – kidnappings, bloodshed and piracy '– committed in the Gallinas river. A few months later, Denman was in England giving evidence to a Select Committee of the House of Commons. He told the committee that he had wanted for a long time to take strong measures with the Gallinas people. One of the boats of HMS *Rolla* was stove, and the men had to bale hard with three buckets and just managed to get alongside an American brig anchored in the river. The American captain kindly hoisted the boat on board and repaired her. For this he was roundly abused by the Gallinas people; they told him he should have left the boat to sink or swim, and if he did that sort of thing again he would lose his trade. After this, several French and American merchant captains who would have liked to give assistance to naval men dared not do so; and the Navy had been much inconvenienced. No doubt Denman spelt out all these occasions to the Gallinas chiefs in much more detail than he did to the committee in Westminster.

The chiefs were aghast. These horrible things had been done by the Spanish slavers using their river, not by their people. The Spaniards had not consulted them or asked their permission; it would be quite wrong to punish them for what the Spaniards had done. Very well, said Denman; since you disown these men, help me to deal with them. I propose to destroy all these factories and slave barracoons and to take the slaves back to Freetown and liberate them there. I want you to fetch back all the slaves that have been taken into the bush and are being kept there; give them to me so that I can take them to Freetown with the others. And I want the slave trade in this river to cease altogether from now on.

The chiefs promised to consider his demands and give him a reply later. When the meeting was resumed next day they agreed to give up all the slaves and to destroy the barracoons. But to stop the slave trade altogether was too big an undertaking for them to give at short notice. This would affect other tribes besides theirs, and there must be inter-tribal consultations. With this, Denman had for the moment to be content.

Next day, the 22nd, the slaves began to arrive, and in the course of five days Denman received 880. Many of them, he learned, had been twelve months in the barracoons waiting for a ship. Some of them had been put into canoes as many as four times, but each time the slave ship had been afraid to load them and had sent them back to the barracoons. Denman seems to have been satisfied that the chiefs were playing fair with him and were not holding back any slaves. The barracoons, we are told, could hold 5,000. No doubt with trade having been so bad for the eight months of the blockade, the dealers had allowed their stocks to run low. As John Ormond had said earlier, what would be the use of keeping slaves in the barracoons eating their heads off when there was no chance of selling them?

While the parties of slaves were arriving, Denman and his men amused themselves with setting fire to the barracoons, while King Siaka's people salved and appropriated the trade goods which were stored in the warehouses. It was reckoned that the slavers lost goods worth £100,000 (some said much more); and moreover, they had already paid in advance for 13,000 slaves, who would now never be delivered to them for shipping. Slaves were not expensive in the Gallinas, but even so this must have meant an outlay of about £70,000, and the slavers were compelled to forego an expected profit of ten times that sum. Even a tycoon like Pedro Blanco would feel the weight of a blow like this. A wave of apprehension ran up and down the coast. Theodore Canot, who owned the barracoons at New Cess, had been blockaded by HMS *Termagant*. When he heard the sequel to the Gallinas blockade, he got in touch with Lieutenant Seagram and handed over 104 slaves; moreover, he promised to give up the trade altogether and turn respectable. Away in the Rio Pongas on the other side of Freetown, the Lightburns and Lawrences were thankful that they had already turned to coffee and cattle. John Ormond of Bangalang had died, and his slaves revolted and declared themselves free; they moved away from the river, built themselves a village and fortified it with a stockade.

All the Spanish slavers had retired inland, and neither they nor the Gallinas chiefs had any intention of giving up a lucrative trade if they could help it. The slaves were handed over in driblets. Denman wrote from his base at Dombocorro to a chief named Lamina on the 23rd, who had so far handed over no slaves. This letter produced a batch of thirty. Denman knew quite well that Lamina had others, and he wrote again: 'Prince Manna will deliver this letter to you, and unless you give up every one of these slaves immediately I will burn your town.' This produced seventy more, and Denman's intelligence service seems to have convinced him that King Lamina had no more to send. There was no satisfying Denman; he had received the slaves, he had burned the factories, and yet the man was still at Dombocorro and would not go away; what did he want now? The treaty, said the inflexible Denman: the treaty by which you promise to give up the slave trade. There was no escape; Manna and the chiefs agreed to the treaty, and the slave trade was formally abolished in the Gallinas river.

Denman had been completely successful in his operations, and the Admiralty were delighted; he was promoted captain, and instructions were sent to the naval officers on the Coast to follow the Denman formula: make war against the Spanish and other slave dealers, not against the African people; destroy the factories, liberate the slaves, and induce the African chiefs to agree to a treaty by which they bind themselves (in return for a small stipend) to prohibit the renewal of the traffic.

Denman was not so innocent as to expect the Gallinas chiefs to abide by the treaty unless they were compelled to. The barracoons were light constructions of poles and palm-leaf thatch; they could be rebuilt in a few days. The warehouses were somewhat more substantial; but in a country where every man was accustomed to build his own house, a week's communal effort would suffice to erect a warehouse. The blow he had struck in the Gallinas was heavy, but it would need to be repeated. He had captured the papers of the Pedro Martinez agent in the Gallinas:

'The tone of several of these letters from the Gallinas to Havana, dated in September and October last, is most depressing; the writers declare that their prospects have been nearly ruined by the vigilance of the British squadron.'

So reported James Hook from Freetown to Lord Palmerston. As Captain Matson, RN, explained in his evidence to the Select Committee, the Admiralty

'gave orders that wherever we found slave barracoons erected we should endeavour to obtain the sanction of the native chiefs to destroy them; failing to obtain that consent we were in certain cases to do it without. However, it was never difficult to obtain that consent, for it was always readily obtained for a very trifling subsidy; and most of the barracoons on the coast were destroyed. That had such an effect on the slave traders located on the coast of Africa that they gave notice to the native chiefs that they would not be any longer enabled to carry on the slave trade, and they prompted the chiefs to enter into treaties with us to allow us to destroy their barracoons, or at any rate to suppress the slave trade; and in every one of those treaties there was a stipulation that we were authorized to employ force, failing the execution of the treaty by the chief. Most of the chiefs in Africa, in fact all the principal ones, entered into the treaties with us.'

The Navy found these orders most congenial. Commander Hill of HMS *Saracen* had been with Denman in the Gallinas operation. Soon afterwards he went to the Shebar. He wanted fresh water for his ship, and he also had a copy of the model treaty which the Admiralty had sent him; he wanted the local chief, 'king Harry Tucker', to sign it. Tucker demanded an exorbitant price for water, and would sign no treaty. So Hill landed, and found a slave factory belonging to Mr Henry François (no doubt the man mentioned in Fry Norman's letter). The factory was deserted, and there was no sign of Tucker. But a few armed men appeared out of the bush. They said they were slaves of François, and he and Tucker had armed them and told them to fight against the Navy. But for their part they much preferred to give themselves up and obtain their freedom: why should they fight for the right to remain in slavery? François had beaten them and fettered them in his barracoons. There were about fifty of them, out of some 300 to 400 who had been imprisoned there. Hill suggested that before coming away with him, they might like to burn their barracoons, and they gladly did so.

Captain Blount of HMS *Pluto* was also with Denman in the Gallinas. After a while he was quite sure that the treaty was not being observed. The *Pluto* was a shallow-draught steamer, designed for river work. The naval officers all hated her. She was very slow; her maximum speed was seven or eight knots.

She could carry coal for ten days steaming, and if she had to fire her boilers with wood instead of coal (as on the West African coast at that time she often must) a full load of wood would carry her for only three days. One of her commanding officers described her tersely as 'one of the worst vessels in the Navy'. Still, for river work she had her uses; she could go where sailing ships could not. Blount took her much higher up the river. He found several factories fifteen or twenty miles from the sea. One of them was well armed, and fired at him with a battery of guns ranging from 3-pounders to twelves. Blount got the local chief to help him. He found 159 slaves, all chained with iron chains round their necks, which he had to cut off with a cold chisel. Then he destroyed all the factories and the goods they contained, and threw their ammunition in the river. Some of the factories near the mouth of the river had been rebuilt, so Blount destroyed them again.

The naval men were feeling thoroughly savage against the slave dealers. They drew a distinction between the European dealers like Pedro Blanco or Theodore Canot and the African chiefs who supplied them with slaves. Without being sentimental towards the chiefs, they felt that they were more sinned against than sinning. Denman said that the Gallinas was a good country, and it had formerly had a good trade before the Spaniards came and spoilt it all. It produced camwood and ivory, and there was some gold further inland. There was cotton, indigo, pepper, oil palm, sugar and tobacco; all of these might be commercially developed, and there were chances of a cattle industry. But the Spaniards had ruined all this by concentrating on the slave trade. As James Hook had said, the slave trade would always kill other trade if it was allowed to do so. It was only the Navy that kept the slave trade down and allowed other trade to develop. The naval men had no sympathy whatever for the European slavers, whether dealers or blockade-runners. Denman said,

'I conceive that the destruction of barracoons and slave places not in settlements belonging to European Powers would be justifiable all over the coast . . . upon the footing that the law

VII. (a) SLAVES ON THE MAIN DECK

They have been removed from the slave ship to ease the congestion there, and are on their way to Freetown in comparative comfort. Note the restricted space and light. *(From a painting by Lieutenant Meynell, RN.)*

VII. (b) CAPTAIN JONES IN THE SOLYMAN RIVER

'The foliage on the banks is thick and luxuriant to the water's edge. The explosion was terrific; a constant fire of musketry was kept up from the bush, answered by volleys from the four boats, with grape from brass guns.' *(From an officer's letter.)*

VIII. THE 'GRAPPLER' AND THE 'SECUNDA ANDORINHA'

HMS *Grappler*, launched in 1845, was one of the Navy's first iron steamships. Her commander, Lieutenant T. H. Lysaght, reported on April 24, 1848, 'I beg to inform you that I this day, being in lat. 5° 30′N, long. 4° 7′E, captured the new pilot schooner *Secunda Andorinha*, under Brazilian colours, with a crew of 26 persons and 500 slaves. I sighted her at daylight and took her at 9.40 a.m.' This slave ship had left Bahia in Brazil on March 22, 1848. *The watercolour from which this plate is reproduced is by Captain William Buck who served on the West African coast in the eighteen-forties and 'fifties.*

of nations can afford no sort of recognition of the dealing in slaves by Spaniards in a foreign country. And secondly, that those persons were criminals by their own laws, and could not look for protection to their own government.'

In this sort of language, Denman was expressing the general opinion in the squadron. In the early days, the crews of captured slave ships had been taken to Sierra Leone; but in the 'forties, Lieutenant Levinge told the Select Committee that the Navy put them straight ashore and left them to fend for themselves. In the Niger delta, he said, many of them died. Those landed near Whydah were lucky, for Da Souza would look after them and would send them back to Rio or Havana when he had a chance. The Select Committee was shocked: 'Is not this very inhumane?' asked one member. Levinge was unmoved; 'They know the risk,' he replied. A merchant captain named Midgley gave evidence that in the delta these men could not live for more than two or three months. The Africans would do nothing for them; he had often seen officers and men alike starving on the beach, and he and other merchant captains had helped them. He had spoken about it to Captain Tucker, RN, but Tucker, like Levinge, was quite callous on the subject. 'They must bake their own bread,' said Tucker; 'they know the risk, and I have no compassion on them at all.'

If to us, as to some members of the Select Committee at the time, this seems inhumane, we must remember that we, like the members of the committee, have not seen the sufferings which these men caused in order to line their pockets: the flogging, the chains, the branding, the stench and disease and suffocation and death on the overcrowded ships, the women leaping into the shark-infested sea, the living and healthy slaves being thrown overboard in their fetters when the ship was being chased, in order that the naval officer who boarded her should not be able to testify in court that she was carrying slaves when he set foot on her decks. The naval men had seen these things, and they felt that men who did such things for money had put themselves outside the scope of human compassion. For Captain Midgley it was very well; he did not live with the slave trade as the Navy did.

So there began a period of active treaty-making and burning barracoons. Eight treaties were signed during 1841 by various chiefs from the Cameroon river to the Gambia, and the treaty-making continued into 1842.

LORD ABERDEEN'S LETTER

And then there came a blow. The cautious Lord Aberdeen consulted the law officers of the Crown. He submitted to them the reports of Denman's operation in the Gallinas and the instructions which the Admiralty had subsequently sent to the West African squadron. The point which particularly worried Aberdeen was the looting or the destruction of the trade goods in the warehouses, on the assumption, but without proof, that their European owners intended them for buying slaves. How was Denman to know that this cloth and rum and tobacco were to be bartered for slaves, and not for camwood or ivory? Denman's reply was that everyone knew that no camwood or ivory was now obtainable in the Gallinas; the Gallinas now produced nothing but slaves. But this was *ex parte* evidence, which could not satisfy a court.

The Advocate-General, however, took a wider view. He held that all this blockading and burning was legally unjustifiable. He regarded the African chiefs as friendly and independent powers; and you really must not blockade rivers or use armed force in the territory of a friendly power unless you are specifically authorized to do so by treaty, which certainly had not been the case when Denman crossed the Gallinas bar.

So Lord Aberdeen had to write to the Admiralty (May 20, 1842) to haul the Navy from its victim just as it was getting a good grip:

'Her Majesty's Advocate-General, to whom these papers have been submitted, has reported that he cannot take upon himself to advise that all the proceedings described as having taken place at Gallinas, New Cestos and Seabar are strictly justifiable, or that the instructions to Her Majesty's naval officers, as referred to in these papers, are such as can with perfect legality be carried into execution.

The Queen's Advocate is of opinion, that blockading rivers, landing and destroying buildings, and carrying off persons held in slavery in countries with which Great Britain is not at war, cannot be considered as sanctioned by the law of nations, or by the provisions of any existing treaties; and that however desirable it may be to put an end to the slave trade, a good, however eminent, should not be attained otherwise than by lawful means.

Accordingly . . . it is desirable that Her Majesty's naval officers employed in suppressing the slave trade should be instructed to abstain from destroying slave factories and carrying off persons held in slavery, unless the power upon whose territory or within whose jurisdiction the factories or the slaves are found should, by treaty with Great Britain, or by formal written agreement with British officers, have empowered Her Majesty's naval forces to take those steps for the suppression of the slave trade; and that if in proceeding to destroy any factory, it should be found to contain merchandise or other property which there may be reason to suppose to belong to foreign traders, care should be taken not to include such property in the destruction of the factory. . . .'

Denman had confidently cited the law of nations in his support; the Advocate-General dissented.

The Navy staggered under this blow. In his evidence before the Select Committee, Commander Matson described its effects. We have already quoted the evidence he gave on the effect of Denman's bold action. But when Lord Aberdeen's letter became known on the Coast,

'the slave traders altered their tone very much towards the chiefs; instead of assuring them that they would never be able to bring more goods (in fact, they were winding up their affairs) they represented a false report. In the first place, they said that there was a revolution in England: that the people had risen, and obliged the Queen to turn out Lord Palmerston, because he wished to suppress the slave trade; that there was now a revolution going on in England to oblige the Queen to carry on the slave trade, as they expressed themselves, "all the same as they had done one time before". This was believed all along the whole line of coast, not only by the chiefs but by the slave traders themselves – the people who were in the interior collecting slaves. . . .'

'SIR R. H. INGLIS: "Was it believed by such men as Pedro Blanco?" – No, he was just one of the very men who propagated the falsehood. Two of the principal chiefs with whom we obtained those treaties were those of Congo and Ambriz; they export, I suppose, half the slaves that go to Brazil; there are an immense number annually exported. Cabinda, Congo and Ambriz: it includes a very large extent of coast. One of the stipulations in those treaties was, that we should subsidize those chiefs (it amounted to a very small sum); and that failing their faithful execution of the treaty, we should put down the slave trade ourselves. Before the first annual subsidy arrived, Lord Aberdeen's letter made its appearance; and when Captain Foote, the commodore on the station, presented the first year's subsidy, they refused to receive it,[1] and declared that

---

[1] Two letters in Adm. 1/5541 in the Record Office throw light on this. One is a letter of June 6, 1843, from Lieutenant Pasco of HMS *Kite* to the commodore. Lieutenant Pasco reports that he has visited the Cameroons, and has obtained satisfactory assurances, not only from the local chiefs but from British traders, that no slaves had been exported from the river during the preceding twelve months. That being so, he has paid over the subsidy to the chiefs: 3,600 yards blue calico, 120 muskets with bayonets and scabbards, 2,000 gun-flints, eight barrels of rum, one case of gin, four barrels of powder, and sundry fine garments.

The other is the original letter, written in Portuguese with an English translation, from the chief of Ambriz to Captain Foote, refusing to receive the subsidy. It is dated August 17, 1843, and the English translation reads: 'I feel extremely happy to learn that both you and all your companions have arrived in perfect good health. I have received your estimable letter, by which I am informed of the presents that the King of England' (the chief has evidently not heard of Queen Victoria) 'has been pleased to send me. I collected immediately all my noblemen and the ambassadors of my king. And I have to inform you that you can send for your goods, and that

they would not ratify the treaty – although it had been ratified, because it had been signed by the kings and the chiefs. It then became a question with the British Government whether they should enforce this treaty in virtue of one of the stipulations; and it being referred to some of the law officers of the Crown (I believe Dr Lushington among others) it was at last decided that it should not be enforced. Since that, of course, they have carried on the slave trade; and have refused not only to enter into any treaty, but they prevent the English landing whenever they can.

MR GLADSTONE: "Upon what ground did they decline to execute the treaty?" – Because they prefer the slave trade to any other trade. It is not to be supposed that a chief of Africa will enter into a treaty with the Government until he has relinquished every hope of carrying on the slave trade; and it is that feeling which caused them to agree to the treaty with us.'

No new treaties were signed in 1843. But then the Navy began to recover from the blow. Lord Aberdeen's letter seemed to offer a loophole. The Navy was not to destroy factories and barracoons unless the African chiefs concerned had authorized it to do so. But the Navy had already found that there was no great difficulty, for a consideration, in obtaining a treaty giving this authority. Many of the treaties already signed covered this point; and when a chief had accepted a stipend and authorized the Navy to burn factories, it was no longer a legal but purely a political question whether it should do so.

I feel myself very much obliged but will not accept your presents, for such is the will of my people, and also because I have been made poor by the King of England and consequently I can use very well my slaves. You can accordingly send for your presents, as I will not receive presents from you who are not a friend of the Negroes, and will not consequently give you ivory as I do to the Portuguese.

P.S. I send you two pigs for your dinner.'
Courteous, but firm.

THE NAVY RENEWS THE ATTACK

The essential preliminary was to obtain a treaty. The African chiefs were realists. If the slave dealers were telling the truth when they said that there had been a revolution in England, and that the Government was being compelled to relax its ban on the slave trade, the Navy should very soon be sailing away and leaving their coast clear. But this did not happen. The warships were still there, blockading the rivers and making life generally uncomfortable, but at the same time offering a subsidy – small, but worth having if there was no hope of selling slaves. And so after a while the African chiefs came to fear that the slave dealers had misled them, and that it might be better to cut their losses and accept the subsidy.

It was highly desirable that the treaties should follow a common form and should be registered. In the early days of the treaty-making, captains devised their own forms, and a certain amount of mild scandal was sometimes caused because one captain thought he could improve on his predecessor's treaty, and tried to make the African chief tear up the treaty and sign a new one. The whole process needed to be regularized. Only three new treaties were made during the three years 1844-46; but then the Admiralty took its courage in both hands, and new treaties came in a flood: eleven in 1847 and nine more in 1848. Some of them were important: two treaties in 1847 between them covered fifty-two miles of coast, and several of the 1848 treaties covered a degree or more each. By the end of the 'forties, most of the main centres of the traffic, including the Gallinas and Shebar, Bonny, Calabar and the Cameroons, were covered by treaty, though there were large gaps in the treaty network on the coast running southward through the Congo and Angola. Whether the treaties were to be observed depended on whether the Navy was prepared to show its teeth and enforce them. This, as we have said, was now a purely political question.

In spite of Blount's successful following-up of Denman's visit to the Gallinas, the traffic there revived again after Lord Aberdeen's letter. In 1849 the newly arrived commodore, Sir

Charles Hotham, determined to end it for good and all.

Hotham was a different type of man from Denman, and he preferred different methods. Denman had insisted on the tightest possible blockade. 'When I took charge of the station,' he said,

'the orders I issued to the other cruisers (as well as what I practised myself) were, to maintain the principle of blockade; and if they chased a vessel off a certain port where slaves were shipped, never to lose sight of that port; but if they could not catch the vessel without losing sight of it, to go back again, for she was sure to come back again and there was no harm done. If, on the other hand, the chase is continued to any distance, other vessels might slip in and ship slaves, and even the very one pursued might dodge the cruiser at night, and run in and effect her escape with a cargo.'

Hotham did not like this scheme. For one thing, the squadron was not strong enough to blockade all the likely ports. For another thing, the system was terribly hard on the crews of the blockading ships. They were to stay for weeks on end within sight of the one spot of coast, often at anchor, incessantly rolling in the Atlantic swell. He found morale very low at the end of a spell of close blockade, and there was no shore station where the men could be really refreshed by a spell of leave. He much preferred to keep his ships cruising from thirty to sixty miles off shore.

But he agreed with Denman that there was only one way of dealing with the Gallinas people. One of the first things he did on assuming command was to send the Gallinas chiefs a warning, which they disregarded. He did not warn them a second time. He assembled a squadron of no fewer than seven ships, and at 7.30 on the morning of February 3rd the flotilla of boats, with 300 men on board, crossed the Gallinas bar.

They landed on Dombocorro island, and took possession of the rebuilt factories and barracoons there. Captain Jones took the boats of HMS *Penelope* up the south-eastern creek as far as a trading post called Solyman. Here he found three factories; he destroyed all three of them, with their contents, and returned to the base at Dombocorro soon after dark, having met with no resistance except an occasional straggling fire from the bush, by which one African prisoner was wounded, Captain Murray went up another creek and destroyed the factories at Tineh. On the morning of the 4th, all the factories on the islands in the main basin were destroyed, and in the afternoon those on Dombocorro itself. By sunset on that day all the men were back on their ships. The Navy had abandoned its old reluctance to spending a night ashore; and it had ceased to worry itself by asking who owned the goods in the factories, and whether they were intended for virtuous use in buying camwood and ivory, or for the immoral purpose of buying slaves. It acted on Denman's assumption, that no one took thousands of pounds worth of goods to the Gallinas for any other purpose than buying slaves.

On this occasion Hotham did not trouble, as Denman had done, to demand the immediate delivery of any slaves that the Spaniards or the African chiefs might have in stock. He knew that his wholesale destruction of the trade goods on shore had rendered the slaves unsaleable. He interviewed two of the principal chiefs, and obtained from them a written confession:

'Kittam and John Siaka, son of the late King Fortune, voluntarily declare that the measures this day adopted by Commodore Sir Charles Hotham, and the destruction of the barracoons, are right and proper; that on the part of the chiefs of Gallinas they are empowered to say that they have erred and done that which is wrong; that they have violated the treaty concluded by Captain Denman, and merit punishment.'

And they promised to hand over all the slaves.

Hotham knew that even this would have no permanent effects; so he followed it up by declaring a blockade of the whole of that part of the coast:

'I have notified, according to the form already transmitted, the existence of the blockade between Solyman Point on the south and Cazee on the north, lat. 6° 57′N., long. 11° 35′w., and lat. 7° 5′N., long. 11° 45′w., and I have the pleasure of informing Their Lordships that the commanding officers of the French and American forces have expressed their satisfaction.'

This blow finally broke the spirit of the Gallinas chiefs. They acted just as the chiefs in the Rio Pongas had done thirty years earlier: they turned on the Spanish slave-dealers and told them to go. They had ceased to be profitable and were bringing the river nothing but trouble. The British had abandoned their legal scruples, the French and American navies were supporting them in the blockade; the game was played out. And so, very soon a pathetic letter came to one of the officers of the blockading squadron:

'We the undersigned merchants and others, lately residing within the territories of the chiefs of Gallinas, having been ordered to depart therefrom by the said chiefs, and considering that our lives would be in danger if we were obliged to enter the territories of any of the surrounding chiefs, have requested Commander Hugh Dunlop, of HM sloop *Alert* . . . to permit us to be received on board of one of HM ships under his orders and so allow us to be conveyed . . . to Brazil.'

They may well have had reason to fear for their lives. The inland chiefs were intensely jealous of the wealthy and sophisticated chiefs of the waterside, who were doing so well out of the slave trade. The inland chiefs were the primary producers; they had to do all the fighting and raiding to collect the slaves. The waterside chiefs were the prosperous middlemen. The Spaniards were the retailers, and gross profiteers at that. They had their agents in Cadiz, Havana and Rio; everyone knew that they were piling up immense fortunes. They could not expect the primary producers to make them welcome.

And so, by the end of the year, James Hook in Freetown was able to report that all foreign slave dealers had been expelled from Sherbro and from the Gallinas.

About a year earlier, in February 1848, the Navy was

greatly encouraged by a legal decision in the courts at home. One of the Spanish slave dealers in the Gallinas was a certain Señor Buron. When Denman carried out his successful raid on the Gallinas barracoons, Señor Buron suffered a good deal of financial loss, both from losing slaves he had already paid for and from losing trade goods with which he would have bought more slaves. He sued Denman in the English courts, claiming damages of no less than £180,000. The Government at first took the line that this was Denman's private affair and that he must fight his case as best he could. But Denman and his friends fought the Government on this issue, pointing out that Denman's action in the Gallinas had been carried out in the course of his duty, and that the Admiralty had subsequently approved what he had done and promoted him for it. Thus it was now a State action, and the State should defend it. The Government grudgingly gave way, and the Attorney-General appeared for Denman.

The case did not come on for trial until the beginning of 1848. The Attorney-General, for Denman, argued that since Buron was a Spanish citizen, he was bound by the laws of Spain. But by the laws of Spain, no Spaniard was permitted to buy or sell slaves; and Spain had a treaty with Britain which gave British naval officers the right to arrest any Spaniard doing so. It followed that Buron did not lawfully own the slaves he had lost, and could not claim compensation for them. As for his trade goods, they were being kept in his Gallinas warehouses for the sole purpose of buying slaves; there was nothing else in the Gallinas to buy. They were on land ruled by King Siaka, and King Siaka had specifically authorized Denman to destroy the warehouses; the goods in the warehouses had been appropriated by Siaka and his people, not by Denman. If Señor Buron had a claim against anyone for the loss of these goods, it should be against King Siaka, not against Denman.

This argument convinced the court; the jury found for Denman. It must have been a great relief to him after seven years of anxiety; and other naval officers were encouraged to take similarly decisive action, provided they acted within the terms of a treaty agreed to by the African chief of the locality.

The Navy had at last smoked out this particular wasps' nest; and the spread of the treaty network was bringing new hopes that the slave trade on the Guinea coast might before long be effectively put down, though Ambriz, Cabinda and the Angola coast were another matter. But meanwhile, throughout the 'forties the wearisome routine went on, only occasionally broken by the excitement of a chase or some other incident. Hotham was right when he said that the Denman system of close blockade was hard on the crews. In 1843 HMS *Ferret* spent four months patrolling the coast from the Gallinas to Cape Mesurado, a stretch of about seventy miles. The log entries are eloquent in the brevity of their formulas. 'Trimmed sails as required', 'People employed variously', 'Made and shortened sail'; they appear over and over again, and always with a careful record of the amount of water remaining in the ship's tanks. Like a wise man, the *Ferret*'s captain took care to keep his people busy, constantly exercising a division at the great guns, or with small arms, or with cutlasses. Even to knock a floating cask to pieces with a 24-pound shot added a welcome fleck of colour to the day. Two years later, Commander Layton in HMS *Cygnet* was doing the same thing; in one morning's exercise he expended twenty-one shot from his 32-pounders.

In the midst of their routine, they must always keep a sharp look-out, even in 1845, for the unusual. In January 1845, Layton detained a Brazilian schooner off Badagry; she was partly equipped for slaving. In April, near Lagos, he had a less pleasurable experience. In the heat of the late morning something was seen floating in the distance. Layton sent the gig and the jollyboat to see what it was, and hove his ship to and waited for them. They came back an hour later, having picked up from a raft Lieutenant Wilson of HMS *Star* and five men of the prize crew which he had commanded. The *Star* had taken a slave schooner and sent her to Sierra Leone. About March 16th, near the equator, she capsized. For nearly three weeks Wilson and his men had been adrift on their raft under the tropical sun. Luckily for them the current, aided by what wind there was, had carried them northward into the bight and into the trade route. That afternoon, one of the rescued men died, but Wilson and the others were restored to their own ship next day. They had had a terrible experience; but they were more fortunate than a prize crew from HMS *Wasp,* which about that time was murdered to the last man when the vessel's crew rose against them and recaptured her.

On this cruise in 1845 the *Cygnet* seems to have been an unlucky ship; the sailmaker was perennially employed in repairing one or other of her sails, which had been torn when she was taken aback in a squall. Perhaps it was simply that her sails were worn out and she needed a refit. Some of her provisions were in that state. The log entry is oddly impressive through its very lack of punctuation; one can see the compressed nostrils and the tight lips:

'*5 May* . . . Held survey on 16 lbs of flour and 9 lbs of cocoa threw it into the sea being stinking and a nuisance in the ship.
......
7 May . . . Held survey on 804 lbs of bread found it maggotty mouldy and unfit to issue threw it into the sea.'

A few days after these clearances, the *Cygnet* turned and headed south for the refreshing breezes of St Helena, where at last her crew could get some shore leave in decent conditions. But she was still unlucky. Commander Layton, always sparing of punctuation, allows himself the rare luxury of an exclamation mark in his log:

'*22 May.* Michael Kelly ord(inary seaman) whilst furling the main topgallant sail fell overboard! Let go the life buoy hove to lowered the jolly-boat to pick him up she got under the counter and was upset and smashed by ship falling on her lowered the gig to pick up the crew gig returned with Mr Carrington mid(shipman) one boy and one man John Jarvis AB who was completely exhausted. The man Kelly had sunk. Sent gig to pick up jolly-boat tacked working up for gig at noon gig returned with jolly-boat which was so smashed and the wind and sea so boisterous that it was considered necessary to cut her adrift.'

A very heavy morning's work for them all. And next day John Jarvis died.

THE ATTACK IN PARLIAMENT

Thirty years of hard work, both by the diplomatists and by the fighting men, had brought the Navy to a point where it seemed to be gaining control of the slave traffic on the Guinea coast. Legitimate trade, especially in palm oil, was expanding greatly, though James Hook's warning was wise, that the slave trade would soon reassert itself if the Navy were to relax its vigilance. In 1830 the explorer Richard Lander completed the work that Mungo Park had begun: he went from Badagry overland to Bussa on the Niger, where Mungo Park had died, and went down the river by canoe from Bussa to the sea.

Lander thus discovered that the Oil Rivers were not a meaningless labyrinth of creeks, but were the delta of one of the great rivers of the world. His discovery gave rise to a new effort of exploration. The shipbuilder Macgregor Laird built the world's first ocean-going iron steamship, and he and Lander headed an expedition which ascended the new route which Lander had opened. From the health point of view the expedition was disastrous; of its forty-eight Europeans, thirty-nine died. Nevertheless, the steamship had proved its value for this sort of river work, and British merchants began to hope that with its aid they might be able to push up the Niger beyond the fever-ridden mangrove creeks to healthier lands beyond. Life was wretched on the trading hulks moored in the creeks, dealing with the canoemen of the coastal villages. The Europeans were anxious to cut out the middlemen's profits and trade directly with the producers of the palm oil; no doubt the producers were just as anxious to trade directly with them.

The Lander-Laird expedition lasted from 1832 to 1834, and during those years the abolitionists in Britain succeeded in their long struggle to have the status of slavery abolished throughout the British Empire. For the next five years after the Emancipation Act, they concentrated their attention on a sort of neo-slavery which followed emancipation in the West Indies: freed slaves were attached as 'apprentices' to their former masters. In 1838 the apprenticeship system was abolished; and the anti-slavery men, now led by T. Fowell Buxton, turned their attention to the state of West Africa.

They were horrified to learn that in spite of all the Navy's efforts, the traffic in slaves had actually increased, and that the more difficult the Navy made things for the slave traders, the greater were the sufferings of the slaves. The anti-slavery patrol was occupying about one-fifth of our naval strength. In 1836, for example, one-third of the Navy, 104 vessels with a complement of over 17,000 men, was serving on foreign stations. Of these, fifty-six vessels and over 6,000 men could be regarded as wholly or partly occupied in anti-slavery work: fourteen vessels and 1,100 men on the Cape and West Africa station, sixteen vessels and 2,000 men on the South American, and twenty-six vessels and 3,100 men on the North American and West Indies station.

Buxton drew the conclusion that more ships, and especially more steamships, should be allotted to the anti-slavery squadron; but he feared that no naval patrol, however strong, could stop the traffic entirely. The system of anti-slavery treaties must be extended; but even this would not stop it. Treaties and patrol ships must be supplemented by energetic pioneer work in developing legitimate trade.

'Central Africa possesses within itself everything from which commerce springs. No country in the world has nobler rivers, or more fertile soil; and it contains a population of fifty millions. This country, which ought to be amongst the chief of our customers, takes from us only the value of £312,938 of our manufactures, £101,104 of which are made up of the value of arms and ammunition and lead and shot.'

(What, we may ask, did Buxton know about African soils?) He goes on to list some of Africa's principal products: gold, iron, copper, hardwoods, palm oil, shea nuts and ground nuts. He continues:

'Africa, notwithstanding the annual and terrible drain of its inhabitants, teems with population; but for the slave trade, there is no reason to doubt that it would be as densely peopled as any part of the globe. Can labour be obtained there as cheaply as in Brazil, Cuba and the Carolinas? We have some light on this subject. We know that a slave fetches, in Interior Africa, about £3; in Brazil, at least £70; when seasoned, as an African is in his own country, £100. Why then should the inhabitants be torn from Africa, when her native labourers upon her native land might hold successful competition with any slave state?'

He proposes that agricultural settlements should be established at Fernando Po, Lokoja and elsewhere. Here, British technical instructors would teach the Africans modern methods of agriculture, and British businessmen would organize new and profitable commerce routes. Lured by the glittering hopes of vastly increased profits, the African chiefs would gladly sign treaties abolishing the traffic in slaves, and the American and Brazilian slavers would anchor in the creeks in vain.

Buxton's optimism was not quite unrealistic. He knew that slaves were by far the most profitable commodity that Africa had to sell. He cites a case in which the slave trade had killed the palm oil trade:

'the cultivation of the palm trees, which was giving occupation to thousands, has not only become neglected, but the native chiefs have been incited to blind revenge against British influence, and have set fire to and destroyed 30,000 palm trees.'

He knew that the naval patrol must be strengthened if his agricultural projects were to succeed.

Nor was he advocating imperialism. He was not proposing to hoist the British flag and provide Africa with the apparatus of colonial rule. He was proposing something very much like what Livingstone later proposed: a system of Christian agricultural mission stations, living in Africa as guests of the African chiefs, and helping Africa with education and with technical and commercial advice.

Still, Buxton did underestimate the problem. To begin with, in spite of the record of the Lander-Laird expedition, he seriously underestimated the risk of disease. Next, no one in England knew anything about West African soils and crops, and whatever the British tried to grow at Lokoja, it would be years before they made a commercial success of it. The coastal chiefs would certainly do all they could to prevent British traders from going behind their backs in this way. The Oil Rivers by now were far from being the main source of slaves. The Navy had the traffic along the Guinea coast more or less under control; the main source of slaves was further south, in Cabinda, the Congo, Angola, and even round the corner in Mozambique. Settlements at Lokoja and Fernando Po, however successful, would have very little effect on the traffic south of the line. Many more such settlements would be needed.

Buxton, however, was right to this extent: a naval squadron which was adequate for controlling the trade along the Guinea coast could not cover the Congo and Angola as well. More ships were needed. One merchant seaman, Captain Seward, who gave evidence to the Select Committee, thought that one stretch of the Guinea coast, from the River Volta to Calabar, would need fifty cruisers to itself. There was, of course, no hope at all of providing a fleet on anything like such a scale as that.

Buxton was the leader of the anti-slavery movement, and his view was accepted by the Government. A large expedition was sent to the Niger to begin the first settlement of the kind he proposed. It was a failure. All the 145 Europeans were attacked by malaria, and forty-eight of them died. The shock of the disaster killed Buxton; the West Coast intensified its reputation as 'the white man's grave'; and the British public realized that as long as the slave markets across the Atlantic remained open, the Navy was the only means we had of stopping the trade.

The Lokoja expedition took place in 1841, and the news of its failure was quickly followed by Lord Aberdeen's letter putting a brake on the Navy's activity in destroying the barracoons. A wave of weariness and disillusionment came over the country. Many people began to say that the Navy was engaged in an impossible task, that the money and lives spent in putting down the traffic were being spent in vain. Mr (later Sir) William Hutt, MP for Hull from 1832 to 1841 and for Gateshead from 1841 to 1874, was the chief spokesman of this view in parliament. In 1845 he moved and carried an address requiring a return of the cost of the patrol for the five years 1839-44. The direct cost in wages, victuals, and wear and tear of ships totalled over £655,000, and the annual cost was rising. The expenses of the mixed courts in the five years totalled £103,000. During the five years, 385 officers and men had died or been killed in action, and 495 had been invalided out of the service, a total loss in manpower equivalent to the crews of five sloops. The squadron was thus losing about one-third of its manpower in five years. Moreover, the ships were constantly weakened by disease. In 1850, one commanding officer reported that he and his whole ship's company were 'laid up with fever from recent boat service up the Gallinas rivers'.

In 1845, Mr Hutt was appointed chairman of a Select Committee to inquire into the anti-slavery operation on the West Coast. We have already cited some of the evidence given to the Committee. The Committee juggled with the figures and satisfied itself that the country was spending about £600,000 a year on putting down the slave trade; though some people thought that this sum was greatly exaggerated.

Several lines of thought led members of parliament to call for the abandonment of the naval patrol. The abolitionists had always assumed that other countries would gladly co-operate in putting down the traffic. They were bitterly disillusioned when they found that France, Spain, Portugal, Brazil and the United States would join in eloquent condemnation of the slave trade but would take no effective steps to put it down.

Everything was left to the Royal Navy, and the Navy's task was made unnecessarily difficult by French and American touchiness. It seemed as if, in spite of the Navy's efforts, the total export of slaves was increasing, and the slaves were suffering more through their long wait in the barracoons and the overcrowding in the ships. If the trade was put down in one place, it broke out in another. Buxton's scheme of agricultural and commercial development seemed unworkable because of disease. Britain had miscalculated; she was engaged in a hopeless task; why not admit the fact and give it up?

These were the arguments of disappointed idealists. But there were other arguments. First, there was the characteristic British reluctance to increase the size of the Navy estimates. Again, Hutt himself was a keen Free Trade man, and Free Trade was coming into fashion. If Britain was to go on being the workshop of the world, she must have cheap food and raw materials. Sugar was both food and raw material; the British sugar refiners hoped to control the European market. In 1846 the preferential duties which gave an advantage to British West Indian sugar were removed. Cuba and Brazil were now able to export to Britain as much sugar as they could produce. What right had we to reject their sugar because it was slave-grown? For the matter of that, Lancashire was thriving on raw cotton from America. That too was slave-grown. We could ruin our cotton and sugar-refining industries by rejecting their raw materials on moral grounds, but our noble gesture would do nothing to diminish slavery or the slave trade; the cotton and sugar would go instead to France and be manufactured there.

There was still another argument, not respectable enough to be put forward openly, but none the less strong. No British firm was openly engaged in shipping slaves. That was much too dangerous; it was a hanging matter. But British firms and individuals were involved in the trade in various less direct but still profitable ways. We have already met the Englishman, Jennings, who bought ships from British builders for the Spanish slaving firm of Martinez. The court at Sierra Leone reported cases in which British firms were concerned in

Spanish slaving ventures. 'It has been clearly proved in many instances that the property was not Spanish; the *Dolores* proved to be English; the *Paz*, English and American; the *Teresa*, English and French.' The property here referred to was usually the cargo of trade goods, but it was not unknown for a British firm to possess, through a Spanish dummy company, a share in the vessel herself. As time went on, even this became too risky. We need not discuss flagrant criminality like that of the Englishman who was Pedro Blanco's agent for the supply of slaving equipment: shackles, food boilers and other Birmingham hardware. But there was one form of indirect participation in the slave trade which could not be stopped. Over long stretches of the African coast the slave trade was the only trade, and everywhere it was far more lucrative than the trade in any other African produce. The slaves had to be paid for; and they were paid for in cloth, liquor, firearms, knives and axes and all kinds of manufactured goods. Wealthy slave-dealing chiefs like Siaka lived in considerable luxury, with fine furniture and silver plate. Stop the slave trade, and you stopped this market for Birmingham, Sheffield and Manchester manufacturers and Liverpool shippers. No one openly advocated allowing the slave trade to continue so as to encourage British industry; but there must have been many in England who had this secret reason for supporting Hutt when he urged that the naval squadron should be withdrawn.

As we read the proceedings of Hutt's Select Committee, we see its members fall clearly into two groups. One group holds that the naval operations are terribly expensive, liberate only a small proportion of the slaves shipped, involve much interference with private property (remember Señor Buron's claim for £180,000) and are likely at any time to bring about international incidents; they should therefore be abandoned. The other group holds that (even if the financial estimates are accepted) it is absurd to say that the wealthiest country in the world cannot afford these operations; that we could liberate more slaves if the squadron were strengthened; that no honest men's private property is in any danger, Señor Buron and his colleagues being criminals by the laws of their own country and dealing in nothing but slaves; that international incidents must be risked in a good cause; and lastly, that England's honour is at stake.

The witnesses also fall into two groups. The close-blockade school says that the Navy has shown that it can stop the traffic completely at Whydah and the Gallinas; carry on with burning barracoons and making treaties, and (provided France and America co-operate) the traffic can be stopped elsewhere, and that without a great increase in the size of the squadron. Sir Charles Hotham and others say that the system of close blockade will ruin the squadron. Cruising at sea is the only way of keeping the squadron healthy and happy; but this method admittedly needs many more ships than the close blockade: more ships than the Admiralty is likely to make available. Each member of the committee made great play with the evidence which supported his own view, ignored the evidence which told against him, and came out with his opinions unchanged.

Hutt's Select Committee eventually resolved: (1) The traffic in slaves was continuing on a large scale in spite of all that a strong British naval squadron could do, and that, even though for the time being the French and American navies were co-operating. (2) In the years 1846 and 1847, only about four per cent of the slaves shipped from the African coast were liberated by British cruisers. (3) The price of slaves in Brazil was declining. (4) The anti-slavery operations were costing this country about £600,000 a year. (5) The Brazilian slave trade was still extremely profitable. (6) The size of the African slave trade was governed mainly by the European demand for the produce of slave labour, especially sugar. (7) The sufferings of the slaves were worse than ever, and were increased, not diminished, by the Navy's efforts to stop the trade. (8) The Navy had no hope of stopping the trade altogether.

Very well, but what then? Had the Select Committee any alternative proposal? No, none.

On March 19, 1850, Hutt followed up this report by moving an address to the Crown, praying that negotiations should begin for releasing this country from all the treaties it had made with foreign states for maintaining a naval anti-slavery squadron on the African coast.

Moving the address, Hutt said that in spite of all our naval efforts, the export of slaves was increasing. He admitted that the trade had suffered a temporary setback in 1840, but that was not because of any success by the Navy. At that time there had been a general trade recession; and, moreover, both Cuba and Brazil had made momentary efforts to stop their imports. The figures had soon risen again. In 1842, there were 30,000 slaves imported; next year, 55,000; in 1846 the figure had risen to 76,000, and in 1847 to 84,000. Slaves were now cheaper in Brazil than they had been even when the import had been unrestricted. We were still employing thirty to forty ships in the anti-slavery patrol, and spending some £700,000 a year. No other state would co-operate with us, and we were continually on the edge of quarrels with France and the United States through incidents on the high seas involving their flags. He objected to carrying on a campaign which produced so little result for so much effort.

Mr Baillie seconded. We had abandoned our tariff restrictions on Cuban and Brazilian sugar, and so were openly profiting by the produce of slave labour. It was merely hypocritical to claim a moral purpose in putting down the slave trade.

Mr Evans opposed the motion. He queried Mr Hutt's facts and figures, and asked what was the alternative to continuing the struggle. If it was to leave the whole coast of Africa open to a general resumption of the slave trade, this he thought would be a terrible thing.

Mr Labouchere agreed. He thought we were bound to continue our efforts, not only from motives of humanity but for the sake of our national honour. No one could expect the Navy to suppress the traffic completely. But it had already had a good deal of success, and Africa was beginning to make progress in civilization. If we now abandoned our efforts to suppress the slave trade, Africa would lose the advance it had already made and would relapse into chaos.

Mr Grantley Berkeley, supporting the motion, thought that if we seriously desired to stop the traffic altogether, we ought to stop all imports into Britain of slave-grown produce. Nothing short of that would suffice.

Sir G. Pechell agreed that the Navy could not altogether stop the slave trade, but at all events it was doing a good deal to hinder it. In any case, we had a valuable and increasing legitimate trade along the African coast, and we must maintain some sort of squadron there to protect our ships against pirates.

Mr Anstey agreed with Mr Hutt that so far from diminishing the export of slaves and the sufferings in the barracoons and the slave ships, the Navy's efforts had actually increased both export and suffering. We were blockading the African coast for a Utopian purpose, and our blockade was contrary to the law of nations.

Sir R. Inglis disagreed with Mr Hutt's estimate of £700,000 a year; he thought £300,000 would be near the truth. He agreed with Sir G. Pechell that our West African trade must be protected. A squadron adequate to protect it would cost at least £150,000 a year. The supporters of the motion were thus proposing that we renounce our treaty obligations merely in order to save some £150,000 a year. And why belittle the Navy's achievements? Some 600 slave ships had been captured, and that was no slight service rendered to humanity.

Lord H. Vane said that our Spanish and Portuguese treaties were quite ineffective, and to suppress the traffic would need a far stronger naval force than we could even consider providing.

Mr Cardwell agreed with Mr Labouchere that in giving up our attempts to stop the slave trade, we should be giving up all hope of ever civilizing Africa. We could afford the cost of the campaign, and the struggle was not a hopeless one. No one ever claimed that the naval patrol alone could completely suppress the traffic. There were at least two other agencies which would in time bring it to an end: legitimate commerce, and Christianity. But the Navy was the essential shield behind which these two agencies carried on their work; take away the Navy, and how long would they last? Make the slave trade easy, and it would be in the power of black, or Spanish, or Portuguese savages to obtain better returns in human flesh than in palm oil. If we gave up our efforts, we should be leaving Africa open to a recurrence not only of the slave trade but of piracy.

Mr Gladstone agreed that the slave trade was detestable, but he saw no hope of our being able to stop it. Armed repression was futile. Sir Charles Hotham had admitted that if the trade were stopped in one place it broke out in another. Things were getting worse, not better. Now that we had repealed the preferential sugar duties, no other country would ever believe that we maintained our naval patrol for humanitarian reasons. If we really felt it our duty to put down the slave trade at all costs, we should repeal the Sugar Duties Act, persuade France and America to allow us to search their ships, double the strength of our naval squadron, and be ruthless in using force against Spain and Brazil. Nothing short of this comprehensive programme would produce results.

Lord John Russell, the Prime Minister, replied to the debate. He remarked that whatever the weakness in our naval patrol, no one had been able to suggest any alternative method of stopping the slave trade. If we abandoned our French treaty, for example, all the slavers would at once hoist French colours and go about their business unhindered. The motion was in effect a motion in favour of Free Trade in slaves. He quoted against the movers their favourite naval witness, Sir Charles Hotham, who had agreed with Captain Matson that if the trade were left unrestricted, the sufferings of the slaves on the voyage would be increased. Lord John agreed that we must maintain a naval squadron on the African coast to protect our legitimate trade, and that to remove the Navy would be to abandon all hope of civilizing Africa. He went further, and used an old-fashioned argument: the unrestricted import of slaves into Brazil would complete the ruin of our West Indian colonies.[1] He was sure that if our cause was good, other nations would gradually come to support it, and nothing would destroy it except lack of moral courage on our part.

The motion was defeated by 232 votes to 154.

[1] As if their ruin had not already been completed by the recent Sugar Duties Act!

The debate had not been conducted on party lines. The House was agreed that we must do all we could to put down the slave trade. Hutt's weakness was that he could propose no alternative to the naval patrol; and this in itself was enough to doom his motion to defeat. Nevertheless, his motion called in question a great part of British foreign policy from the time of Castlereagh onward, and the Prime Minister himself felt called on to reply to the debate. To that extent, the defeat of the motion was a Government victory.

All the same, over a third of the members who took part in the division had given the Government warning that they thought its anti-slavery measures inadequate. If the Government could do no better, this proportion was likely to increase. The House was clearly prepared to see the Navy given more stringent orders, perhaps even strengthened in ships and gunpower. When this motion was debated in March 1850, Admiral Reynolds and his squadron were already at work off the Brazilian coast. The debate strengthened Palmerston's hand in dealing with the Brazilian protests; it was in the latter half of 1850 that Reynolds became really ruthless. In African waters, too, the Government became more ready for strong measures; next year the Navy was authorized to attack and capture Lagos. Thus, the ultimate result of Hutt's parliamentary attack was to strengthen the Navy's hand. Hutt told the Government, 'You are not hitting hard enough to hurt; give it up.' The reply which the House and the Government made was quite the opposite: 'Not hitting hard enough? Then we will hit harder!'

This period of a little more than ten years – say from the Act of 1839 to the parliamentary debate of March 1850 – may be regarded as a period in which the Navy's fortunes swung high, then dropped low, and then began to recover, slowly at first but with increasing speed. The period begins with the general adoption of the equipment clause and the inauguration of a new collaboration between the British and American navies as a result of the Ashburton treaty. On the African coast, we have Denman's highly successful attack on the Gallinas barracoons, which seems to set the pattern for a whole series of offensive operations. Then comes disaster and bitter anxiety: Lord Aberdeen's letter discourages all attacks on barracoons, Señor Buron brings his action for enormous damages against Denman, the African chiefs begin to repudiate their treaties, Buxton's scheme for an agricultural settlement miscarries, and the Select Committee recommends the discontinuance of naval action.

All seems dark; but then the Navy begins to pluck up heart again. The Admiralty encourages treaty-making, and by the end of the 'forties long stretches of coast are covered by treaty, so that the Navy is authorized to take strong measures of the Denman type against any resumption of trading in slaves. American naval collaboration is by no means the success that was hoped; but at all events, the Royal Navy finds it possible to intercept quite a number of American vessels without causing an international incident. The Navy's increasing vigour brings about a drop in the morale of the slavers, so that they begin to run themselves ashore at the sight of a British cruiser. Then Hutt's motion is defeated in parliament, and Russell and Palmerston take the hint that the House will back them in strong measures. And so the stage is set for the strongest of all measures: the attack on Lagos and the high-handed methods of Reynolds in Brazilian waters.

Chapter Nine

THE WEST COAST IN THE 'FIFTIES

By this time, the new fast sailing vessels and the improving steamers had begun to shorten the time-scale on which the Navy operated. The normal passage from Cape Coast to Freetown had been cut to 18 or 20 days, and even less than that in December and January, when the harmattan (the north-east trade wind) reached down from the desert as far as the Guinea coast. We must add another week or so for the passage from Lagos to Cape Coast; so a captain could now reckon on making the coastwise passage from Lagos to Freetown in four weeks or less, compared with the six weeks that it usually took thirty years earlier.

No one in the 'fifties thought of establishing colonial possessions in West Africa, except that the French were beginning to push inland from their posts on the Senegal coast. The scramble for Africa was still thirty years ahead, and the British were impressed with the idea that West Africa was 'the white man's grave'. Nevertheless, as treaty was added to treaty, British influence on the coast was steadily increasing. Britain was exercising a very informal sort of protectorate over the Gold Coast, and in 1850 bought out the Danish castles and influence there. The oil trade was increasing so much in the Niger delta that many of the prominent chiefs there accepted treaties banning the slave trade. In 1849 a British consul was stationed at Fernando Po to watch over British trading interests in the delta and to deal with disputes; and soon afterwards, another consul was stationed on Sherbro island. The British Government was still determined to acquire no colonies in West Africa if it could help it, and it was not until the 'sixties that Sierra Leone was allowed to expand its territories eastward. The prevailing opinion in Britain was that trade itself was a civilizing and pacifying influence. If only the slave trade could be replaced by legitimate trade in oil, gold, ivory, hides, and anything else that Africa might be able to produce, there was no need to undertake the expense of conquering and administering colonies on African soil.

Legitimate trade was expanding so much that in 1852 the African Steamship Company of Liverpool began running a regular mail service to West African ports as far down the coast as Fernando Po. This great expansion in legitimate trade helped to squeeze out the traffic in slaves. But legitimate trade would not have had the chance to expand so much had not the Navy (both in African waters and on the other side of the Atlantic) harried the slavers to the point of making them decide to give up the business and turn to a trade less lucrative but safer. From 1839 onwards, when the equipment clause was in full operation, the slave trade was greatly hampered at the great centre of Whydah, which was an open roadstead. The slavers had their own way of trying to evade the equipment clause. The moment they arrived, they would dash into port and land all their slaving equipment. They would then wait off shore, immune from arrest, while their slave cargo was being gathered; then they would hastily load both the equipment and the slaves, and be away. This trick could often be worked in the shelter of a river. All the river-mouths had bars of mud or sand, and there were always friendly canoes to pilot the slavers across the bar, whereas the Navy had to sound the channel and feel its way in unaided. But the trick was more difficult in an open roadstead like Whydah; and once Denman's system of close and constant blockade was applied, any open roadstead became unusable. From Whydah, as we have seen, the slavers had the habit of bolting straight down southward across the equator, and then claiming that they had loaded their slaves at Cabinda or some other port south of the line, and so were exempt from seizure. This device was stopped in 1838 by an ingenious decision of the mixed court at Freetown. Admitting that the treaties exempted Portuguese slavers from being seized south of the line, the court proceeded to ask the purpose of this exemption. It found an answer by recalling that the purpose of the proviso was to reserve to Portugal the right of supplying slaves to Brazil, which was then a Portuguese colony. But Brazil was now independent and had prohibited the import of slaves. Thus the grounds of the exemption had lapsed, and Portugal had no more right than any other nation to smuggle slaves illegally into Brazil or Cuba. The court adopted a legal fiction that a slaver captured under Portuguese colours, whether north or south of the line, could not be Portuguese; he must be Brazilian or Spanish. In 1842, Lieutenant Levinge, RN, told the Select Committee that for the last two years and more he and his colleagues had been authorized to take slavers south of the line.

Cabinda, Ambriz and Benguela were now the chief centres of the trade. Even after the closure of the Brazilian market in 1853, the export from these places was considerable. In September 1859 the British consul at Loanda reported to Lord John Russell that the American squadron was quite ineffective in that region:

'Since January 1st of this year, three heavily armed American corvettes have made their appearance at different times in this quarter; and running along the coast from this port to the Congo or Cabinda, immediately returned again to the Cape Verde islands. After these cruises, or more properly speaking, voyages, an interval of three or four months usually elapses, during which no cruiser is seen on the coast; and the slave-traffickers then redoubling their efforts, numerous vessels escape.'

He adds that 'although Her Majesty's cruisers have been more than ordinarily successful', seventeen slavers (thirteen of them American) have sailed in the last eight months, carrying away 12,750 slaves. We have to remember that an American ship on this stretch of coast was some 2,000 miles from its base, so that a lengthy cruise was hardly possible. But Captain Totten,

USN, the American commanding officer at that time, seems to
have been a very different sort of man from his predecessor
Commodore Perry. When he called at Loanda, the British
consul gave him a list of the American vessels which had
recently taken on cargoes of slaves. Totten snubbed him
severely:

'. . . I must content myself by simply reminding you that the
Government of the United States claims to be quite competent
to correct any deplorable or flagrant abuses of their flag on
this or any coast; and also, that the commanders of the United
States vessels on this coast need no other advice or inducements
than are contained in the instructions received from their own
Government for the performance of their duties.'

THE ANNEXATION OF LAGOS

On the Guinea coast, the slave trade was now on its last legs.
Lagos was the last important remaining centre. There were
special reasons for this, both political and geographical. Lagos
is not in the Niger delta, but it lies in the centre of a large
system of creeks and lagoons about 150 miles long. Just beyond
the western end of this system is the port of Whydah, which
was the chief port of the kingdom of Dahomey, both for slaves
and for palm oil. Whydah being put out of action as a slave
port by the Navy's blockade, any port along this line of creeks
could be developed as an alternative; and Lagos, being an
island some little distance from the sea and protected from
the Navy by the usual sand-bar, was more useful than any
open roadstead.

Directly inland from Lagos there lived two nations, the
Egba and the Yoruba. They were often at war, and the Egba
were often at war with Dahomey, their western neighbour.
The Yoruba kingdom, moreover, was falling to pieces in long
years of civil strife. Lagos was thus the natural outlet for the
slaves from three sources. It could, of course, be closely
blockaded, as Whydah and the Gallinas had been. But in the
temper of the 'fifties, long-continued close blockade was not

favoured; a treaty with the local chiefs was the method preferred.

But here the Navy came up against the political difficulty of Lagos. The Lagos chiefs would sign no treaty.

For some years the government in Lagos had been unsettled. When King Idewu died, many years before, he should normally have been succeeded by his younger brother, Kosoko. But Kosoko had mortally offended one of the chiefs, whose high rank made his consent to the succession indispensable. This chief refused to accept Kosoko. The Lagos chiefs then went back to the previous generation and recalled a man named Adele, uncle of Idewu and Kosoko; Adele had already been king, but had been deposed. Adele died in 1836, his son and successor Oluwole died in 1841; and then the chiefs again passed over Kosoko and selected Adele's younger brother Akitoye, who, of course, was Kosoko's uncle.

All these years, Kosoko had been kept off what he considered his rightful throne by the enmity of one man, and his exile had not improved his temper. Akitoye was amiable and peaceful; he received warnings that Kosoko was dangerous, but he ignored them. He invited Kosoko to return to Lagos. Kosoko came, worked up a party of adherents, and in 1845 was strong enough to carry out a *coup d'état*. Akitoye fled, first to the Egba capital of Abeokuta and then to the port of Badagry, and all his relatives and supporters in Lagos were massacred by the victorious Kosoko faction. Kosoko belonged to the old school. There were large numbers of slaves to be exported; Whydah could not export them; let Lagos therefore benefit from its favourable position and become the centre of the trade.

Kosoko took over the government of Lagos at a time when European contacts in the Bight of Benin were becoming closer. The Church Missionary Society sent its first missionaries to the Egba country in 1842, and the Methodists and the Baptists followed soon afterwards. Legitimate trade was developing, and Lagos was as much a natural centre for palm oil as for slaves. In 1849 the British Government appointed John Beecroft as its consul in Fernando Po, with jurisdiction over the

traders in the Bights of Benin and Biafra. Kosoko and his group
of Portuguese slave dealers were becoming something of an
anachronism in the Nigeria of the 'fifties, when the new mail
steamers were taking only six weeks for the journey between
Lagos and Liverpool.

One of Beecroft's first enterprises was to visit Dahomey
and try to persuade its king to give up the slave trade and
concentrate on trading in palm oil. King Gezo politely
declined, and he gave two main reasons. One was that there
was much more money in slaves than in palm oil. The other
was that his capital of Abomey was eighty miles from the sea,
whereas Lagos was only four miles. It surely was not reasonable to expect him to give up the trade while such a petty
king as Kosoko, almost within gunshot of the sea, was allowed
to carry it on in such a big way.

It was no part of Beecroft's plan to allow Kosoko to continue the trade; in fact, one of his objects in visiting Dahomey
was to cut off one source of Kosoko's slave exports. Kosoko
was impervious to hints, so Beecroft wrote to Palmerston in
London, and suggested that we might strike a bargain with
Akitoye, who was still living in fear of his life at Badagry. If
we helped Akitoye to return to Lagos as king, he might agree
to sign a treaty of the usual kind prohibiting the slave trade.
Palmerston agreed that the proposal should be made to him,
and Akitoye jumped at the idea. He was in considerable
danger, for Kosoko was intriguing in Badagry. Badagry was
the port through which Abeokuta obtained most of its supplies, and Kosoko was trying to put a stranglehold on Abeokuta by cutting this route and controlling all its trade. The
Egba people were terrified, and were eager to have the formidable Kosoko replaced by the peaceable Akitoye. Beecroft took
Akitoye from Badagry to the safety of Fernando Po, and
there Akitoye formally accepted the bargain which Beecroft
proposed. There is no reason to suppose that Akitoye was
troubled by any humanitarian scruples over the slave trade,
or that if we had left him alone he would have exported fewer
slaves from Lagos than Kosoko did. But the abandonment of
the slave trade seemed to him a price worth paying for his

reinstatement as king of Lagos. Akitoye was henceforth regarded by the British as the rightful king, and Kosoko as an usurper. This assumption suited British convenience; but the question involved a fine point of Lagos constitutional law, which the British were quite incompetent to judge.

Beecroft now sent to Kosoko, proposing that he should come to Lagos to discuss the whole position. The palaver was held on November 20, 1851; Kosoko sat in state with his chiefs and councillors, and Beecroft was accompanied by three naval officers, Commander Wilmot of the *Harlequin*, Commander Gardner of the *Waterwitch*, and Lieutenant Russell-Patey of the *Bloodhound*. Beecroft offered a trade-and-friendship treaty of the usual kind, including the prohibition of the slave trade and the expulsion of the slave dealers. Kosoko and his people refused it, and added plainly that 'the friendship of England was not desired'. Not, at all events, on such terms as those.

The British retired, and Beecroft wrote to the senior naval officer in the Bights, Commander Forbes of HMS *Philomel*. 'I have no alternative,' he wrote, 'but to apply to you (as senior officer in the Bights) for a sufficient force to compel him to make a treaty, or dethrone him and replace the rightful heir Akitoye.' On November 23rd Beecroft met Forbes and his commanding officers, and discussed the position with them. He produced a despatch he had received from Palmerston, which instructed him to try and make a treaty with Kosoko. If he failed, he was to ask the Navy for an escort strong enough to secure his personal safety, and was then to obtain a second interview with Kosoko. At this second interview, he was to point out to Kosoko how weak his position would be if Britain decided to screw down on the Lagos slave trade at all costs and to back his rival Akitoye. The despatch did not authorize Beecroft (as he had implied in his letter to Forbes) to take action to dethrone Kosoko and instal Akitoye, but only to hint to Kosoko at the possibility. The interview was in fact to be a demonstration in force, covering a barely veiled ultimatum. The naval officers agreed that Palmerston's despatch exactly met the circumstances of the case. Beecroft had had his first interview without success; the Navy was bound to provide him with an escort for the second.

The commodore, Captain Bruce, was away; but like Captain Leeke thirty years earlier, Forbes was ready to take the responsibility for action. The sequel was the biggest flotilla engagement ever to take place on the Guinea coast, bigger even than Hotham's at the Gallinas.

On November 25th, the steamer HMS *Bloodhound* entered the Lagos lagoon, towing no fewer than twenty-one boats with a complement of 306 officers and men. Two hundred yards ahead of her went a naval gig, carrying Beecroft and Commander Wilmot and flying a white flag. Another white flag was flown on the *Bloodhound* herself.

The lagoon was imperfectly charted, but it was expected that the channel would be deep enough for the *Bloodhound*. Lagos island, like Manhattan, is long and narrow, and turns its narrow end to the sea. The approach is along the west face; the channel on the east face, like New York's East River, is of less importance. Kosoko's palace and Lagos town were at the northern end of the island, some four miles from the sea.

As soon as the flotilla began to enter the channel which had been surveyed for it across the bar, it came under musketry fire from the mainland. The naval officers looked at each other, and hoped that this unpromising beginning might be the result of faulty staff-work by Kosoko's officers: excited and undisciplined tribesmen opening fire without orders. When the boats came abreast of Lagos island, more musketry fire opened on them from the island; which, of course, was not returned. The *Bloodhound* reached a point nearly opposite the town at the north end of the island, and then she grounded. As soon as she was stationary, a battery of heavy guns opened fire on her. It certainly seemed as if Kosoko was disinclined for any more interviews. The British stood this fire in silence for twenty minutes; then they hauled down their white flags and returned it. A landing party went ashore with the idea of capturing the battery; but it was attacked by strong forces of the Lagos men and had to retire after setting fire to a few houses. The demonstration was a failure; and having refloated

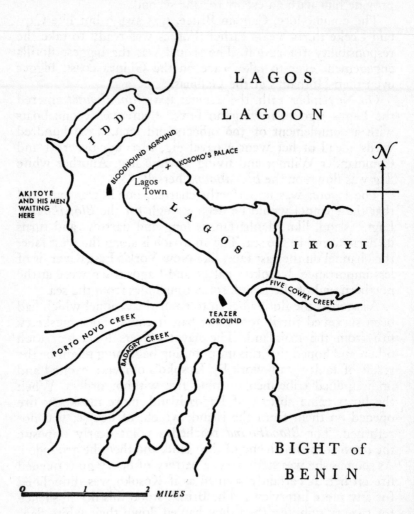

THE ATTACK on LAGOS

LAGOS

LAGOON

IDDO

BLOODHOUND AGROUND

KOSOKO'S PALACE

Lagos
Town

AKITOYE
AND HIS MEN
WAITING
HERE

LAGOS

IKOYI

N

FIVE COWRY CREEK

TEAZER
AGROUND

PORTO NOVO CREEK

BADAGRY CREEK

BIGHT of
BENIN

0   1   2
MILES

the *Bloodhound*, the expedition withdrew to the ships, with a loss of two officers killed and two officers and fourteen men wounded.

Only success will justify a measure of this kind. Had Kosoko held his fire and been duly impressed with the British power, Beecroft and Forbes would have been brilliantly successful. Forbes would have been promoted captain, Kosoko would have signed a treaty, slaving would have been more or less completely stopped at Lagos, the British would never have occupied the town, and perhaps Western Nigeria might in due time have been absorbed into the French colony of Dahomey. But failure altered the whole situation. Beecroft was reprimanded. He had been authorized to sound Akitoye and to warn Kosoko, but not to undertake this large-scale operation; and if such an operation were essential, he should certainly have consulted Commodore Bruce. However, the situation could not be left as it was; we must try again, and this time we must succeed.

Commodore Bruce now took charge. On November 30th a landing party went ashore on the mainland to the east of the river entrance, and burned a village and some large slave barracoons. A combined attack on Lagos island was planned for Christmas; the Navy would attack from the sea and Akitoye would lead a force of troops overland from Badagry.

Kosoko and his Portuguese advisers had not been idle. They knew that another attack must certainly be made, and that it must be made along the same route. They had fortified the whole western face of the island with a bank and a ditch, and at intervals had planted batteries of big guns, protected by stout stockades: double rows of tree trunks with the space between them filled with earth. They knew all the places where the water was deep enough to allow the boats to come close inshore; and these places they had fortified with double double rows of bamboo stakes planted in the water.

The attack was made shortly before dawn on December 26th by a force of 400 officers and men in the boats of the squadron under Captain L. T. Jones. The flotilla was protected by the shallow-draught steamers HMS *Bloodhound* and

HMS *Teazer*, and by the consul's iron galley the *Victoria*, which had been fitted out for this occasion as a rocket-boat, armed with 12-lb. and 24-lb. rockets. As before, the attack was carried out under heavy musketry fire from the whole length of the waterfront, and the shore batteries joined in as the boats came into their field of fire. The *Bloodhound* again went aground when near her destination at the north end of the island, and only her forecastle 18-pounder would bear on the enemy. She was within musket-shot of a shore battery, but the battery was silenced by the gunfire from the boats in her division. The *Teazer*, leading the second division of boats, went aground near the south end of the island. She at once came under heavy fire from a shore battery of two 12-pounders, and she was aground in such a position that none of her guns would bear. Captain Lyster saw that if this went on the ship would be destroyed. 'My men,' he called, 'those guns must be taken; man the boats and follow me!' He led a force of over 200 men. They were lucky enough to strike on a beach which the enemy had not staked, and in the face of a heavy but not very accurate musketry fire they made their landing. They drove the Lagos men from their first line of defence; but there was a second line some sixty yards further back, and the Lagos men retired to this line, keeping up a heavy fire all the time. However, the battery of two guns was left deserted, and Lieutenant Corbett rushed up and drove a spike into each of them.

The landing had achieved its object, and the enemy fire had so far caused but little damage. But there could be no question of pressing the attack, and Lyster gave the order to retire to the boats. As soon as the Lagos men saw the British retiring, they swarmed out of the bush in great numbers and attacked the British party on all sides. And now men began to fall fast. Lyster and Corbett were both wounded, and the landing party suffered heavily in hand-to-hand fighting before it got back to the beach. The enemy made a determined effort to capture the boats, and some of the men left in charge were killed. But the party reached the boats in time to save them all, except one. This boat had been left in charge of a gunner's mate and

some Kroo seamen. The seamen panicked and fled; the
gunner's mate stayed on board alone to try and save the boat.
He was attacked in force and wounded; his comrades tried in
vain to cut their way through to him; and he had to jump into
the water and swim for safety, leaving the boat to the enemy.
The landing party tumbled into the remaining boats and pulled
away under heavy fire; they picked up the wounded gunner's
mate and fired a rocket into the captured boat, causing heavy
casualties among the Lagos men on board.

Meanwhile the *Bloodhound*, though still aground, had been
busily firing at the neighbouring batteries with her one available gun, and the boats in her division went round the northern
end of the island and silenced some more enemy guns. One
battery was a particular nuisance, and at two o'clock the boats
of HMS *Sampson* organized another landing party to spike its
guns. They met one of the enemy's staked patches; the
bamboo stakes were planted fifteen feet out from the shore in
nine feet of water. The men hacked savagely at the stakes
with axes and cutlasses under heavy musketry fire; but they
could not force the obstacle, and had to retire with heavy
losses. Late in the afternoon, Captain Lyster succeeded in re-
floating the *Teazer*, and he arranged for burying the dead and
sending the wounded down the harbour to the ships outside
the bar. There was no fighting during the night.

At daylight on the 27th, the *Teazer* and her boats moved
up to join the *Bloodhound* at the north end of the island. The
whole day was spent in bombarding the town, the *Bloodhound*'s single available gun being reinforced by the *Teazer*'s
18-pounder carronade and long thirty-two, as well as by the
guns in the boats. No further attempt was made at landing.
The gunboats fired shells at Kosoko's palace, and the rocket-
boat also did good work, one of its rockets being lucky enough
to explode the enemy's main powder-magazine. In the course
of the day, the enemy's fire gradually died down, and by
sunset all was still.

Next day was Sunday. The British were in no hurry to
resume firing, and an uncanny quiet hung over the town.
During the morning, the headman of one of the neighbouring

hamlets came to tell the British commanders that Lagos was empty; Kosoko and his people had abandoned it during the night.

All this time, Akitoye with his forces, several hundred strong, had been waiting on the west bank of Lagos harbour. The intention had been that they should take an active part in the fighting, and each man had been given a strip of white calico to tie round his neck, so that the British could tell friend from foe. As things turned out, they had not been used. The course of the action had been determined by the grounding of the two gunboats; the British attacking force had been thrown tactically on to the defensive. The two boats had grounded nearly two miles apart, so that the whole operation had split into two separate actions, each designed to preserve the gunboat from being destroyed by enemy gunfire before she could be refloated. It is to be presumed that if the operation had gone according to plan and the whole attacking force had been able to concentrate at the north end of the island, there would have been a bombardment of the enemy position, and when the enemy guns had been silenced Akitoye's men would have been ferried over and they and the British together would have landed to attack the town. But things did not work out thus, and so Akitoye's people took no part in the fighting. On Monday the 29th, however, Akitoye and his people were brought over and landed, and Akitoye was left to persuade the chiefs and elders of Lagos to return and to instal him as king in place of Kosoko. This he succeeded in doing. All that day, while Akitoye and his people were engaged in these negotiations, the British were busy with dismantling Kosoko's fortifications and dismounting his big guns, no fewer than fifty-seven in number. On Tuesday the guns were loaded into the boats, taken out to sea and dumped into the water. The armed boat which had been abandoned to the enemy was recovered nearly intact.

The British loss in this affair was three officers and twelve men killed and five officers and seventy men wounded. It need hardly be said that many individual deeds of gallantry were performed. The carpenter from HMS *Sampson* distinguished himself when leading the way in hewing at the bamboo stakes in the water, and we have mentioned the gunner's mate who defended the boat single-handed. The rocket-boat *Victoria* helped to carry Lyster's landing party ashore. She also was left with a guard of Kroo seamen. They did not panic; but one of them took it into his head to drop the anchor. When the landing party returned and wanted to push off in a hurry, the anchor could not be moved; and Lieutenant Corbett, who was already wounded, dived over-board to cut through her chain cable with a cold chisel, receiv-ing five more wounds while doing so. 'I have done it,' he said as he emerged, 'and I am still alive.' No doubt equally gallant deeds were performed by Kosoko's men defending the island; but they have not been recorded.

We had done our part and had restored Akitoye to his throne. We now called on him to carry out his share of the bargain and sign an anti-slavery treaty. The treaty was signed on HMS *Penelope* on New Year's Day 1852. The export of slaves was forbidden, and no slave dealer was to live in Lagos. Slave dealers already living there were to be expelled, and any slaves awaiting export were to be handed over to the British for liberation at Sierra Leone. British officers were to suppress the slave trade by force if it ever revived at Lagos. Human sac-rifices were to be abolished. British subjects were to be free to trade, and missionaries from any country were to be free to preach. A special article in the treaty provided that France might accede to it if she wished. The treaty was signed by Bruce and Beecroft, and by Akitoye and two of his chiefs.

Three weeks later Akitoye died, and his son Dosumo was installed as his successor. In February 1852, Dosumo made a commercial treaty with a group of five European merchants (only two of them British) to regulate customs duties and other matters of commercial routine; this treaty was witnessed by Lieutenant Bedingfield of HMS *Jackal*.

So Lagos, still nominally independent, settled down under the watchful eye of a British consul and the informal protec-tion of the Royal Navy. Dosumo plainly owed his position to the Navy; without the Navy's protection, it was very likely that Kosoko would return. No one expected the Lagos people to forego the profits of the slave trade without a sigh.

Unfortunately, Dosumo was not a strong ruler, and though trade developed under his rule, Lagos did not greatly prosper. There were too many rumours and ripples of anxiety. The Portuguese slave dealers were expelled in March, but they begin trickling back in September. By April 1853 there was a small surreptitious revival of the slave trade, and next month Dosumo loyally stamped on it and imprisoned some of the traders.

The Portuguese reply was to send to Kosoko and invite him to return for another attempt on the throne. He came; in August there was civil war in Lagos, and naval forces had to be landed to restore order and maintain Dosumo in power. Even after this, Kosoko's war canoes were often hanging around the island and keeping it in a state of anxiety. In January 1854 the British consul, Campbell, presided over a formal palaver which arranged a compromise: Kosoko was recognized as chief of Palma and Lekki (two neighbouring towns on the mainland) and in return gave up his claims to Lagos.

This was all very well; but no one supposed that Kosoko, who was clearly a stronger man than Dosumo, would remain content with Palma and Lekki if he thought he had a chance of regaining Lagos. Dosumo was a British puppet, and the slaving interest among the Portuguese and some of the Lagos chiefs was too formidable to allow him to set up a strong administration. And there was always this York-and-Lancaster doubt (though it did not worry the British) whether Kosoko was not in fact the rightful ruler?

So things went on; and in April 1860 the British consul, Brand, wrote to Lord John Russell:

'There is a measure which if adopted would tend to put an end to the slave trade and increase the legal commerce and industrial prosperity of this line of coast to an unlimited extent: the occupation of Lagos, either as a possession or by way of protectorate. Lagos, from being a haunt of piratical slave-dealers in 1851, has from its geographical position and the great resources of the countries adjoining, of which it is the natural outlet, become the seat of a most important and increasing legal trade. . . . This place is the natural entrepôt of an immense country abounding in unlimited resources; and it is also the natural basis of operations for extending the blessings of industry, commerce and Christian civilization to this portion of Central Africa, but it can never fully serve these purposes under the Native Government. The increase of trade, of civilized ideas, and European interests and habits, demand that there should be such an administration of government as to give an efficient protection to property. . . . Lagos at present may be said to have no Government; there is no effective protection to property, no mode of enforcing the payment of debts applicable to Europeans; and the wonder is that in such a state of things there are so few disturbances. . . .'

It seems as if Mr Consul Brand was longing principally for an efficient police to stop thieving and an efficient system of magistrates' courts to enforce debt judgments.

On June 22, 1861, more than a year later, Lord John Russell replied. He agreed that Lagos should be occupied, but his priorities were somewhat different:

'It is not without some reluctance that Her Majesty's Government have determined by the occupation of Lagos to extend the number of British dependencies on the African coast; but they have been induced to come to this determination because they are convinced that the permanent occupation of this important point in the Bight of Benin is indispensable to the complete suppression of the slave trade in the Bight, whilst it will give great aid and support to the development of lawful commerce, and will check the aggressive spirit of the king of Dahomey, whose barbarous wars and encouragement of slave trading are the chief causes of dissension in that part of Africa.'

Lord John Russell went on to explain that we had no quarrel

217

with Dosumo (or Docemo, as the name was usually spelt at that time). He was loyally co-operating as well as he could. He must cease to be an independent ruler, but he must receive an adequate stipend; Russell seems to have thought that a stipend would be sufficient compensation.

'You will carefully explain to King Docemo the motives that have induced Her Majesty's Government to take this step. You will inform him that Her Majesty's Government are not actuated by any dissatisfaction with his conduct, but that on the contrary they have every wish to deal with him in a liberal and friendly spirit; and that their object in taking this step is to secure for ever the free population of Lagos from the slave traders and kidnappers who formerly oppressed them; to protect and develop the important trade of which their town is the seat; and to exercise an influence on the surrounding tribes which may, it is to be hoped, be permanently beneficial to the African race.'

These instructions came to Brand's successor, Foote; but they were carried out by Foote's deputy, the acting consul William McCoskry. Like Beecroft and others, McCoskry was a trader of long experience on the West Coast; and Dosumo and his chiefs were not too pleased at finding him now invested with official authority.

On July 30th, McCoskry and Lieutenant (now Commander) Bedingfield invited Dosumo to visit them on board HMS *Prometheus*; and there they explained to him what was to happen. Dosumo could, of course, make no reply except that he would discuss the matter with his council and let the British officers know the council's views in due time.

Two days later, on August 1st, McCoskry and Bedingfield called on Dosumo to hear his reply. He said that he could not accept the proposals. They did not come from the British Government; they were probably drawn up by McCoskry and Bedingfield on their own authority. The two British officers earnestly explained that he was wrong; that they were speaking with the full authority of Lord John Russell and the

Queen. Dosumo and his chiefs still demurred, so they gave him an ultimatum. He must accept the proposals or take the consequences; and they would give him until August 6th to decide. The ultimatum was accepted. On August 6th, with HMS *Prometheus* at anchor in the lagoon and with a strong escort of armed marines round the council chamber, Dosumo and four of his chiefs signed the treaty of cession. The British flag was hoisted, the children of the local mission schools sang 'God Save the Queen', and McCoskry assumed the title of acting Governor of Lagos. There followed the inevitable protests and petitions and financial haggling, but Dosumo finally bowed to fate and accepted an annual stipend of 1,200 bags of cowries, worth £1,030 sterling, a considerable sum in those days.

The whole affair was an exercise in power politics. As the Irish Jacobite said after the battle of the Boyne, 'Change kings with us and we will fight you again.' It was a pity that the strong man, Kosoko, made the wrong choice and decided to back the slavers. If he had put down the slave trade and fostered legitimate commerce, Lagos would have kept its independence for another generation or so. The British parliament in 1861 would not have sanctioned the annexation merely as a means of opening up the trade of Lagos and its hinterland. Four years later, in fact, the House of Commons passed a resolution calling on the Government to abandon Lagos and its other African possessions as soon as it could be assured that abandonment would not mean the resumption of the traffic in slaves.

In African affairs, the British people on the spot have often been readier to push forward than the Government in London. McCoskry had been many years a merchant in Lagos, and no doubt he welcomed the solidarity of British rule there; Bedingfield and the naval men must have been equally glad to have this leak plugged. But the Government in London could only justify the annexation to parliament by showing that it was necessary for stopping the traffic in slaves on the Guinea coast, and that this annexation need not lead to others.

With Lagos in British hands, the Navy could concentrate its main effort south of the Line.

Chapter Ten

THE CLOSE OF THE CAMPAIGN

Throughout the 'forties and 'fifties and into the 'sixties the routine patrolling went on: the usual tale of cruising; exercising the crew at the great guns or the marines at small-arms; a strange sail sighted; firing a gun to order her to heave to; a lieutenant away in the jolly-boat to inspect her papers; stranger proving to be the brig So-and-So; anchoring in Such a bay, finding there certain ships which were duly examined; water remaining in tanks, twelve tons. Only occasionally was the monotony broken by a capture or an exciting chase. But one always lived in hope. Thus, on April 30, 1841, Captain Butterfield, whom we met in 1830 as lieutenant on HMS *Primrose*, had an enjoyable day. He was in command of HMS *Fantôme*, and he chased a stranger for twenty-four hours, during which his ship covered 257 miles. In the end he caught her; she was the brigantine *Josephine* from Havana, which had already been chased by the *Wolverine*, *Bonetta*, *Cygnet* and *Lyra*, and had outsailed them all. Her American skipper reckoned there was no ship in the whole British Navy that could catch him, except perhaps Commander Gardner's *Waterwitch*, for which he seems to have had great respect. Captain Butterfield was a happy man that day; but joys like that came but rarely.

As far back as 1816, Sir James Yeo had commented that 'the black chiefs will bring their slaves from every extremity of Africa as long as there is a nation that will afford them a slave market'. The experience of the next forty years had shown how right he was. The Navy had nearly stifled the trade along the Guinea coast, but the successful export of more than

12,000 slaves in 1859 showed that it was still being profitably carried on further south. The only sure way of extinguishing it altogether was to deprive the slave dealers of their markets.

At the beginning of the 'fifties there were three main slave markets in the New World: Brazil, the United States and Cuba. Palmerston's high-handed action in sending the Navy into Brazilian waters closed one of the three. There remained Cuba (still a Spanish colony) and the United States. In both countries the trade had long been illegal. In the United States, though not in Cuba, the crime of importing slaves was legally equivalent to piracy, and carried the death penalty. But no American citizen had yet been executed for this crime.

THE UNITED STATES

As time went on, the South clung more and more tenaciously to its 'peculiar institution', and on the other hand the abolition movement in the North gathered strength. In 1854 the Republican party was founded as an abolitionist party, and the slavery question lay very near the root of the bitter arguments which led in the end to the secession of the Confederate States.

The war between the States was fought on a constitutional issue: had, or had not, a State the right to secede from the Union? But after the great slavery debates and discussions of the last forty years, it was inevitable that this point of constitutional law should be overshadowed by the greater moral question of slavery. The South claimed the right to extend its 'peculiar institution' into the new territories of the West. The North held that, as Lincoln said, 'this Government cannot endure permanently half slave and half free'; and so holding, found itself led on to abolish slavery in order to preserve the Union.

Though Lincoln himself was an opponent of slavery, nevertheless for the sake of peace he would have been prepared to allow slavery to continue in the States where it already existed. But he and his predecessor, President Buchanan, were determined to enforce the federal law against slave-running, and the changing climate of opinion in the North enabled them to do so. In 1861, towards the end of Buchanan's presidency, Nathaniel Gordon was skipper of the American slave-ship *Erie*. He was running with a full cargo of slaves from the Congo to Cuba, but was intercepted by the USS *Mohican*, which landed his slaves in Liberia and took Gordon and his ship to New York for trial. Gordon was convicted and sentenced to death, and his appeal was dismissed. He contrived to take a lethal dose of strychnine before his execution, but the prison doctor saved him for the gallows. On February 21, 1862, he was hanged, the first American to suffer the death penalty under the law of 1820.

Early in April 1862, while McClellan and Joseph E. Johnston were manoeuvring in tidewater Virginia, and the Confederate and the Union armies of the West were mauling each other in the bloody battle of Shiloh, Lincoln signed the reciprocal search treaty with Britain; it was unanimously ratified by the Senate before the end of the month.

Emancipation was first decreed by President Lincoln as a war measure. Slavery was to remain lawful in the four slave States (Kentucky, Missouri, Maryland and Delaware) that supported the Union; but it was to be abolished in the States, or parts of States, which were in rebellion. (Parts of Virginia and Louisiana were occupied by the Union forces and so were unable to continue their rebellion against the Union.)

BY THE PRESIDENT OF THE UNITED STATES OF AMERICA

A PROCLAMATION

I, Abraham Lincoln, President of the United States of America and Commander-in-chief of the army and navy thereof, do hereby proclaim and declare . . . that on the 1st day of January, in the year of Our Lord 1863, all persons held as slaves within any State, or designated part of a State, the people whereof shall then be in rebellion against the United States, will be then, thenceforward, and for ever free; and the Executive Government of the United States, including the military and naval authority thereof, will recognize and maintain the freedom of such persons. . . .

Done at the city of Washington, this 22nd day of September in the year of Our Lord 1862, and of the Independence of the United States, the 87th.

BY THE PRESIDENT   *Abraham Lincoln*
William H. Seward, Secretary of State.

On January 1, 1863, the rebel States and counties were proclaimed and designated, and Lincoln proclaimed:

'I do order and declare that all persons held as slaves within said designated States or parts of States are, and henceforward shall be, free.'

The emancipation of the slaves in the Confederate South necessarily led in due time to the emancipation of slaves throughout the country. This was carried out after the end of the war by a constitutional amendment. President Lincoln was murdered in April 1865. His successor, President Andrew Johnson, was anxious to restore the machinery of the Union as quickly as possible. He invited the Southern States to repeal their ordinances of secession, repudiate the Confederate war debt, and abolish slavery. Any State fulfilling these conditions might elect its representatives in Congress. The Southern States accepted the offer, and in December 1865 the Thirteenth Amendment was ratified.

'*Resolved by the Senate and House of Representatives of the United States of America in Congress assembled (two-thirds of both Houses concurring)* That the following article be proposed to the Legislatures of the several States as an amendment to the Constitution of the United States, which, when ratified by three-quarters of such Legislatures, shall be valid, to all intents and purposes, as part of the said Constitution: namely,

Article XIII, Section 1. Neither slavery nor involuntary servitude, except as a punishment for crime whereof the party shall have been duly convicted, shall exist within the United

States, or any place subject to their jurisdiction.
    Section 2. Congress shall have power to enforce this Article
by appropriate legislation.'

The proclamation goes on to list twenty-seven States that have
ratified the amendment, which makes exactly three-quarters
of the total of thirty-six States then existing:

'Now therefore be it known that I, William H. Seward,
Secretary of State of the United States . . . do hereby certify
that the amendment aforesaid has become valid, to all intents
and purposes, as a part of the Constitution of the United
States.'

The United States was thus closed as a market for slaves;
and with the fate of Nathaniel Gordon as a warning and a
victorious Republican Government in power, no American
skipper was likely to risk his life to smuggle slaves into the one
remaining market, Cuba.

CUBA

The planters of Cuba would continue to import slaves as long
as the Spanish Captain-General and his officials could be persuaded to connive at the smuggling. This connivance was
usually available, but not always. No expatriate official can
expect an easy life if he refuses to conform to the ideas and
customs of the closely-knit and hospitable community to
which he is posted; but occasionally the Spanish Government
appointed as Captain-General a man who refused to accept
Cuban ideas on the slave trade. When this happened, the
island's import dropped heavily. In 1839, for example, Cuba
imported 25,000 slaves; in 1845 the figure was reduced to
1,300. Meanwhile, the planters worked and prayed for the
replacement of such a governor by someone more sympathetic
and understanding.
    In the 'fifties, the Cuban import of slaves rose again to its
normal figure of around 20,000 a year. In May 1860, the

British consul-general in Havana reported gloomily to Lord John Russell:

'Every Spaniard being imbued with the idea that the prosperity of Cuba depends on the slave trade being continued, the pressure on the Government at Madrid, as well as here, is such that they are apprehensive that disorder would ensue did they not tolerate its being carried on, and they dare not make any efforts for its suppression. It is hopeless therefore to expect anything from them.'

But a new Captain-General was appointed, Don Francisco Serrano, and in September 1860 we find Mr Crawford, the consul-general, writing home more hopefully. General Serrano has warned all his officials that he will hold a strict inquiry whenever he hears that a slave cargo has been landed. Any official who cannot show that he did all in his power to prevent the landing will be suspended from duty; any who is suspected of corruption will be sent for trial. 'I need scarcely point out to Your Lordship,' says Crawford, 'that if this measure is strictly enforced, it will go a great way towards putting down the slave trade; but I fear that General Serrano's good intention will be often thwarted by the cunning of the traders.'

Part of the trouble was that Spain had not made slave-running a crime punishable by death or a heavy prison sentence. A Spanish slaver who was caught lost his ship and cargo but was free to resume his business and hope for better luck next time. Lord John Russell made representations on this matter to Madrid, who always replied patiently, avoiding this point and explaining how difficult it was to intercept slave ships. Yes, yes, replied Russell:

'Her Majesty's Government are quite willing to admit that there are difficulties arising from various causes in the way of the entire extinction of this odious traffic. Still, the facts remain. Other nations have, like Spain, made treaties for the suppression of the slave trade, and have been able to effect their object, whilst Spain has not done so.'

So things went on in 1861 and 1862. In 1863, General Serrano was recalled to Spain, but he was promoted to high place in the home government, and his successor in Cuba, General Dulce, was as anxious as he had been to put down the trade. The Cuban import began to decline. In 1860 the island had imported 18,000 slaves, but by 1864 the number had been reduced to less than 3,000. In 1865, General (now Marshal) Serrano declared that slave running ought to be condemned as equivalent to piracy; and his chief, Marshal O'Donnell, spoke in the Senate with unaccustomed vehemence and directness; he said that 'the slave trade must and shall be put an end to'. In 1866, the British ambassador in Madrid reported a change in public opinion. More and more people were coming to realize the evil of the slave trade, and the opinion was being expressed that if Cuba continued to import slaves, Spain might lose the colony.

No doubt this change was brought about mainly by the result of the American war. For one thing, a nation which had paid such a heavy price to put down slavery in its own land was not likely to tolerate indefinitely a slave economy almost within sight of its own shores. For another, there would be no more American ships and American skippers to carry slaves to Cuba. The slaves must now be brought in Spanish ships with Spanish crews; and the British cruisers had no scruples about violating the Spanish flag and treating Spanish slave captains with but scant consideration.

The final step was taken in 1869. There had been a system in Cuba whereby all slaves taken from captured slave ships were nominally emancipated, but were kept in the hands of the Cuban Government and hired out in labour gangs to any estate owner applying for them. In 1866 the Cuban Government was forbidden to extend this system. All slaves taken off a captured ship were to be taken back either to their African homes or to some Spanish colony where slavery did not exist; and the choice was to be theirs. In 1869, all these 'emancipados' were declared free and the system of labour gangs was abolished. The officials in the British Foreign Office had the unusual task of drafting a letter for the Ministerial signature expressing the Government's gratification at this final closure of the Cuban slave market.

In setting out to suppress the Atlantic slave trade, the Navy was endeavouring a very great matter: a far greater matter than was realized by Wilberforce and his friends. Sir Winston Churchill writes,[1] 'The moral surge of the age had first suppressed, by naval power, the slave trade on the seas, and thereafter – the young Mr Gladstone notwithstanding – abolished the status of slavery throughout the British Empire.' Sir Winston is not quite correct. That is what Wilberforce and the abolitionists expected would happen, for who could resist the Royal Navy? But it did not happen like that. The abolitionists had not realized how naval power could be thwarted by diplomatic and legal obstruction. They did not expect other nations to be so reluctant to forego their profits. They did not expect that many countries would not accept the equipment clause until after Britain had abolished slavery in 1833. Nor did they expect the French and American insistence on the rights of their flags: the chicanery and corruption by which governments cynically made laws condemning the slave trade without lifting a finger to enforce them: or the scruples of British lawyers over the rights of Señor Buron and his friends, who were carrying on a business which was illegal both by international treaty and by the laws of Spain.

All these obstructions sorely hampered the Navy in its task; and though it did a great deal to make life unpleasant for the slave traders, the Navy did not succeed in completely suppressing the trade. Suppression was a gigantic combined operation. Foreign Secretaries who negotiated the treaties, and the ambassadors and consuls who carried out the ceaseless battle against diplomatic evasiveness, spent a great part of their time in striving to set the Navy free to do its work. What freedom the Navy was given, it used so successfully that in later years many a slaving captain ran his ship aground and

[1] *A History of the English-speaking Peoples*, Vol. 4, page 123.

took with his crew to the bush at the mere sight of a British cruiser. Whenever the Navy was allowed to fight slavers, to burn barracoons, to blockade rivers, to make treaties and enforce them, it carried out its duties with patience and diplomacy, as well as with its traditional gallantry. Had the Navy been given full freedom of action, the story of the Atlantic slave trade would have been shorter, and the hopes of the abolitionists would have been amply fulfilled. Under the limitations imposed upon it, the Navy fought a campaign against the trade which brought glory to the officers and men engaged in it, and to the Fleet in which they served.

1792 Denmark passes law abolishing the slave trade, to take effect 1802.

1802 Slave trade illegal in Denmark.

1807 Abolition Act: slave trade illegal in Britain.

1808 First cruise of HMSS *Solebay* and *Derwent*.
Slave trade illegal in United States.

1810 First Anglo-Portuguese treaty: Portugal to load slaves only at her own ports.

1811 Naval squadron of five ships on regular patrol.
Slave trading becomes a felony in Britain.

1812-15 American war.

1814 Slave trade illegal in Holland.

1815 Second Anglo-Portuguese treaty: the equator the boundary line.
Congress of Vienna issues a general condemnation of the trade.

1817 Spain prohibits slave trading north of the equator.

1818 Stiffer American law against slave trading: master of a ship has to prove his innocence.

1820 Slave trade illegal in Spain, south as well as north of equator.
Slave trade equated with piracy in United States.

1822-23 Empty Spanish, Dutch, Portuguese vessels can be condemned on proof that they have been slaving.

1822 Holland accepts equipment clause.

1824 Slave trade equated with piracy in Britain.

1826 Brazilian treaty: slave trade to be illegal after 1829.

1828 French navy begins an anti-slavery patrol.

1830 Lander's exploration opens the Niger route.

1832-34 Lander-Laird expedition to the Niger by steamship.

1833 Reciprocal search treaty with France.
Emancipation Act: status of slavery abolished in British Empire.
United States refuses to discuss proposals for an anti-slavery treaty.

1835 Spain accepts equipment clause.

1836 American slavers begin sailing openly under American colours.

1839 Under heavy pressure from Palmerston, Portugal acquiesces in equipment clause.

1840 USS *Dolphin* on the African coast. Several American slave ships condemned.

Denman's action against the Gallinas barracoons.

1841 The disastrous Lokoja expedition.

The *Creole* affair heightens tension between Britain and America.

The first anti-slavery treaties with African chiefs.

1842 Portugal formally accepts the equipment clause.

The Webster-Ashburton treaty: a regular American squadron is established and there is good Anglo-American co-operation.

Lord Aberdeen's letter produces a serious set-back in the campaign.

1845 Brazil closes the mixed commission at Rio and protests against the Navy's interference with Brazilian shipping.

Growing strength of feeling in parliament opposed to naval anti-slavery operations: Hutt's Select Committee appointed to investigate.

1847 Large-scale revival of treaty-making with African chiefs.

1848 Decision in *Buron v. Denman*: Denman wins case.

1849 Hotham's action in the Gallinas.

Beecroft appointed consul in the Bights of Benin and Biafra.

1850 Hutt moves address in parliament for ending of the naval anti-slavery patrol: motion defeated but obtains considerable support.

Admiral Reynolds, after five years of unsuccessful negotiations with Brazil, hunts down slave ships in Brazilian waters.

1851 British capture of Lagos.

1852 Regular service of mail steamers begins from Liverpool to Fernando Po and intermediate West African ports.

1853 Brazilian slave market finally closed.

The Progress of the Campaign

1861 British annexation of Lagos.

1862 Execution of American slaving captain, Nathaniel Gordon. Lincoln's emancipation proclamation: slavery to be abolished in the Confederate States.

1863 Lincoln's proclamation takes effect.

1865 Thirteenth Amendment to American Constitution: slavery abolished throughout United States.

1869 Final closure of Cuban slave market and abolition of slavery.

barque – a vessel of three or more masts, the aftermost mast fore-and-aft rigged and the other masts square rigged.

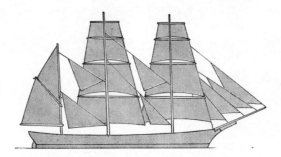

BARQUE. Under all plain sail with royals set.

beam – a vessel's maximum width. This is normally at the middle of the vessel; hence, *abeam*, or *on the beam*, directly opposite the middle of the vessel. Wind *abeam*, or wind *on the beam*, wind blowing at right-angles to the vessel's course.

between wind and water – a level on the hull which is alternately covered and left bare by the waves or the ship's rolling.

boatswain's call – the pipe on which the boatswain pipes orders.

bow, bows – the front end of the vessel.

bowsprit – a spar projecting forward from the bows; fore-and-aft sails are rigged between bowsprit and foremast.

brace – a rope attached to the end of a yard, by which the yard can be moved into different positions round the mast. See *rig*.

brig – a two-masted vessel, both masts square rigged.

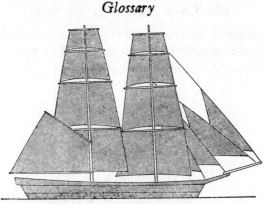

BRIG. This brig carries four jibs: flying-jib, outer-jib, inner-jib and jib. All are fastened to the *bowsprit* at their foot.

brigantine – a two-masted vessel, the foremast square rigged, the mainmast fore-and-aft rigged.

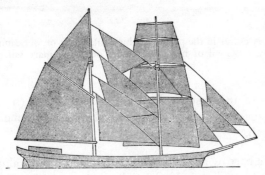

BRIGANTINE. This vessel carries four staysails.

bulwarks – the solid wall protecting the top deck from the sea.

cable's length – one-tenth of a nautical mile.

chains – the place where the leadsman stood to cast the lead for the purpose of taking soundings; forward near the bows and outside the bulwarks, directly over the water.

counter – the overhanging part of a vessel's side just forward of the stern.

cutter – a single-masted vessel with more than one headsail. Cutters today are usually fore-and-aft rigged, but formerly used sometimes to set a square sail as well.

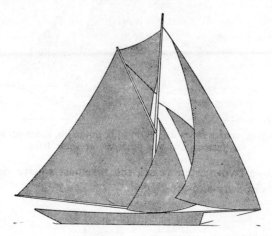

CUTTER. A cutter in the period of this book might on occasion replace some or all of her headsails by one big square sail.

fathom – (a) in measuring depth of water, six feet; (b) in measuring distance, one-tenth of a nautical mile, the same as a cable's length.

fine – at a narrow angle; fine on the starboard bow, almost directly ahead but slightly to the right.

gaff – in a fore-and-aft rigged vessel, the largest sails are set between two spars, one at the top and one at the bottom. The gaff is the spar at the top.

gunwale – the upper edge of a small boat.

haul up, haul his wind – to tighten the sails and turn more closely into the wind.

headsail – a fore-and-aft sail set forward of the foremast.

Glossary

heave to – to stop; a sailing vessel stops by turning into the wind and arranging the sails so that they counteract each other, shortening sail if necessary.

helm – Small boats are steered by a tiller which is rigidly fixed in the same plane as the rudder, so that when the helmsman turns the tiller one way, the rudder turns the other way. Thus, to make the boat turn to starboard (to the right), the helmsman must put the tiller to port (to the left). In this connection, *up* means toward the wind and *down* means away from the wind, always referring to the tiller; to *put up* the helm means to turn the tiller towards the wind so that the boat turns away from the wind, and to *put down* the helm means to make the boat turn into the wind. By the beginning of the anti-slavery patrol, all large ships were already steered by a wheel, but the old terminology was retained, as if they were still steered by a tiller. It was only in 1933 that this terminology was abandoned, by international agreement. The modern order 'Port ten', for example, means that the vessel is to alter course ten degrees to port.

jib – one of the fore-and-aft headsails set between foremast and bowsprit. *flying jib*, the uppermost of three jibs.

larboard – the left-hand side of a vessel, looking forward. Obsolete, replaced during the nineteenth century by the word *port*.

lee – the side away from the wind. In the *lee* of the land, sheltered from the wind by the land. A *lee shore*, a shore towards which the wind is driving the vessel. On the *lee bow*, ahead of the vessel, but somewhat on the side which is away from the wind. The opposite of *lee* is *weather*.

leeward – see *windward*.

mainmast – in a two-masted vessel, the rear mast; in a three-masted vessel, the middle mast of the three. (This assumes that the two masts are about equal. There are rigs, such as the ketch

235

and the yawl, in which the rear mast is much smaller than the mast further forward. In this case, the forward mast would be the mainmast, and the rear mast would be called the mizzenmast.)

mizzenmast – in a three-masted vessel, the rearmost of the three.

offing – in the offing, further out at sea from the land; to *gain an offing*, to get far enough away from the land to have room for a necessary manoeuvre.

port – the left-hand side of a vessel, looking forward; the modern term replacing *larboard*.

quarter – towards the stern; on the *port quarter*, behind the vessel but to the left.

reaching – sailing with the wind abeam. A sailing vessel *beats* against the wind, *runs* before the wind, and *reaches* with the wind abeam.

reef – to reduce the area of a sail by folding it and tying down the fold.

rig – There are two types of rig used in European sailing vessels, the square rig and the fore-and-aft rig. A square-rigged vessel sets her sails on horizontal spars called yards, set on the masts roughly at right-angles to the long axis of the vessel. The yards and sails can be turned to suit the wind by slackening the braces on one side of the vessel and tightening them on the other.

A fore-and-aft sail is set roughly along the vessel's long axis, but can be adjusted to suit the wind by tightening and slackening ropes. Neither square-rigged nor fore-and-aft rigged vessels can sail directly into the wind (see *tack*), but fore-and-aft rigged can sail closer to the wind than square rigged. For this reason, square-rigged vessels nearly always carried fore-and-aft sails as well, set between the masts, between foremast and bowsprit, and behind the mizzenmast.

rigging – A ship's ropework. *Running rigging*, ropes used in trimming sails; *standing rigging*, fixed ropes holding masts in position.

schooner – a vessel with two or more masts, completely fore-and-aft rigged. But see *topsail schooner*.

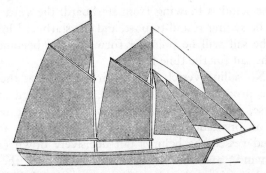

SCHOONER. This is the ordinary schooner, both masts rigged alike, as distinguished from the staysail schooner.

ship – often loosely used to mean any biggish vessel. But strictly, it means a vessel of three or more masts, all of them square rigged.

shorten sail – to reduce the sail area by reefing or furling some of the sails.

sloop – In the period of this book, originally a small full-rigged ship, but later used more loosely to include a naval brig.

slip the cable – to leave an anchorage hurriedly by abandoning anchor and cable instead of taking the time to weigh anchor.

starboard – the right-hand side of a vessel, looking forward.

stay – a rope holding a mast in position.

staysail – a fore-and-aft sail, set on one of the stays between the masts of a square-rigged vessel.

stern – the rear end of the vessel.

studdingsail – a small square sail set on an outward extension of the yard; only used in fine weather.

stove – with a plank damaged so that she leaks.

tack – (a) the forward lower corner of a sail. The tack of a square sail is the lower corner which for the time being is forward. If the wind is blowing from starboard, the yard and its sail will be swung round to port, and the starboard lower corner of the sail will be pointing forward; this becomes the tack of the sail for the time being.

(b) No sailing vessel can sail directly against the wind. To make progress against the wind, she must sail in a zig-zag course, going first as close to the wind as she comfortably can on one side, and then on the other. In a fore-and-aft rigged vessel, the helm is put decisively down (away from the wind), and the vessel turns sharply into the wind and overshoots it, so that the sails swing over and fill again on the opposite side. This operation is called tacking; the vessel *tacks*, or is *tacked*. A square-rigged vessel uses a different method : see *wear*. A vessel sailing with the wind on her starboard side is said to be sailing on the starboard tack; if the wind is blowing on her port side, she is on the port tack.

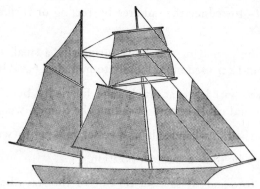

TOPSAIL SCHOONER. The masts are set so close together that the foresail overlaps the mainsail. The braces of the square topsails are carried to blocks on the main mast.

Glossary

topsail – in a fore-and-aft rigged vessel, the triangular sail set between the gaff and the mast; in a square-rigged vessel, the sail immediately above the lowest and biggest sail on a mast.

topgallant sail – in a square-rigger, the sail immediately above the topsail.

topsail schooner – a schooner with one or two square-rigged topsails on her foremast.

trim sails – alter the angle of the sails to suit a change of wind.

trysail – a triangular sail set immediately abaft the foremast.

warp – to move a vessel by fastening a rope from the vessel to a fixed point on shore and hauling on it.

wear – a square-rigged vessel is not so handy in turning into the wind as one that is fore-and-aft rigged. When she is sailing, the wind is blowing on the after face of her sails. If she turns directly into the wind, the wind suddenly blows on the forward face of the sails and checks her motion. This is called being taken aback, and a vessel taken aback in a strong breeze may split her sails. Consequently a square-rigged vessel does not tack; she wears. Instead of turning into the wind she turns right away from it and comes up to it on the opposite tack, a much slower and more laborious operation than tacking.

weather – on the side facing the wind; the opposite of *lee*.

windward – nearer the place from which the wind is blowing. If vessel A is north of vessel B, and the wind is from the north, A is to windward of B, and B is to leeward of A. On the Guinea coast, the prevailing wind is westerly, so the westerly section, from Cape Verde to Cape Palmas, is called the Windward coast. From Cape Palmas eastward is the Leeward coast.

yard – the horizontal spar to which a square sail is attached.

Some of the materials for this story come from files in the Public Record Office in London. Naval officers on the West African station kept in touch with the British settlements on the West Coast, and the Colonial Office files of the C.O.267 series contain some of their despatches. Captain Irby and Captain Lloyd in 1812, for example, are in C.O.267/35; the affair of the *Thistle*'s boat is in C.O.267/51. To come to a much later date, Commander Sotheby's search in the Rio Grande is in C.O.267/228.

The Admiralty series 51 contains the Captains' logs; thus, the log of HMS *Bann* is Adm.51/2180, of HMS *Cygnet* Adm.51/3570. Other useful Admiralty papers are the Adm. 1 series of letters from Captains to the Admiralty, and the Adm. 2 series of letters from the Admiralty to its Captains. The orders to Sir James Yeo are in Adm. 2/1327; the letters between Captain Foote and Commodore Perry, USN, are in Adm. 1/5541.

But it is not necessary always to go to the original papers in the Public Record Office, for many of the most interesting are printed in the annual volumes of State Papers. These volumes contain slave trade material indexed separately. The courts at Freetown, Havana and Rio reported regularly to the Foreign Office, and always provided full documentation in cases of unusual interest or difficulty. The cases of the vessels *Aurora, Gaviao, Midas, Netuno, Rosalia, Sylphe, Veloz Pasagera, Voladora* and many others are taken from these reports; so are the attacks by Denman and Hotham on the Gallinas barracoons and the capture of Lagos. The State Papers contain diplomatic correspondence (but not the office minutes thereon) between the Foreign Office and our ambassadors and consuls abroad, and enable us to follow the diplomatic struggle to secure for the Navy its freedom of action. They contain the correspondence with our long-suffering consuls in Rio and Havana, the texts of the Webster-Ashburton treaty and of Lincoln's emancipation proclamation, and all kinds of incidental items, such as an 1812 speech by the American Secretary of the Navy giving particulars of the armament of American frigates and sloops of that day.

The full proceedings of the various parliamentary committees on the slave trade and West African affairs generally are available as printed parliamentary papers.

The passages from T. Fowell Buxton are taken from his book,

List of Authorities

The African Slave Trade and Its Remedy, published in 1840. Other contemporary books from which I have taken some details are Howard Douglas's *A Treatise on Naval Gunnery* and W. O'Byrne's *Naval Biographical Dictionary.*

More recent books include the following:

R. and R. C. Anderson: *The Sailing Ship*
E. Keble Chatterton: *Sailing Ships and Their Story*
R. Coupland: *The British Anti-Slavery Movement*
Kenneth Dike: *Trade and Politics in the Niger Delta*
Warren S. Howard: *American Slavers and the Federal Law*
Michael Lewis: *A History of the British Navy*
Michael Lewis: *A Social History of the Navy 1793-1815*
Christopher Lloyd: *The Navy and the Slave Trade*
Daniel Mannix and Malcolm Cowley: *Black Cargoes: A History of the Atlantic Slave Trade*
W. L. Mathieson: *Great Britain and the Slave Trade*
Eric Williams: *Capitalism and Slavery*

Index

Aberdeen, Lord, Foreign Secretary, 149, 162-4, 178-82

Abolition Act, 19, 43, 102

Adams, John Quincy, US Minister in London, 161

Accra, Gold Coast port, 154

Activo slave ship, expensive capture of, 122, 123, 146

Akitoye, king of Lagos, 206-8, 214, 215

Alecto, HMS, paddle steamer, 37

Alert, HMS, stops suspected slaver *Uncas*, 156, 157; removes slave dealers from Gallinas river, 185

Ambriz, slaving port, 180, 187; chief declines subsidy, 180

Amelia, HMS, unprofitable cruise, 50-3

Angola, Portuguese colony, 44, 77, 158, 182, 187, 192

Anna Maria, slave ship taken in Bonny river, 103-6

Arsenia, slave ship converted to naval tender, 128

Asp, slave ship unsuccessfully claims American nationality, 143, 144

Atholl, HMS, financially disastrous capture by, 122, 123

Aurora, slave ship taken off Gallinas, 91-4

Badagry, port in Dahomey, 86, 120, 167, 206, 207

Badgley, Lieut., RN, fails to convince court, 123

Baker, American merchant captain, detained, 147, 148

Bangalang, slave depot, 67, 70, 71

Bann, HMS, voyage times, 44, 45; takes slavers *San Antonio*, 59, 60, and *Rosa*, 112, 113; good gunnery, 113

barracoons, built in Gallinas, 133, 141, and New Cess, 141; American officer suggests destroying, 141; destroyed by Denman, 172, 173, by Hill, 175, by Hotham, 184

Bathurst, Lord, Secretary of State, 52

Bedingfield, Lieut., RN, witnesses treaty, 215; Cdr., negotiates annexation of Lagos, 218, 219

Beecroft, John, British consul, 206-11

Belcher, Lieut., RN, prize-master of pirate *Virgen*, 110; drives suspected slaver ashore, 110

Bella Dora, slave ship taken by HMS *Myrmidon*, 111

Benin, 122

Benguela, Portuguese colony, 44, 45, 122

Bingham, Lieut., RN, boat action in Bonny river, 105-7

Black Joke, slave ship converted to naval tender, 128, 130

Blanco, Pedro, slave dealer, 132, 133, 170, 176, 180, 195

Bloodhound, HMS, in action at Lagos, 209-13

Blount, Capt., RN, in Gallinas action, 175, 176

Bom Caminho, suspected slave ship, warned, 50

Bonny, port and river, 60, 86, 95, 103-7, 148, 182

Bosanquet, Cdr., RN, deals with suspected slaver *Uncas*, 156, 157

bounty for liberating slaves, 90, 91, 94, 102, 103, 141

Bourbon, see Réunion island

Braima, Mungo, paramount chief, 68, 69

Brand, British consul, 216, 217

Brazil, 120, 121, 124, 126, 129, 133, 163-6, 191, 197, 200, 204, 221

Brazen, HMS, reports slaver *Principe de Guinea* at Whydah, 115

Broadhead, Capt., RN, low opinion of Seppings brigs, 27; catches American slaver *My Boy*, 154

Broughton, Capt., RN, action against slaver *Veloz Pasagera*, 129-32

Bruce, Capt., RN, commodore, organizes attack on Lagos, 211-15

Buchanan, James, President of the USA, 221, 222

Bullen, Sir Charles, RN, commodore, 128

Index

Buron, slave dealer, fails in action for damages, 186, 195, 227

Bussa, village on Niger, 189

Butterfield, Lieut., RN, action with slaver *Veloz Pasagera*, 129-32; Capt., takes slaver *Josephine*, 220

Buxton, T. Fowell, plans for stopping slave trade, 190-2

Buzzard, HMS, convoys American slavers across Atlantic, 145-7

Cabinda, Portuguese slaving port in Africa, 87, 122, 154, 155, 187, 192, 203

Calabar, Nigerian slaving port, 53, 84, 85, 123, 135, 182

Calhoun, American slave ship, driven ashore, 157, 158

Campbell, British consul, 216

Cameroons river, 116, 180, 182

Camperdown, pirate brig, takes two Government vessels, 107

Canning, George, Foreign Secretary, 76, 79, 80, 89, 114

canoes, needed for open beaches, 50, 51, 120

Canot, Theodore, slave dealer, 173, 176

Cape Coast, British headquarters on Gold Coast, 50, 51, 57, 202

Cape Mesurado, 46, 187

Cape Mount, 91, 99

Cape Palmas, 53

Cape Verde, 44, 45

Cape Verde islands, US naval base, 150, 151

Carolina, pirate beaten off by British prize, 116-18

Carrington, midshipman, RN, lucky escape, 188

Castlereagh, Lord, Foreign Secretary, 59, 76, 79

Chisholm, Capt., 2nd West India Regiment, 65-8

Clara, slave ship escorted across Atlantic, 144-6

Cock, Simon, administrator, 52

Collier, Capt. F. A., RN, commodore, takes slaver *La Fanny*, 123; boards slaver *Mulata*, 136; buys tender, 128

Collier, Capt. Sir George, RN, commodore, commands frigate *Surveillante*, 64, and frigate *Tartar*, 65, 70, 103-5; approves plans for attack on Rio Pongas, 66; case of slaver *Gaviao*, 84-6; reports difficulties to Admiralty, 84, 86, 121, 122; with Lieut. Hagan in Bonny river, 103-5

Congo, 135, 157, 158

Conny, Yando, sub-chief in Rio Pongas, 68

Corbett, Lieut., RN, gallantry in attack on Lagos, 212, 215

Corisco island, 101

Courtenay, Lieut., RN, hazardous boat action in Gallinas river, 92-4, 143, 171

Crawford, British consul in Havana, 225

Crawford, Richard, RN, prize-master, beats off attack by pirate, 116-18

Creole, slave ship, mutiny of slaves on, 144

Crozier, Alexander, AB, mortally wounded, 93

Cuba, slave market, 114, 124, 125, 133, 191, 197, 221, 224-6

Curtis, slave dealer in Rio Pongas, 64-70

Cygnet, HMS, dealings with American vessels, 154, 155, 157; drives suspected slavers ashore, 158, 159; incidents of cruise, 187-9

Cyrene, HMS, successful action does not qualify for bounty, 91-4.

Dahomey, African kingdom, 63, 205, 207, 217

Dale, USS, 150

Da Souza, slave dealer at Whydah, 114, 177

Davidson, British prize-master, 155

Denman, Capt. Joseph, RN, commands brig *Wanderer*, 27, 28; operations in the Gallinas, 167-74, 200; strong views on slave dealers, 176, 177; wins legal action, 186; favours close blockade, 183, 203

Denmark, abolishes slave trade, 76

Derwent, HMS, preliminary cruise, 43

Deschamps, midshipman, RN, boat action in Bonny river, 106

Dichosa Estrella, slave ship, no bounty awarded for capture, 90, 91

disease, 47, 53, 60, 87, 88, 100, 134, 189, 193

Disunion, British prize destroyed by pirate, 116

Doherty, Richard, Governor of Sierra Leone, 167-9

Dolphin, USS, commander criticizes Royal Navy, 141, 142

Dombocorro island, 171, 183, 184

Dosumo (Docemo), king of Lagos, 215-9

Douglass, American ship unwisely detained, 147, 148

Dulce, Captain-General of Cuba, 226

Dunlop, Cdr. Hugh, RN, removes slave dealers from Gallinas, 185

Eagle, slave ship, unlucky voyage, 143-6

Eden, HMS, cannot get suspected slaver condemned, 123

Eliza, vessel containing only one slave, 81, 82

Emancipation Act, 123, 124

Emilia, slave ship, incredibly swift passage from Cabinda, 87

Ephraim, Duke, African chief in Calabar, 84, 85, 135

equipment clause, 119, 120, 123, 126, 132, 143, 162, 200

Erie, American slave ship, master hanged, 222

Erne, HM sloop, 61

Esk, HMS, captures slaver *Netuno*, 116

exploration, 65, 189

Fales, American slaving captain, abandons ship, 158

Fama de Cadiz, slave ship, disastrous voyage, 133, 134

Fanshawe, Capt., RN, commodore, 150

Fantôme, HMS, great speed overhauls slaver *Josephine*, 220

Felony Act, 52, 58, 166

Fernando Po island, 145, 191, 202, 203, 206, 207

Ferret, HMS, boards American vessels, 154; sloop or brig?, 158; monotonous patrol by, 187

Fisher, Capt., RN, successful command of HM sloop *Bann*, 59, 112, 113

Fitzgerald, Lieut., RN, unpleasant convoy duty, 144-6

Foote, Capt., RN, commodore, 151-3, 157, 180

Foote, British consul in Lagos, 218

Forbes, Cdr., RN, unsuccessful attack on Lagos, 208-11

France, 79-81, 119, 121, 123, 125, 126, 162

François, slave dealer at Shebar, 168, 175

Freetown, British naval base, 44, 46, 53-5, 58, 96, 99, 107, 110, 116, 122, 123, 167, 168, 172, 202

Frexas, Don Pablo, Spanish slave dealer, 148

Gaboon river, 46, 55, 101

Gallinas river, 73, 91-4, 111, 132, 133, 141, 167-76, 182-5, 187, 196, 200, 205

Gallon, Louis, slaving captain, 93

Gaviao, slave ship, legal complications over, 84-6

Gendema (Ghindamar), town in Gallinas, 170

Gezo, king of Dahomey, 207

Gladstone, William Ewart, MP, 181, 199, 227

Gold Coast, 44, 58, 63, 77, 166, 202

Gomez, slave dealer, 82

Gordon, Nathaniel, hanged for slaving, 222

Grace, Capt., RN, does not qualify for bounty, 91-4

Grampus, USS, good relations with Royal Navy, 141, 149

Gray, Lieut., RN, speaks highly of American colleagues, 152, 153

Gregory, Commodore, USN, 150

Guadeloupe, 95

Hagan, Lieut. Robert, RN, in Rio Pongas, 64-70; detains slavers *Eliza*, 81, 82, *Rosalia*, 88, 89, *Anna Maria*, 103-5

Havana, mixed court in, 79, 139, 140; slaver *Fama de Cadiz* returns to, 134; slaver *Minerva* chased into, 124, 125; slavers *Voladora* and *Midas* taken into, 135-7; American vessel *Uncas* clears from, 156

Hill, Cdr., RN, action in the Shebar, 175

Hook, James, judge at Freetown, 174, 185

Hoop, slave ship, chequered career of, 128, 129

Hotham, Sir Charles, commodore RN, on Americans, 151, 160; dislikes close blockade, 183; in the Gallinas, 183-5; is not prepared to abandon naval patrol, 199

Hunn, Capt., RN, injudicious handling of slaver *Sylphe*, 94-6

Hutt, Sir William, MP, leads parliamentary attack against naval operations, 193-201

Hypolite, slave ship taken off Gallinas, 92

Inconstant, HMS, flagship of squadron, 60, 112

Inglis, Sir R. H., MP, 180, 198

Inman, Robert, midshipman, RN, killed in action, 65, 69, 70

Invincival, British prize taken by pirate, 115, 116

Iphigenia, HMS, boat action in Bonny river, 108-10

Irby, Capt., RN, unprofitable cruise, 50-3

Jackson, British prize-master missing, 116

Jarvis, John, AB, dies, 188, 189

Jellicoe, Lieut., RN, wounded in action, 101, 102

Jennings, British agent for Spanish slaving firm, 133

John Adams, USS, 150

Jones, American merchant ship unjustifiably detained, 147

Jones, Capt. L. T., RN, destroys factories at Solyman, 183, 184; action at Lagos, 211

Josephine, slave ship overhauled and taken, 220

Kangaroo, HMS, unprofitable cruise, 46, 53-8

Kearney, British slave dealer in Gallinas, 73-5, 105, 132, 133

Keith, surgeon, RN, wounded in action, 112

Kelly, Capt., RN, unsuccessful action, 101, 102

Kelly, Michael, seaman, RN, lost overboard, 188

Keta, Gold Coast port, 155; can one get palm oil there?, 123

Kittam, Gallinas chief, 184

Knight, Capt., RN, takes slaver *Dichosa Estrella*, 90, 91

Kosoko, claimant to kingdom of Lagos, 206-16

Kroo seamen in Navy, 102, 103, 212, 213, 215

La Fanny, slave ship captured, 123

Lagos, 46, 53, 120, 144, 167, 201; first attack on, 205-11; second attack on, 211-15; annexed, 216-19

Laird, Macgregor, shipbuilder and explorer, 189

Lamina, chief in Gallinas, 173

Lander, Richard, explores Niger, 189

Lawrence, retired slave dealer, 71

Layton, Cdr., RN, cruises in HMS *Cygnet*, 154-9, 187-9

Leeke, Capt., RN, in Rio Pongas, 65-8; in Bonny river, 105-7; takes pirate *Virgen*, 110

Lekki, coastal village, 216

Levinge, Lieut., RN, no sympathy with marooned slave dealers, 177; working south of the line, 204

Liberia, 167

Liebray, Benjamin, slaving captain, 93

Lightburn, slave dealer and coffee planter, 72-4

Lincoln, President Abraham, 221-3

Lloyd, Capt., RN, unfruitful cruise, 46, 53-8

Lokoja, projected plantations at, 191

Los, Isles de, 45, 64

Lyons, midshipman, RN, takes slaver *Anna Maria*, 104, 105

Lyster, Capt., RN, leads landing party in Lagos action, 212, 213

MacCarthy, Lt.-Col. Charles, Governor of Sierra Leone, 65, 66, 73, 75

McCoskry, William, British trader and acting Governor in Lagos, 218, 219

MacHardy, Lieut., RN, takes slaver *Voladora*, 135, 136

Maclean, George, British Governor on Gold Coast, 166

Maidstone, HMS, flagship of squadron, 115

Manna, chief in Gallinas, 168-71, 173

Maria, slave ship runs herself ashore, 134, 135

Martinez, Pedro, Spanish slaving firm, 132, 133, 144, 174

Matson, Capt., RN, evidence to Select Committee, 174, 175, 179-81, 199

Mends, Sir Robert, RN, commodore, 97, 100, 107-10

Merchant, American vessel, trouble on board, 154, 155

Miami, action off, 137

Midas, slaver taken by HMS *Monkey*, 137

Midgley, Capt., kind heart of, 177

Mildmay, Lieut., RN, takes five slavers in Bonny river, 108-10

Minerva, slave ship lands cargo at Havana, 124, 125

missionaries, 166, 206

mixed commission courts: Freetown, 79, 81-6, 89-91, 133, 194, 195, 203, 204; Havana, 79, 139, 140; Rio de Janeiro, 79, 163; Surinam, 79

Mohican, USS, takes slaver *Erie*, 222

Molemba, Molembo, slaving port in Angola, 122

Monkey, HMS, takes slaver *Midas*, 136

Morgiana, HMS, 61; in Rio Pongas, 65-8; takes slavers *Emilia*, 87, and *Dichosa Estrella*, 90, 91

Murray, Capt., RN, expensive disregard of equator by, 122, 123

My Boy, slave ship, outwitted by Navy, 154

Myrmidon, HMS, 61; in Rio Pongas, 65-8; general alarm caused by, 74, 75, 101; detains slaver *San Salvador*, 82; in Bonny river, 105-7; takes pirate *Virgen*, 110, and slaver *Bella Dora*, 111

Nash, Lieut., RN, unpleasant twenty minutes, 111

Netuno, slave ship and British prize, 116-18

New Cess, Liberian slaving port, 153, 173, 179

Norman, Mrs Fry, kidnapped and rescued, 167-71

Palma, coastal village, 216

Palmerston, Lord, Foreign Secretary, 120, 140, 143, 148, 149, 162, 164, 165, 174, 200, 208, 221

palm oil, 19, 120, 146, 147, 189, 191, 206

Park, Mungo, explorer, 189

Parliament, debates in, 13-19, 196-200; Select Committee of, 151, 171, 174, 175, 177, 179-81, 193, 195, 196, 204

Pasco, Lieut., RN, welcome visitor to Cameroons, 180

Paul Pry, naval tender, 128

Penelope, HMS, boat action in Gallinas river, 183, 184; at Lagos, 215

Perry, Commodore, USN, good relations with British, 151-4, 205

Perry, USS, 150

Petite Betsy, slave ship taken in Bonny river, 109, 110, 115

Pheasant, HMS, 61, 86; unsuccessful action, 101, 102

Pickle, HMS, takes slaver *Voladora*, 135, 136

piracy, pirates, 107, 110. 116-18, 134, 135

Pluto, HM steamship, 128; in Gallinas river, 175, 176

Pongas river, 64-73, 141, 167

Popo, slaving port in Dahomey, 57, 135, 136, 155, 159

Porpoise, USS, 150, 153; arrests slaver *Uncas*, 157

Porto Novo, port in Dahomey, 53, 63

Portsmouth, USS, 150

Portugal, 78, 121, 122, 129, 162; *see also* treaties

Primrose, HMS, captures slaver *Veloz Pasagera*, 129-32

Princes island, 54, 77

Principe, *see* Princes island

Prometheus, HMS, at Lagos, 219

Protector, HMS, brings encouraging news, 53

Proctor, British trader, 64, 65, 69

Purchas, Capt., RN, takes slaver *Netuno*, 116

Quicombo, slaving port in Angola, 158

Quiz, London privateer, fools HMS *Kangaroo*, 57, 58

Rattler, HMS, screw steamer, 37

Redwing, HMS, arrests slavers *Sylphe*, 94-6, and *Invincival*, 115, 116

Réunion island, 43, 96

Reynolds, Admiral, RN, in Brazilian waters, 164, 165, 200

Rio de Janeiro, 79, 114, 116, 163, 164

Rio Pongas, *see* Pongas river

Rosa, slave ship, poor gunnery of, 112, 113

Rosalia, slave ship, unwarranted arrest of, 88, 89

Russell, Lord John, Prime Minister, 199, 200, 217, 218

Sampson, HMS, ineffectual gallantry of boats' crews, 213

San Antonio, slave ship, overloaded, 59, 60

Sao Joao, slave ship, captured, 50

Sao Joao Voador, suspected slave ship acquitted, 123

Saracen, HMS, operations in the Shebar, 175

Sarah Anne, slave ship handed over to US Navy, 141

Sao Tomé, *see* St Thomas island

St Thomas island, 45, 47, 53-5, 77, 95, 116

Seagram, Lieut., RN, injudicious arrest by, 147, 148; blockades New Cess, 173

Seabar, *see* Shebar

Sealark, HMS, assiduously searches creeks, 47-9

Seamew, American vessel wrongfully detained, 147

Select Committee of Parliament, 151, 171, 174, 175, 177, 179-81, 193, 195, 196, 204

Seppings, Sir Richard, chief naval designer, 27

Serrano, Captain-General of Cuba, 225, 226

Shebar channel, 167, 179, 182

Sherbro island, 167, 170, 185, 202

Sherer, Lieut., RN., takes slaver *Maria*, 134, 135

Siaka, John, Gallinas chief, 184

Siaka, king, pleads alibi, 92, 93; supplies slaves, 133, 170; represented by his son, 171; destroys Spanish warehouses, 173, 186; lives in luxury, 195

Sierra Leone, 43, 113, 115, 147, 167, 187, 202; *see also* Freetown

Skipjack, HMS, action with slaver *Maria*, 134, 135

Smith, Lieut., RN, unpopular in Havana, 124, 125

Snapper, HM brig, 61, 65-8, 113

Solebay, HMS, takes preliminary cruise, 43

Solyman (Sulima), attack on, 183, 184

Sotheby, Cdr., RN, pertinacity in searching creeks, 47-9

Souza, Da, slave dealer at Whydah, 114, 177

Star, HMS, unlucky prize crew of, 187, 188

Stellwagen, Lieut., USN, handsome conduct of, 152, 153

Stevenson, US Minister in London, tactful diplomacy of, 148, 149

Sugar Duties Act, 194, 199

sugar, 19, 20, 194, 196, 199

Sulima, *see* Solyman

Surveillante, HMS, frigate, 64

Sybille, HMS, takes slaver *La Fanny*, 123; acquires tender, 128

Sylphe, slave ship, international incident over, 94-6

Symonds, Sir William, chief naval designer, 28

Tartar, HMS, visits Rio Pongas, 70; visits Bonny river, 103; visits Calabar, 84

Teazer, HMS, in attack on Lagos, 212, 213

Tellus, American vessel, suspicious loitering of, 155

Termagant, HMS, blockades New Cess, 173; unwisely arrests American vessel, 147, 148

Thistle, HMS, 61, 64, 113; in Rio Pongas, 65-8; arrests slavers *Eliza*, 81, 82, *Rosalia*, 88, 89, *Anna Maria*, 103-5

Thornton, Henry, MP, 17

Tineh, village in Gallinas, 184

Totten, Capt., USN, requires no advice, 204, 205

Trade Town, Liberian port, 90

treaties: with African chiefs, 174, 175, 178, 180-2, 215; with Brazil, 120; with Denmark, 78; with France, 121, 139; with Holland, 78, 96, 119, 120; with Portugal, 45, 53, 58, 77, 78, 96, 119, 120, 132, 162; with Spain, 78, 96, 119, 120, 132; with Sweden, 78; with United States, 149

Trist, US consul at Havana, 139-41, 161

Tucker, Capt., RN, no sympathy with marooned slave dealers, 177

Tucker, Lieut., RN, takes slaver *Principe de Guinea*, 115

Tucker, Harry, king at Shebar, 175

Turner, Charles, Governor of Sierra Leone, 167

Tweed, Lieut., RN, boat action with slaver *Rosa*, 112, 113

Uncas, American vessel, shifty behaviour of, 156, 157

United States and the slave trade, 58, 76, 77, 115, 126, 138-61, 221-3

United States, civil war, 160, 221, 222

United States Navy, 76, 115, 149-54, 161, 200, 204, 205

Urania, slave ship captured, 57, 58

Ursula, slave ship captured, 109, 110

Van Buren, President of the USA, 138, 139

Van Sirtema, Dutch judge, 81, 82

Vecua, slave ship captured, 109, 110

Veloz Pasagera, slave ship, action against HMS *Primrose*, 129-32

Vengador, slave ship taken, 129

Vienna, Congress of, disappoints Castlereagh, 38, 78

Vigilant, slave ship taken in Bonny river, 109, 110, 115

Virgen, pirate schooner put to good use by British prize crew, 110, 111

Voladora, slave ship caught when nearly home, 135, 136

Walsh, legal agent at Freetown, small assistance to client, 85, 86

Wasp, HMS, disaster befalls prize crew, 188

Webster-Ashburton treaty, 149, 162, 163, 200

White, Edward, British Governor in Cape Coast, 50-3

Whydah, slaving port in Dahomey, 47, 53, 57, 58, 63, 78, 86, 113, 114, 120-2, 155, 177, 196, 203, 205

Wilberforce, William, MP, 17, 18, 20, 100

Willes, Capt., RN, despondency of, 115

Wilmot, Cdr., RN, at Lagos, 208, 209

Wilson, British merchant in Rio Pongas, 66, 68

Wilson, Lieut., RN, terrible ordeal of, 187, 188

Ycanam, slave ship taken in Bonny river, 109, 110

Yeo, Capt. Sir James, RN, commodore: Admiralty orders to, 43, 44; reports by, 60, 61, 100, 101, 220; eagerly sought for, 61, 112

Yorktown, USS, spoken by HMS *Cygnet*, 155

VERMONT COLLEGE
MONTPELIER, VERMONT